An Introduction to
Popular Culture in the US

An Introduction to Popular Culture in the US

People, Politics, and Power

Jenn Brandt and Callie Clare

BLOOMSBURY ACADEMIC
NEW YORK · LONDON · OXFORD · NEW DELHI · SYDNEY

BLOOMSBURY ACADEMIC
Bloomsbury Publishing Inc
1385 Broadway, New York, NY 10018, USA
50 Bedford Square, London, WC1B 3DP, UK
29 Earlsfort Terrace, Dublin 2, Ireland

BLOOMSBURY, BLOOMSBURY ACADEMIC and the Diana logo are
trademarks of Bloomsbury Publishing Plc

First published in the United States of America 2018
Reprinted 2018 (twice), 2019 (twice), 2020, 2021

Copyright © Jenn Brandt and Callie Clare, 2018

For legal purposes the Acknowledgments on p. viii constitute an
extension of this copyright page.

Cover design by Louise Dugdale
Cover images © iStock

Bloomsbury Publishing Inc does not have any control over, or responsibility for,
any third-party websites referred to or in this book. All internet addresses given
in this book were correct at the time of going to press. The author and publisher
regret any inconvenience caused if addresses have changed or sites have ceased
to exist, but can accept no responsibility for any such changes.

A catalog record for this book is available from the Library of Congress

ISBN: HB: 978-1-5013-2058-3
PB: 978-1-5013-2057-6
ePDF: 978-1-5013-2056-9
eBook: 978-1-5013-2059-0

Typeset by Integra Software Services Pvt. Ltd.
Printed and bound in the United States of America

To find out more about our authors and books visit
www.bloomsbury.com and sign up for our newsletters.

For our students, teachers, and democracy

Contents

Acknowledgments

The writing of this book was a fun, collaborative process that would not have been possible without a number of people and support. Katie Gallof, Susan Krogulski, Gogulanathan Bactavatchalane, and the team at Bloomsbury have been incredibly supportive and enthusiastic about this project from start to finish. Additionally, we would like to thank early reviewers of this text, including Nick Witham and Jordan McClain. To all our friends from Bowling Green, the Department of Popular Culture, and the Popular Culture Association, we thank you for the inspiration and good times, with special shout-outs to our teammates on Nothing But Diamonds, our rivals-turned-friends the ASC Shockers, as well as Mark Bernard, Colin Helb, Mike Lupro, and Marilyn Motz.

Jenn would like to thank Alain-Philippe Durand for his continual mentorship and support; Jody Lisberger for her wisdom and invaluable writing advice; and the faculty and staff at High Point University, particularly the English department, women's and gender studies program, and colleagues Cara Kozma, Kirstin Squint, and Scott Wojciechowski. A special thank you to all my wonderful and supportive friends, including Laurie Carlson and Eva Jones for maintaining the best work-related group text; Nancy Caronia for her unending willingness to play online Scrabble; and Beth Ann Semeraro and Natalie Whaley for keeping me up-to-date with celebrity-related news. Lastly, to my family for instilling an early love for and appreciation of popular culture, and to Stephen for his love, encouragement, and for reminding me that we don't do normal.

Callie would like to thank Lucy Long, Pravina Shukla, Henry Glassie, Vivian Halloran, and the Department of Folklore and Ethnomusicology at Indiana University for all they teach and their guidance; the faculty and staff at Siena Heights University, which fosters a supportive work environment, particularly the wonderful people in the Humanities Division; and Yasue Kuwahara for her professional mentorship and encouragement. Finally, a big thank you to all the people in my personal life: my friends who inspired examples in the book, who sat with me in coffee shops while I worked, offered retreats in their beautiful homes, and are proud of me; and my family who have always supported me, never limited me, and love me, not only because they have to.

Preface

In 1973 Ray Browne founded the Department of Popular Culture at Bowling Green State University with the goal of creating a space in academia to explore the amusements, texts, and practices that constituted the leisure activities of average Americans. Believing that elitism was a construct, Browne's emphasis on popular culture as the practice of everyday experience was an attempt to democratize the study of culture in a way that was about the people and for the people. Drawing from the fields of American studies, folklore, and literary studies, the study of popular culture in the United States branched out into a number of different disciplines, including Sociology, Anthropology, and Communication Studies. Similarly, the Centre for Contemporary Cultural Studies (CCCS) at the University of Birmingham, established in 1964, was dedicated to the history of cultural studies, relying heavily on the theories of the Frankfurt School of philosophical, political, economic, and social thought. Until its closing in 2002, the CCCS heavily influenced the field of cultural studies, with an emphasis on subcultures and countercultures, audience reception theory, and media studies.

With each of these foundations for the study of popular culture, the number of schools offering courses, concentrations, and degrees in popular culture has grown. Few of these offerings, however, are housed in full-standing popular culture departments, and are instead found in a variety of programs and departments across campuses globally. The diversity of methods in approaching popular culture is one of its strengths, and this book embraces a number of different theories in exploring the study of popular culture in the United States.

As the study of popular culture has grown and diversified, other disciplines have appropriated the subject matter, most often through the lens of media studies, without acknowledging, understanding, or taking into account the historical underpinnings of the field. While there are a number of texts that provide an introduction to the study of popular culture, the majority of them are UK-based and do not offer an explicit understanding of the study of popular culture as it has developed in the United States. Others focus more on contemporary media, and tend to be a collection of articles rather than an introduction to the theories that support the analysis of media texts. In 1992, Jack Nachbar and Kevin Lausé published *Popular Culture: An Introductory Text*; Nachbar was a professor in the Department of Popular Culture at Bowling Green State University and Lausé was affiliated with the university through teaching classes and library research. As a textbook offering an introduction to the study of popular culture coupled with chapters written by contributors illustrating the theory in practice, the book defined the undergraduate study of popular culture at Bowling Green and was adopted at other universities throughout the country. Learning to teach through this approach and using the textbook in classes ourselves, we find great value in this work. However, after twenty-five years, the book is older than most of our students, and so the quest for a new text began.

This book is the result of that quest. It is meant to be a textbook for introductory courses that examine the study of popular culture in the United States today. Beginning with the democratic approach adopted by Ray Browne, the text situates the academic study of popular culture into larger conversations that have evolved over the second half of the twentieth century into the twenty-first century. The theories are presented in such a way as to make them accessible for first-time students, but also to engage with those who already have a familiarity with the field. Though there are examples running throughout each of the chapters, we limited ourselves as the nature of popular culture is always changing.

Our goal is to provide a foundational examination and various lenses to approach the study of popular culture in the United States and to allow room for each individual student and teacher of popular culture to supplement with their own experiences and observations. With this book as the launching-off point, the study of popular culture can be catered to one's personal needs and interests. Various edited volumes with contributions from scholars in the field exist as natural complements to this textbook. Current events, news articles, and contemporary examples from popular culture are also invaluable supplements to this study, and lists of such collections and examples are available on our companion website.

Our focus on the United States is a conscious one. Throughout the text, when referring to the nation, we purposefully use "United States" as opposed to "America" in order to differentiate and be respectful of the multiple nations that comprise the American hemisphere. When "America" or "American" is used, it reflects the vernacular used by citizens and those living in the United States to define themselves and their culture. In the democratic spirit of the founding of the academic study of popular culture, we also recognize that the language and examples used in the text should be accessible to most readers. While the purpose of our study is certainly serious, we also want this work to be fun, and, at times, our tone is playful and light where appropriate. At the same time, though, our emphasis on the people, power, and politics of popular culture is intentional, as we stress the legitimacy and seriousness of this study at a time when, perhaps more than ever, it is needed.

Jenn Brandt and Callie Clare
May 31, 2017

Introduction

Don't give up. The beginning is always the hardest.

—Chinese Fortune Cookie

On February 1, 2015, the Seattle Seahawks and New England Patriots stormed into the University of Phoenix Stadium for Super Bowl XLIX. The weeks leading up to the game brought us the great "Deflate Gate" scandal, creating added fervor to the highly anticipated East Coast–West Coast battle. New England Patriots' quarterback Tom Brady and head coach Bill Belichick were forced to defend their balls after accusations surfaced that the team used underinflated footballs in their playoff victory against the Indianapolis Colts. The near shutout game, where the Patriots beat the Colts forty-five to seven, made them the AFC champions, securing their spot in the Super Bowl. Suspected tampering during the regular season would have been one thing, but the Patriots heading into the most anticipated game of the year as possible cheaters made it that much more outrageous. On social media, #deflategate trended for days, discussed by both sports enthusiasts and casual observers.[1] Videos and memes poking fun at the scandal quickly emerged to supplement the opinions and add fuel to the trending fire. Seattle Seahawks star running back Marshawn Lynch did his part in making the week leading up to the Super Bowl interesting by refusing to answer questions at the required media sessions with anything other than the phrase, "I'm just here so I won't get fined."[2] Again, fans and critics weighed in with their opinions online, and varied news sources, ranging from opinion-piece blogs to the major corporate media outlets, reported on Lynch's refusal to give them anything on which to report.

On game day, people gathered all over the United States to watch the battle. By the time it was over, media sources proclaimed that the over 114 million viewers made it the most-watched show in US television history.[3] Even those who claim to not care for the sport of football, the teams, or the outcome still watched. Perhaps they wanted to see Idina Menzel perform the National Anthem and get all of the words right. Maybe it was to see Katy Perry headline the halftime show. Not only did she ride in on a lion and fly through the stadium on a shooting star, but she also made Millennials realize that Lenny Kravitz is an actual musician (and not just a stylist from *The Hunger Games* films) and that Missy Elliott still has "it," her raw talent and strengths transcending modern-day trends in music. And, of course, Left Shark became an instant Internet sensation, proving himself to be not the hero we need, but perhaps the one we most deserve. No one knows exactly why, but everyone pretends to have enjoyed it, making it one of the highest rated halftime shows in several years.

Viewers who find no pleasure in the sport of football or the peripheral entertainment of the halftime show at least have the advertisements to fall back on. There are always at least a few guests at every Super Bowl party who say they are watching "just for the commercials." And those people, I'm afraid, were most likely disappointed because rather than the usual abundance of funny, irreverent commercials, this particular year gave us profound sadness and loss as we were asked to buy insurance by the ghost of a dead child.[4]

So why do so many people tune in to watch these games? Why do people momentarily decide to like commercials and not fast-forward through them during the Super Bowl? Why do so many people care to make fun of or blindly praise the mainstream musical halftime show, which, as expected, is always full of surprises? Why do more people care about this event than any State of the Union Address, presidential debate, or news coverage of important current events? What is so important and unifying about this one game?

The answers to these questions are the purpose of our study. Wrapped up in the Super Bowl are the elements of competition that keep our society moving. It is about heroes we look up to and aspire to be. It is about entertainment and money. It is about ritual and coming together as small groups of friends and families. It is about defining ourselves as members of a nation, and the variations that occur within this larger national identity. By examining what it is that we as a culture preoccupy ourselves with on a daily basis, we can better understand that culture and our place within it. We can recognize the patterns and structures of power and how we interact with that power, at times accepting it and at other times resisting it. This is the study of popular culture.

Popular culture in the academy

What kind of book tells you to "pick up your smartphone"?

Well, this one does.

Pick up your smartphone, or your tablet, or go to the nearest computer. Now, do a web search for "popular culture major" or "popular culture college." Some of the results are about actual academic programs and departments across the country or world that teach courses in popular culture. Perhaps your school is mentioned.

But keep looking at some of the other results.

Click to look at some of those opinion articles questioning the validity of popular culture being taught in higher education. Pay attention to how some of them may brush off the programs as worthless, as not valid areas of study, and/or as degradation of the modern university. Sometimes there is an article saying that it is "cool" and not immediately slamming the classes, but overwhelmingly, well, they're bad.

Perhaps someone thought the same thing about you taking this course. Responses to the study of popular culture range from either "Popular culture, cool!" or "Popular culture, why would you study that?" More often than not, the study of popular culture is greeted with the level of intolerance that our nation typically reserves for gluten. But this disdain, or at the very least these conflicting responses, fuels our quest for understanding.

Judging by how the mainstream media regards the study of popular culture, the reason we get these reactions is because people don't fully understand what studying popular culture is actually about. The term "popular culture," or, worse for our case, "pop culture," is regularly used to describe media distractions. What is on television, popular in movie theaters, trends and fads, or what is being reported on *E! News* is what typically comes to mind when most people hear these terms. Although this undoubtedly *is* popular culture, and is therefore included in our study of it, that's not where it ends. The study of popular culture is much more than keeping up with the Kardashians. This book does not contain a history on celebrity hook-ups and break-ups, it doesn't list facts about what actor played which role and to what success, nor does it give plot summaries and qualify which texts are good or bad. This book, and the field of popular culture studies more broadly, examines everyday life. As a nation more and more engrossed with media, entertainment, and corporate products, our everyday life is often preoccupied with these elements of popular culture. Therefore, we must give them the attention they deserve as they prove to be valuable resources in understanding our culture, society, and the world around us. We don't need to memorize the facts of popular culture, and we don't need to evaluate the products of popular culture as good or bad. What we need to do is understand that the aspects of our everyday lives, the amusements, practices, and products that take up so much of our time and on which we focus so much of our attention, are extremely valuable tools for understanding not only ourselves, but the people, power, and politics as well that drive our country. Recognizing and analyzing trends, digging deeper to ask "why?", we can begin to understand aspects of ourselves and our culture hidden just below the surface. Looking critically at our everyday lives is the academic study on which you are about to embark.

Popular culture has been defined in many different ways, and before we jump into how we will use it, it is important to understand the intellectual, academic, and cultural climate that led to the development of this particular study. The study of popular culture in the United States owes a great deal of credit to Ray Browne, who first developed and argued for the academic study of popular culture as "an organization of rebellion, devoted to enlarging cultural and Humanities studies as much as possible."[5] In his 1989 book *Against Academia*, Browne candidly reflects on his personal history as well as the cultural climate in which he was working and establishing this field of study. Born in Alabama in 1922, Browne attended college at the University of Alabama before serving for the US military in Europe during the Second World War. Upon his return home, he pursued advanced degrees in English literature, but his study and scholarship were affected by the cultural climate of the tumultuous 1960s, a decade famous for unrest, rebellion, and the questioning of power structures. Many academic disciplines found themselves responding to this period of time, using different theoretical lenses to examine and find meaning in the chaotic turning of the tides. Influenced by the fields of American Studies, which at the time was moving away from a more textual approach of American culture to a broadened study of the diversity of experiences of American people, and folklore, thriving as a field with the resurgence of interest in folk music and ways of life as a response to the modernization in the postwar era, Browne found himself a rebel in the English Department at Bowling Green State University in Bowling Green, Ohio.

During his first years at Bowling Green, beginning in 1967, Browne established allies and further developed his ideas of popular culture. As a member of the English department, Browne was required to teach from the canon of "great works" throughout history. While he was no slouch when it came to the understanding of classic literature, it occurred to Browne that Shakespeare and those who attended the performances of his plays at the Globe Theatre, Melville and his readers of *Moby Dick*, and the potboilers of now-famed and highly regarded authors such as Charles Dickens, weren't always a part of the "elite" culture they are valued as today. Instead, they were produced for and consumed by the general public and done so mainly for profit. They were "popular" in that they were well known and widely distributed, not limited to the territory of the elite or the academy. Yet, over time they were elevated to the realm of high culture and became seen as valuable works of literature worthy of serious study. If this were the case, if these texts, which were considered "popular" and for everyone in their original context, were worthy of study, why weren't the texts being produced and popularized by the general audiences of the time? If people were reading dime novels, westerns, pulp fiction, gumshoe mysteries, comic books, and other popular fiction and works, shouldn't those be valuable materials to study? They, after all, appeared to be more relevant to the majority of the people. At this same time, television was becoming increasingly more prevalent as more networks were broadcasting more types of programs, effectively changing how people got their information and where they devoted significant amounts of their leisure time. As a folklorist in an English department, Browne began adding more and more popular culture elements to his curriculum. He had the ear of administrators who were willing to take risks, and in a short period of time Browne successfully created the *Journal of Popular Culture*, started the Popular Press, founded the Popular Culture Association in 1970, and began a center for the study of popular culture and a depository for popular culture research materials.[6]

However, shifts in power, retirements of supporting faculty, and curricular rearrangements led to distaste for Browne and his growing study of popular culture. Members of the English Department cited the stigma of popular culture as not a serious academic study, saw Browne's efforts as a waste of time and of money, and wanted him removed from the department. Tensions came to a head, and by 1971 Browne was out of English, but garnered enough institutional support to start his tiny Department of Popular Culture. The founding of the department didn't end the name-calling and attempts to strip the program of its notoriety despite the support Browne was receiving from administrators and colleagues across the United States. His nontraditional approach to the study of everyday life and culture through his focus on a variety of content materials was emblematic of the changes and shifts happening all over the United States at the time. Academic departments in the humanities and social sciences were responding to the radical social upheaval of this era of Civil Rights, women's liberation, and the counterculture revolution. The academy was becoming more democratic, recognizing differences not just between cultures across the globe but cultures within the diverse United States. This quest for democracy and paying equal attention to all groups, particularly those who had been limited to the fringes of mainstream society based on characteristics such as race, gender, sexuality, class, religion, or region, resulted in new academic areas of study to better understand the realities of the US culture and society.

Browne's vision became part of this new reality. The academic study of popular culture is an attempt to study the various cultures and identities that exist within the larger, mainstream dominant culture. It is about focusing on real people and everyday life, rather than what people have traditionally been told is worthy of study. It forces us to be active participants in our own knowledge base, questioning not only what we know, but how and why we know what we know, and what is at stake when we become more than just passive consumers of the world around us. Therefore, our study is driven by a democratic history of popular culture, situated in lived experience, and demonstrates popular culture's potential as a tool for agency.

Defining popular culture

Despite the eventual acceptance of the Department of Popular Culture and the growth of the study to academic institutions and programs across the United States, the term "popular culture" is most commonly used to describe entertaining media forms or other mass-produced cultural products. These false impressions are why some academics criticize popular culture and/ or consider it not worthy of our time and study. Their misconceptions and trivializations are what Ray Browne and the early advocates of popular culture dealt with most of their life, and are what many popular culture departments and programs still respond to and fight against today.

So what is popular culture if it is not to be conflated with the derogatory, superficial connotations attributed to "pop culture"? Once we look past the stigma of "pop culture" as just mediated trivialities and distractions, we can articulate a more accurate definition. Before doing so, however, we need to go further and shake off the idea of popular as something that is merely "well-liked." Instead, let's refer back to the fifteenth-century use of *popularis*, which is directly connected to the *populus*, or people. With this frame of reference, we can correctly identify that something that is "popular" is something that is from or for the people. As a result of its connotation of being affordable, accessible, and intended for ordinary people, "popular" took on the added meaning of being liked, readily available, and/or widespread, which is the way we often think of and define the term today.

Browne's use of the word "popular" to describe culture is therefore slightly deceiving. He doesn't necessarily mean the things that are just "popular" because they are well known, well received, and regularly mediated. What he means by "popular" is this notion of "the people," of "ordinary" folks like you and me. Browne eschewed notions of elitism, and insisted on a democratization of the study of culture and its consumers, encompassing what people do every day as part of their daily lives. An accurate definition of **popular culture**, then, is the activities, objects, distractions, and focus of daily life. The study of popular culture is not only focused on its products, but also what we do with them. It is the study of people, their rituals, beliefs, and the objects that shape their existence. More than just products or media texts, popular culture represents the people, power, and politics that shape our daily existence within contemporary US culture.

The development of this definition of popular culture is in response to two other types of **culture**: elite and folk. Elite culture is historically the culture of the aristocracy, the wealthy, the intelligentsia, and/or those associated with the highest socioeconomic class. In terms of academic study, elite culture is considered part of the traditional humanities curriculum and the "great works" of the masters such as Shakespeare, Rembrandt, or Mozart. Perhaps not coincidentally, elite culture is entrenched in a white, bourgeois, and masculine tradition. Elite culture resides in the ivory tower where individuals who are not part of the populace decide what is worthy of time and study, critics who determine what is the best of Culture. Elite culture tends to ignore the differences and variations between cultures and is overwhelmingly Euro-centric. In order for something to become elite, it must *not* be accessible to all people, and in order for something to remain elite, it tends to be more expensive and/or require a specialized education to be fully appreciated. This restricted access to Culture ignores and purposefully excludes the experiences of most individuals. Elite art is limited to art museums and galleries, praised and studied in art history classes, and used to define shifts in culture. Elite literature consists of the canonical works studied as the classics. Elite music is limited to sophisticated arrangements like orchestras, operas, and now even jazz (which demonstrates how over time, popular culture can become Culture). Elite culture is often time tested; its prestige has endured for decades or even centuries. Its age can also limit how it appears relevant to our culture today, requiring a different code to understand it, a code which comes at a high price—either monetary, or through time and study. Elite culture is not intended for, nor appreciated by, everyone, though those who study it and revere it feel as if it is the height of human capabilities and that we should strive for nothing less as a culture, society, or species. Elite culture and the traditions of the academy are resistant to the study of popular culture and criticize it as something base that will lead to the ultimate dumbing down of our society. The study of popular culture was (and by some still is) seen as lowering society's standards, eventually making it so we no longer work to excel or achieve greatness.

In addition to finding these fears irrational and overblown, Browne and his equally radical contemporaries found elite culture to be out of touch, no longer completely relevant to the human condition, and quite limiting. Still, elite culture remained a touchstone against which other cultures and creations were compared. In response to this persistence, the broader sense of culture was utilized in Browne's conception of popular culture. Rather than the quest for the best of all human Culture, varying cultures were emphasized. Within this widened look at culture, every aspect of human society and everyday life from food to family to creative expression can be studied. While anthropologists tend to focus on the cultures which are temporally or spatially distant from their own, some folklorists and other scholars in the humanities and social sciences realized the need to examine the more mundane (and therefore taken-for-granted and largely ignored) aspects of the practices and elements of everyday life of the vast majority of individuals in the here and now, of one's own country. For popular culture scholars, then, folklore became a useful method and approach in the study of contemporary US culture.

As opposed to elite culture, folk culture is accessible to all. Historically, the usage of the word "folk" has referred to groups that are on the fringes of society. In the European tradition, these were the peasants and rural residents who lived away from urban (and later industrialized) civilization. They weren't fully "savage," but they also weren't "civilized." In the United States, the "folk" being studied were rural residents who maintained some European traditions, African Americans, and Native Americans. As the concept developed, it became wider and grew to encompass all groups of people, not just the rural and illiterate peasants. Famed folklorist Alan Dundes came to define "folk" as "any group of people whatsoever who share at least one common factor" no matter what that linking factor may be.[7] However, implied in the continued use of the terms "folk" and "folklore" is that the study is limited to small groups, more individualized, based on tradition (which ties it to the past), and not necessarily written or presented in mass media, but transmitted through face-to-face interactions. Like the term "popular," "folk" and "folklore" are also commonly misunderstood concepts. Although historically tied to tradition and small groups, this does not mean that folklore and the individuals it studies no longer exist or are outdated. Instead, it is important to understand that the term "folk" can apply to everyone, everywhere. From family traditions related to holiday celebrations or heirlooms, to the connections made between members on a sports team or in a sorority or fraternity, folk and folklore impact everyone, making up a significant part of our daily lives and meaningful connections.

From its origins as a word used to describe rural populations on the fringes, folk came to encompass the majority of people in the world. It isn't the official and recorded history of the literate and more urban minority, but accounts for the everyman. According to folklorist Warren E. Roberts, "written records are often inadequate as sources of data for the folklife researcher,"[8] because those records tend to focus on what the elite, educated, and more financially or politically powerful have had to say. "When one is trying to learn about the common people—about 95 percent of the population—the attempted reliance on written records usually proves futile."[9]

Therefore, the study of popular culture and the study of folk culture are closely related as both are seen in opposition to the study of an elite culture that has traditionally been the focus of the academy. Ray Browne writes:

> All of us in these early days had our own definition, but generally speaking we could all agree that we were talking about all elements of the culture around us except the narrowly elite and narrowly elitely creative. Popular culture to us was the everyday, the vernacular, the heritage and ways of life that we inherited from our predecessors, used and passed on to our descendants. It was the cultural environment we lived in. Popular culture is mainly disseminated by the mass media (word of mouth, print, radio, pictures, movies, television) but not necessarily limited to such media of dissemination. Popular culture probably should not include some ten per cent of so-called elite culture but it should include all folk culture. It is by definition international and comparative in scope, with no time limit; it is not restricted to the present.[10]

Elements of everyday life are not a part of "pop culture" as it is generally described, as they are often unmediated and/or deemed unimportant. From its earliest academic study, though, *popular culture* has included the study of folk culture, uniting against elitism. Looking at how people live, what they eat, how they decorate, what they wear, how they interact in groups, and other elements of folk culture are included in Browne's idea and this text's understanding of popular culture. Everything that average people have always done falls under the umbrella of popular culture. What was once considered folk culture has changed, of course, over time. This is due to a variety of factors such as movements of people, technology, and evolving mindsets, and will be explored more in the coming chapters. Regardless, popular culture today, though usually defined by the presence of media, is really an extension of the folk culture.

Also credited in the foundations of the study of popular culture in the United States is Russel Nye. Nye's focus on popular culture was concerned with cultural texts, and his 1973 study *The Unembarrassed Muse: The Popular Arts in America* is directed at music, literature, art, television, and films made explicitly for the consumption by large and wide audiences. Where Browne and Nye differ, however, is with Nye's claim that popular culture is "new," developing in the United States after 1750 in the age of **industrialization**. Industrialization ushered in an age of mass production, and resulted in, among other things, the emergence of a middle class. This new socioeconomic group had more money to purchase manufactured goods and more leisure time to use them than previous generations. People were no longer working only for the literal fruits of their labor: growing their own food, building their own homes, and making their own clothes. Instead, they were working jobs that paid money. After their basic needs for survival were met, they still had some money and time left over and, therefore, wanted to be entertained. Alongside this industrial shift was a move toward more widespread education, which resulted in greater rates of literacy. Nye felt that these developments were the beginning markers of a new culture, what he also referred to as popular culture.

As was with Browne, Nye also regarded popular culture as different from elite culture and geared toward the average citizen. Nye disagreed, though, arguing that popular culture differentiates more from folk culture than Browne allowed. Popular arts for the masses, according to Nye, do not include the folk arts; folk culture is not as concerned with aesthetics as popular culture and is intended for a smaller audience, he argues.[11] Much of what Nye discusses is influenced and connected to the theories of mass culture. These theories suggest more of the negative aspects of "mass culture" as homogenous and therefore lose the individuality of the much smaller folk cultures. While Browne and Nye were arguing for the rise of popular culture, those who studied folk culture resisted it for that very reason. The thought that popular culture is taking over at the expense of individual folk cultures is still part of the criticism of popular culture today.

Both views are necessary and both make valid points. The fact that industrialization changed all areas of daily life is undeniable. Prior to industrialization, people worked and lived much differently, and the speed of communication and methods of industrialization advanced rapidly. We couldn't have modern society and what we commonly refer to today as "popular culture" without the shift from an agricultural to a manufacturing society. As Browne noted, however, defining what average people do against what elite culture traditionally imposed is an extension of what has typically been considered folk culture, even if the means of cultural production are industrialized. Today folk culture stands apart from popular culture as more individualized and focused on smaller groups, but that does not make it less concerned with audience or aesthetics, as Nye suggested. It should be, and is, included in our study of popular culture. In fact, the things originally intended for smaller groups (craft beers, handmade jewelry, and pretty much anything you can find on Etsy) are becoming more and more conflated with the wider popular culture in today's society. A post, video, or photo intended to be shared among a small group can, with the rise of social media and the new ways in which people are constantly connected, in just a matter of hours be seen by and shared with millions of people. This demonstrates the ways in which the lines between folk culture and popular culture are increasingly blurred. Justin Bieber wouldn't have a career if it weren't for YouTube (*thanks, YouTube*), half of the country wouldn't have debated about whether a dress was white and gold or blue and black if it weren't for social media, and we would still be laughing out loud instead of ROFL if it weren't for text messaging. What were once instances of small group or individual expression have evolved and spread through popular culture.

The 90 percent

In September of 2011, protestors began to collect in Zuccotti Park in New York City to bring attention to economic inequality in the United States.[12] Targeting Wall Street, the symbolic center of US capitalism and finance, the Occupy Movement called for the 99 percent of the population to pay attention to the disparities in income and the connections between those in power of the government, financial, and corporate institutions (the 1 percent) and the rest of the country. Despite the Occupy Movement's focus on these inequalities, since 2011 these trends only continue to rise, and in January 2017, Oxfam International research revealed that the wealthiest 1 percent of the world's population now owns more wealth than the rest of the planet, with eight men owning the same amount of wealth as the poorest half of the world.[13] While the goal of this book is not to point out the financial differences among the wealthiest and poorest residents nationally or globally, it is to talk about the majority, or the 90 percent, and the ways in which popular culture both abets and resists these systems of power.

Although Browne himself did not demonize the culture of the elite, he knew that it was limiting. "High Culture" cannot be considered representative of the majority of the population because, by definition, it is exclusive. In order to recognize the majority, he had to look at the daily lives of average individuals. He wrote:

> If anything is going to unite the nation—and all humanity—it will not be the art museum, not the elite novels, architecture, the so-called legitimate theater, not the conventional humanities and standard approaches to education [...] If anything binds humanity together it will be the arts and humanities that speak about, to, and with the basic voice of the people.[14]

Therefore, the goal of popular culture and its usefulness as an object of study is in its appeal toward democracy. The word "democracy" is most often used to describe our system of government in the United States. By definition, it is a government "by the people, for the people," and its goal is to ensure that not any one person or group has too much power. This participatory form of government requires local and national elections, where individuals are voted into office with the intention to "represent" the majority and their interests. Elected officials are charged with the task of creating and upholding our laws and governance in order to achieve "the greatest good to the greatest number of people."[15] More than just our system of government, democracy has become one of our nation's core **ideologies**. Therefore, as we begin to study popular culture, we need to identify the democratic forms and media that not only reach the most people, but also reflect the values and beliefs that bind us together as a society.

Writing before the rise of the Internet, Browne wrote, "Television—or whatever forms it develops into—because it is the basic medium for the expression of democracy—might well be the medium for the dissemination of democracy."[16] By the mid-twentieth century, television was the height of entertainment and center for daily life, as well as the medium through which most people got the bulk of their information. Given rapid changes in media and modes of communication in a short period of time, Browne anticipated that television and technology would quickly change and evolve. Today it can be argued that television is no longer the major medium for expression and dissemination, and has instead been replaced with the Internet. With rapidly evolving technology that puts the Internet at our fingertips, on our wrists, in our eyeglass frames, and always floating through the air we breathe, this ever-present access to information has changed and shaped the way people communicate.

The Internet provides a platform for everyone's opinion to be heard. It allows for the dissemination of many ideas and conversations. At times, we relish in this opportunity, and at other times, we wish we had a mute button for everyone on our Twitter or Facebook streams. However, the access to information and the capability to say whatever it is that we want to say, whether people pay attention to it or not, is the realest expression of democracy. It supports the promotion of equality inherent in the goal for democracy because it is the voice of the people. While there are still restrictions to access based on factors such as age, income, and location, it is much closer to a democratic platform than what has existed before. Perhaps more than just being an outlet for saying one's opinion or letting one's voice be heard, it is the access to information that makes the Internet such a powerful tool. Knowledge and education are the most valuable resources when it comes to the promotion and follow-through of democracy, and the Internet and other aspects of daily life are where democracy shines. It allows for greater communication, connection, and opportunities for participation, including more people than previous forms of culture. That doesn't mean we have to like all of it. In fact, some of it is absolutely terrible; but, even the terrible stuff is valuable to understanding our culture at various points in time.

What is also key to understanding popular culture is recognizing it as "one of the sites where [the] struggle for and against a culture of the powerful is engaged."[17] This is where the goals for democracy argued by US popular culture studies scholars meet the theories and adaptations of the European cultural studies model. Regarding popular culture as a site of struggle demonstrates that popular culture is, in actuality, about power. In our daily lives, there are many institutions that maintain order. We have guidelines that we must follow to fit into our society. We must obey traffic codes, pay taxes, and abide by all laws. There are rules at schools, at home, and at work. Whether it is religion, family, school, the government, or any other **institution**, there are regulations that keep us all in check. This is necessary for maintenance of a culture and society. Within each of these institutions, there is also a hierarchy and a power structure. If popular culture is a site of struggle, it is where this order of power is negotiated. It is the aspects of our culture that influence us, shaping us into one organized and functional society. We are indoctrinated into the culture, learn our roles, and contribute based on what we are taught by society's various institutions, such as religion, education, and the media. Certain groups maintain their power through this system. Subordinate groups, often distracted by the very means of their subordination, do not regularly question this system of power because it is made to seem natural. This is the theory of **hegemony** as described by Antonio Gramsci in his prison notebooks. We don't make it a habit to question why we must listen to our parents, that the teacher leads the classroom, or that the president runs the country. There are those with authority over us in every aspect of our lives despite living in what we call a "free country" founded on the notion of individual liberty. Of course, this structure isn't necessarily a negative thing. Maintaining order is basic to civil society and is meant to keep us safe, and in ideal circumstances, this system of order works toward equality. This is democracy at its best. In order for such a society to function, though, there has to be willing participants. This is where the American Dream comes in; it enforces the notion we are all equal, even when we aren't. The American Dream works by instilling us with the belief that if we work hard and dedicate our time and energy, we will achieve the cultural definition of success: happiness, a good job, a healthy family. The idea behind the dream is that if everyone is working to better themselves, by extension they are contributing to our society, making us a stronger unit. The elements of popular culture that promote and are related to the American Dream serve as hegemonic tools to this maintenance of power.

Of course, there are many instances of abuses of power that become detrimental to those in subservient positions. When individuals question and challenge existing power structures, power can shift to other groups. This was the goal of the Occupy Movement mentioned above. While it has yet to reach its ultimate goal, it was successful in the fact that it started a national conversation about the distribution of wealth and power in our culture. In doing so, it exemplified popular culture as a site of struggle and an instrument of democracy. Products of popular culture, whether mediated or not, can be strong motivators in helping individuals question power structures and implement desired change.

It's never just a game

Let's think back to the football example from the beginning of the chapter. Professional sports teams and franchises are owned by very wealthy people, and these teams are sponsored by very wealthy companies. These wealthy corporations also have ties to politics. Cities that want good major league teams to represent them need stadiums to attract teams and accommodate fans. In order to build these stadiums, cities need money, which is most readily generated through taxpayer dollars. This money is supposed to "return" to taxpayers in the form of jobs and revenue associated with housing a major-league team. More often than not, however, when rich and powerful individuals and companies are in control of making these alliances with the government, what often emerges are connections that better benefit those teams, owners, franchises, and companies. Despite the fact that the government is supposed to represent the interest of its constituents, quite often in these negotiations, taxpayers benefit the least through these deals. Regardless, residents are expected to root for and support their local teams, to come together and take pride in their wins and mourn in their losses. This support carries an additional financial burden through the purchasing of tickets to games, spending inflated amounts of money at concession stands, and wearing all of the officially licensed sports apparel. When you think about it, the amount of time and money put into professional sports can come off as silly. There are many other places where the government and millions of Americans could spend their money that would help people and not just aid wealthy heads of franchises and corporations in becoming even wealthier. We don't, though, and because of this, those in power tend to stay in power. These are the folks who not only make the most money off professional sports, but they are also the ones who can decide to black out NFL games on local television stations to punish fans who opted to not buy tickets and attend the games in person. However, when people begin to question these power structures, unite, and make decisions based on the more powerful voice of a majority, then things can begin to change. The NFL can lift the black out. Or, they can choose to no longer ignore the instances of brain damage, drug use, domestic violence, and other criminal behavior within its organizations. This is not to suggest the takedown of the NFL or the teams we love to support. It does, though, provide a salient example of the ways in which average Americans support and perpetuate a system which doesn't reward them the same way as it does those in power, or to a lesser extent, those who participate in it (for example, college athletes). The sweet Sunday afternoon sense of victory a fan feels when their team wins is miniscule and cheap compared to what is going on behind the scenes with those who pull the strings. If this is what is happening with sports (it's only a game, right?), it can be too daunting to even consider what might be happening behind the scenes of our government, military, education, food production, the medical field, or other areas with a greater influence over matters of life and death.

Approach to the study

What is important to us in this study is that we examine what it is that "average," "regular" people do. Our task is to study everyday life and the elements that aid in our participation and enjoyment of our immediate worlds. This is where the misconception of popular culture as referring only to the media we consume can be misleading. While this is, of course, a major component of our concern, it is not the only aspect of everyday life that shapes individuals and culture. Throughout this book, we are going to look at all aspects of daily life from a variety of angles, through many different lenses, alongside a host of theories.

As discussed earlier, **folklore** is one of the ways in which we will approach the study of popular culture. The definition of folklore most widely accepted in the field is "artistic communication in small groups."[18] Characteristics that we discussed above connect to this definition, as there is an emphasis on the face-to-face communication of small groups made up of similar individuals. The "artistic" elements of this communication have been examined in varying genres of folklore study made up of verbal art, rituals, and material culture. These smaller groups and closer connections are also a part of daily life and, therefore, an important element of our study of popular culture.

Overwhelmingly, though, "popular culture" is synonymous with the "media" and often the two terms are conflated. Many individuals think that popular culture is *only* media. Because it is very important that we understand what individuals, groups, and larger communities do on a daily basis, we certainly must pay attention to the media. It is the major way we receive information, communicate with one another, form our identities, group ourselves, and discover how we fit into the larger national and global culture. From the moment we wake up in the morning and check Twitter on our phones, through the radio we listen to during our commute, the countless hours binge watching series on online streaming services, and up until we check Instagram on our phones before falling asleep, media surrounds us. It, too, then is a very important way for us to study popular culture.

Understanding the world around us so that we can better understand ourselves as individuals, groups, and a culture is the main focus of this study. We want to "read" all of the activities of daily life as texts, as they provide insight into the larger concerns of individuals and communities as a whole. Allowing them to "speak" and to speak freely is crucial, as are the ways in which we respond to these texts. In framing our responses, we don't want to focus on one particular theory or theoretical framework, as that will not only limit our understanding of the text, but also what we say about it. There is no one theory of popular culture. Various academic departments and their theories have influenced the study of popular culture, but one is not valued or central over any others. For example, a study of genre is influenced by theories of structuralism, also utilizing functionalism. The dominant theory of performance in folklore studies is also influential. The myth-symbol study of culture in the United States, which defined early American Studies, features prominently in our examination of national identity. The struggle laid out above is highly influenced and discussed using Marxist theories, such as hegemony, as well as audience reception theories, which come from British cultural studies. Individual identity can be explored through many other approaches examining gender and race and other theories and frameworks meant to navigate these interconnected channels. It is just a matter of letting the text breath and live on its own before we, as the students of popular culture, attempt to stifle and understand it through forced theoretical frameworks.

This may sound like a lot, and you are not expected to be familiar with these topics at this time. Many of them, however, will be applied in this book as we situate popular culture as an interdisciplinary academic field that examines daily life in the United States.

This book

Take a moment to recall the shape of an hourglass. If you picture an hourglass, it is very wide at the top, tapers to a much more focused center, and then expands wide again at the bottom. In many ways, this book is structured like an hourglass. We will start off broad, discussing our modern culture and society in the United States at large by examining the myths, ideologies, and institutions that shape our collective cultural mindset. The examination of cultural myths asks us to look at everyday life and the texts produced that contribute to our popular culture in order to recognize recurrent themes that shape our understanding and interactions with our culture. These myths, which rely on and reinforce specific ideologies, provide clues for making sense of the world of which we are a part.

Chapter 2 introduces the concept of cultural myth as the means by which sign systems work within a culture to create narratives that situate and perpetuate ideology. Chapter 3 builds upon the concept of cultural myths in its exploration of genre and the ways in which popular media texts rely on formulas in their transmission of cultural meaning. By examining genre in terms of trends, their characteristics, and their changes, we can trace the transformations and shifts of the larger culture and its mindset. While Chapter 3 looks at some of the texts of popular culture, Chapter 4 introduces the concept of the culture industries and examines popular culture production and its relationship to representation and consumption.

The ways in which we as individuals consume cultural objects also add to their meaning, whether these meanings align with, or in opposition to, their intended purposes. This focus on the individual brings us to the second section of this book, the narrow part of our hourglass, which explores identity. To being with, we'll use Chapter 5's focus on heroes and celebrities to consider the people represented in and by popular culture and the values associated with these individuals and identities. After establishing an understanding of how popular culture functions at large, our concentration shifts and becomes much more focused as we look to examine the individual in culture. In these chapters, we explore identity, what it is, and how it is formed culturally and individually. Chapter 6 introduces theories of identity and their relationship to popular culture, and Chapter 7 explores the power dynamics of identity through the process of social construction as it relates to race, class, gender, sexuality, and (dis)ability.

After focusing on identity at the individual level, we then expand back out to the broader base of the hourglass as we consider the role of community and the ways individuals come together to make meaningful connections through cultural expression. Chapter 8 focuses on material culture and the ways in which the objects of our everyday life communicate our identities to others, and how these objects and communication help in the formation of communities. Community is examined in more detail in Chapter 9, as we situate the concept as it has been studied and conceptualized through various lenses from diverse fields. With increasing globalization and continued technological advances, the concept of community has changed significantly. These shifts accommodate diverse subcultures and countercultures, the growth of online communities, and the mainstreaming of fandom. After establishing an understanding of community as an evolving concept, the tenth and final chapter is devoted to the cultural expressions of various communities. These enactments take the form of rituals, ceremonies, and holidays, all with formalized patterns allowing for participants and spectators to communicate group values and cultural identification.

Conclusion

If we return again to the football example that opened the chapter, we can see how the sport embodies popular culture at the three levels we have outlined—myth, identity, and community—and reveals a number of facets of contemporary US culture. Built into the very fabric of life in the United States is our drive for competition. From a young age, we are taught that it is in our nature to compete for limited resources. As a result, it may seem that the moment we enter society, we begin to compete with each other. You may compete with siblings for attention or to be "the favorite," whereas in school we are trained to compete for grades, which teaches us the importance of working hard to excel. Team sports do the same. By directly competing against others, the goal is to make us perform better and to be better versions of ourselves. This is in preparation for the "real world," where we have to compete for jobs and money. The sport of football, which is uniquely popular here in the United States, is a direct representation of this core belief in competition. Baseball may be America's pastime and we experience "March Madness" over college basketball, but football is our favorite sport. It is a militaristic battle where one team literally works to invade another team's territory. The brutality and barbarism of football explains how we as a nation measure strength through physical domination, and where we as Americans take pride in calling ourselves the leading world power. Competition and domination—these are the cultural myths at the heart of the game.

Every myth needs a hero, and football is no exception. In numerous interviews year after year, players discuss the hardships they faced and the difficulties they had to overcome in order to achieve the American Dream (in this case, making it to the NFL). When asked, many individuals respond that their favorite athletes are their heroes. As with celebrities, some athletes emerge as heroes because of their positivity, while others, who may be well-known because of their performance on the field, become more (in)famous or reach a higher celebrity status because of their behavior off the field. The 2014 football season saw the downfall of many NFL players. There was the surveillance video footage of Baltimore Ravens' running back Ray Rice knocking his then-girlfriend unconscious, before dragging her out of an elevator, and Minnesota Vikings' running back Adrian Peterson was suspended due to allegations of child abuse. Thanks to social media and entertainment news, these private matters became very public. The NFL was criticized for its role, or lack thereof, in proper punishment of these men for their actions. Public backlash and the fallout from these scandals resulted in the NFL teaming up with the "NO MORE" campaign to bring attention to domestic violence and sexual assault. At the same time these players were being taken off their pedestals and off the field, the daughter of Cincinnati Bengal defensive tackle Devon Still emerged as a hero in her battle with cancer. The story of Leah Still and the actions of the Bengals (such as donating all the proceeds of Still jerseys sold to cancer research) worked to counteract stories of violence against women, children, and pets, as well as stories of substance abuse, gang violence, and other run-ins with the law.

As with the off-field actions of players, the entertainment and profits associated with football don't end with ticket sales and game attendance. Licensing of official NFL merchandise, for which fans pay exorbitantly, is a huge profit maker for the NFL and the different franchises. Through the consumption of these materials, fans can exert regional loyalty as well as something about themselves. The teams and the merchandise become icons, imbued with meaning beyond the basic function of the materials. Through their added price and official team logos, they mean significantly more.

When it comes to football, it may seem as if the construction of identity is not as clear. However, there are many stereotypes to which players and fans are expected to conform, and accordingly, there are certain traits connected to these identities. Football is about masculinity as exhibited through tough, physical dominance. The hyper-masculinity associated with football leads to overt homophobia in remarks made by coaches and teams, and few NFL players are openly gay or public advocates for LGBTQ equality. Players who do identify as homosexual tend to wait until after they retire from their NFL careers before making their sexual preference publicly known. As with gender and sexuality, race and racial stereotyping are also apparent with American football. Historically there have been prejudices against black quarterbacks, and many racial stereotypes about black male physicality and strength have been made about African-American players. This extends to what is considered "sportsman-like behavior," such as when Seattle Seahawks' cornerback Richard Sherman was labeled a "thug" after he expressed excitement over his team's playoff win. A Stanford graduate, Sherman calmly and intelligently pointed out that "thug" is a watered-down version of a racial slur against African Americans, and suggested that comparable words would not be used to discuss white athletes expressing similar confidence in their own abilities.[19]

How players and fans act on and off the field also leads to stereotypes of the team and of the city. The communities surrounding professional sports are many and diverse. There are communities built among the team members, as well as communities formed by fans and followers of specific teams. On the high school level, these communities are made up of members of the school and the surrounding town. On the college and national levels, fan communities are much larger, more spread out, and less intimate. Some fans take their dedication further and belong to active fandom or online groups. When it comes to football, one type of fan community people can participate in is Fantasy Football. The development of individual leagues with friends and family leads to friendly competition, trash talk, and team names based on past exchanges, all of which build these smaller communities and work to unify the members involved. Football games themselves can be seen as rituals that bring these various communities together. Players may have "superstitions," and teams may have rituals throughout the season, which unite them on their mission toward victory. Communities, both small and large, gather to watch the games in the stadiums. Even smaller groups can gather in public at bars or in private in homes to share the experience. The Super Bowl, as mentioned, annually brings together more people in the United States than any other televised event. It is not only the culmination of a football season, but a spectacle that unites our diverse nation as it reinforces our core values: competition, patriotism, entertainment, and consumerism.

Like the Super Bowl, the purpose of this book is to amuse you, surprise you, and as with all good entertainment, hopefully you will learn something along the way. In order to make sense of popular culture and the world around us, we need to pause and give our serious attention to the often-overlooked aspects of our everyday lives. This requires that we question our beliefs, what we have been told, and how we receive information, and ask why we do the things we do. Once we take the time to consider these questions and complicate the familiar, we can learn not only a lot about our culture, but also ourselves. It is from within this framework that we can begin to record more accurate and well-rounded accounts of the daily life of average citizens and, more importantly, write our own history of ourselves for future generations. In this way, we embrace the true meaning of "popular" as we work toward the ultimate goal of democracy.

Notes

1   Lorena O'Neil, "#DeflateGate Trends on Social Media after Patriots Investigated for Deflated Footballs," *The Hollywood Reporter*, January 19, 2015, http://www.hollywoodreporter.com/news/deflategate-trends-social-media-patriots-764672.

2   Stav Ziv, "Marshawn Lynch Gets Trademark Approved for 'I'm Just Here So I Won't Get Fined'," *Newsweek*, December 31, 2015, http://www.newsweek.

com/marshawn-lynch-gets-trademark-approved-im-just-here-so-i-wont-get-fined-410657.

3   John Breech, "Super Bowl 49 Watched by 114.4M, Sets US TV Viewership Record," *CBSSports.com*, February 2, 2015, http://www.cbssports.com/nfl/eye-on-football/25019076/super-bowl-49-watched-by-1144m-sets-us-tv-viewership-record.

4   NBC, "Nationwide Explains Depressing Super Bowl Ad," *NBC News*, February 2, 2015, http://www.nbcnews.com/storyline/super-bowl-xlix/nationwide-explains-depressing-super-bowl-ad-n298181.

5   Ray Browne, "The Theory Methodology Complex: The Critics' Jabberwock," in *Ray Browne on the Culture Studies Revolution: An Anthology of His Key Writings*, ed. Ben Urish (Jefferson, NC: McFarland & Company, Inc., 2011), 101.

6   Ray Browne, *Against Academia* (Bowling Green, OH: Bowling Green State University Popular Press, 1989), 16.

7   Alan Dundes, *Interpreting Folklore* (Bloomington: Indiana University Press, 1980), 6.

8   Warren E. Roberts, *Log Buildings of Sothern Indiana* (Bloomington, IN: Trickster Press, 1996), vii.

9   Ibid.

10 Browne, *Against Academia*, 24.

11 Russel Nye, *The Unembarrassed Muse: The Popular Arts in America* (New York: The Dial Press, 1970), 1–7.

12 Alan Taylor, "Occupy Wall Street," *The Atlantic*, September 30, 2011, http://www.theatlantic.com/photo/2011/09/occupy-wall-street/100159/.

13 Oxfam International, "An Economy for the 99%," January 16, 2017, https://www.oxfam.org/en/research/economy-99.

14 Ray Browne, "The Many Faces of American Culture: The Long Push to Democracy," in *Ray Browne on the Culture Studies Revolution: An Anthology of His Key Writings*, ed. Ben Urish (Jefferson, NC: McFarland & Company, Inc., 2011), 38–39.

15 This quote is often attributed to British philosopher Jeremy Bentham (1748–1832) and his writings on government.

16 Browne, "The Many Faces of American Culture," 39.

17 Stuart Hall, "Notes on Deconstructing 'The Popular,'" in *People's History and Socialist Theory*, ed. Raphael Samuel (New York: Routledge & Kegan Paul, 1981), 238.

18   Dan Ben-Amos, "Toward a Definition of Folklore in Context," in *Toward New Perspectives in Folklore*, ed. Americo Paredes and Richard Bauman (1972; repr., Bloomington, IN: Trickster Press, 2000), 14.

19   Ryan Wilson, "Richard Sherman: 'Thug' Is Accepted Way of Calling Someone N-Word," *CBSSports.com*, January 22, 2014, http://www.cbssports.com/nfl/news/richard-sherman-thug-is-accepted-way-of-calling-someone-n-word/.

2

Cultural Myths and the American Dream

The reason they call it the American Dream is because you have to be asleep to believe it.

—George Carlin

What is the "American Dream"? The concept is mentioned frequently, whether by our friends and family, or in politics and popular culture. Sometimes we see it as something we want to—and believe we can—achieve. Other times we criticize it or mock it, suggesting that this goal or belief that was once attainable and worthy of our desire is now dying or already dead. When you close your eyes, certainly you have your own picture of what this dream looks like. When I think of the American Dream, I still have the image of the perfect nuclear family in mind. I see a whitewashed and sterilized version of a generically handsome man with light brown hair and a light blue V-neck sweater in his early forties, a comparably attractive wife with shoulder length blond hair, wearing a modest yet flattering skirt and heels standing by his side. They're on the manicured front lawn of their newish suburban home. They've got an eight-year-old daughter, a smaller version of the mother, and a five-year-old son. They're all waving for some reason, as their proud golden retriever sits stoically at their side. Sometimes I add a pristine white picket fence, a shiny new hybrid SUV, and a backyard barbeque to this picture. Although this scene is clear in my mind, I'm not entirely sure where it came from, as I've never actually lived or viewed this image. It is, I suspect, an amalgamation of things I saw as a child: 1950s sitcom reruns of *Leave It to Beaver*; commercials for dish soap that aired during the day; glossy, colorful advertisements I saw when flipping through magazines or the Sunday paper; and billboards advertising new housing developments where there used to be fields of cows. No one showed me this exact image and said, "This is the American Dream." It's just something that I see, even if it is not necessarily something I want to see, when I'm asked to think about the American Dream.

Maybe this picture is similar to the one you envision when asked to think about the American Dream. Or, maybe it isn't like this at all. Perhaps you think more about the promise of the American Dream made to generations of migrants flooding the shores of the United States from the late nineteenth and into the early twentieth centuries. Your American Dream might be the one that describes America as a land of milk and honey, with streets lined with gold and opportunity abound for anyone willing to work hard enough. For many, the American Dream was or is a new beginning, an escape from famine, poverty, persecution, or war. Perhaps beyond the quest of the people looking to come to the United States to settle for a chance at a new and better life, you see the promise of the American Dream as important for all who already live here. Maybe it is the continued belief that if one works hard enough, no matter where they came from or the obstacles in their way, they too can achieve greatness. Hard work, we are told, equals success, and this opportunity is supposedly available for us all.

If none of this sounds right to you, no matter what you think people are trying to tell you about the American Dream, you may not see it as a valid possibility at all anymore, or maybe even ever. It could be that you've spent a lot of time scouring news sources reading about income inequality and the continued stratification of the socioeconomic classes, even beyond racial and regional lines. You may be confused as to how or why anyone would still be talking about the American Dream. And yet, despite these doubts, the American Dream as a concept surrounds us daily from political speeches and promises to popular culture representations of happy families to celebrity interviews, which invariably chronicle journeys from difficult childhoods to platinum albums and Super Bowl rings.

We see this narrative arc regularly in various media forms. These are what Jack Nachbar and Kevin Lause call myth narratives: the stories that express the fundamental belief in a myth and all of its associated ideologies. Popular culture is a great contributor of myth narratives broadly, and certainly in support of the American Dream. *The Blind Side, The Pursuit of Happyness*, fairy tales, and the life stories of figures like Oprah Winfrey and Steve Jobs are all narratives that rely on familiar tropes in demonstrating the power of the American Dream. We see these narratives on television, in theaters, in the news, and on social media regularly. Whether we acknowledge it or not, this common narrative arc of overcoming difficulties and working hard to achieve one's dreams in order to become successful (at least by our national standards) constantly surrounds us. While these narratives aren't hidden from us, they are not necessarily advertised or sold to the general public as a way of selling the continued belief in the American Dream. As audiences, we willingly buy into these narratives as they make us feel good and give us hope.

The question for all of us to ask, then, whether we believe in the American Dream or believe that such a dream is dead, is *why* does it exist? The answer to this question is at the heart of this chapter as we explore myth and the role that it plays in our contemporary society. This chapter foregrounds influential theories of myth and culture before continuing our discussion of the American Dream and its associated myths. In doing so, we introduce the concept of cultural myth as the means by which sign systems work within a culture to create narratives that situate and perpetuate ideology.

What is myth?

Since the time of ancient peoples, mythology, or myth, has been a part of culture. Just as the stories of Zeus and the gang helped the Ancient Greeks make sense of their world, so too does myth function for us today. While the stories we tell ourselves may not literally resemble those of classical mythology, a surprising number of the morals from these tales, as well as the dos and don'ts they prescribe, have filtered down through the ages. In that way, myth is imperceptible in its ability to shape our behaviors, yet is constantly around us, influencing us, and so close to us that we rarely, if ever, acknowledge it or think about it. According to Ray Browne, "The world has always been large and mysterious, and people's efforts to understand it have caused them to create an existence outside themselves."[1] This existence is myth.

In order to understand myth and its relationship to popular culture, we begin by considering the very early uses of myth, which were traditionally shared through oral performance. The oral transmission of myth is important as it unites the individuals who share in the tradition, making it a communal activity that serves a purpose of bringing people together. Key to this uniting of individuals into groups is the shared element of belief. It is this component of myth that, for our purposes, is the most important. Popular culture studies draws from the field of folklore in highlighting "the feature of orality, the community's belief factor in relationship to the myth, and the interpretive qualities that issued from the value the people placed on the myth."[2] Focusing on using the belief factor and interpretive qualities from the value placed on myth produces a more complex understanding. Myth is not something that is just false or about gods playing around and shaping the natural world as we know it. It is also more than stories being told for mere entertainment purposes. What is most characteristic and definitive of a myth is that it is believed, and that through the ways it infiltrates our lives, it gains value for those who believe it. Folklorist Alan Dundes stresses this understanding of myth in contrast to the term "folk idea," which refers to "traditional notions that a group of people have about the nature of man, of the world, and of man's life in the world."[3] Building off these distinctions, for our purposes we define **myth** as a shared belief in the symbolic representation of a culture's mindset, identity, and way of life.

In addition to folklore, our popular culture study of myth is also influenced by the theories of structuralism and semiotics. As its name suggests, structuralism is concerned with structures and the various ways in which the larger institutions of society assemble and shape meaning through social interaction. The focus on structure stresses *how* meaning is produced through cultural practices. Language is emphasized as one way of organizing and making sense of our reality. Related to this notion is **semiotics**, which is the study of sign systems. Swiss linguist Ferdinand de Saussure pioneered the field of semiotics through his study of the structure of language. Referring to it as semiology, Saussure is credited with bringing greater awareness to the deeper meanings of language. This is achieved by thinking about language as a series of signs that produce meaning through the ways in which they are arranged and structured.[4] If you think about language, there are few words that have a direct relationship to the object they represent. For example, right now there is a book in front of you. Is there anything at all in the letters B-O-O-K put together in that order to be written or spoken that would lead any person to naturally, without a learned knowledge of the English language, put that word and that object together? (The answer you hopefully came up with is "no.") Saussure refers to language as a "social institution," one that exists in society and follows an unspoken set of rules or guidelines that we agree to subscribe to and follow with or without our consent.[5] You could call the object in your hands anything you want other than "book," but unless others agree to it, no one is going to know or understand what you're talking about. The words and elements of language are there for our taking to use to express meaning, and what really matters is *how* all of these elements of language are put together. The words you choose, when you choose to use them, and how you use them is what makes meaning. In isolation, these elements are quite meaningless, but put together they wield a great deal of power.

This concept can be difficult if you've never thought about how arbitrary language is, so try this: imagine a jigsaw puzzle. Each one of those strangely shaped pieces does little on its own. If you sit down and begin to put pieces together, however, an image starts to become clear. When you look at this page, each of the words are pieces of a larger puzzle, chosen to be put together in a specific way to express to you a certain idea. This idea is an intangible thought; you can't see it or touch it. However, by giving structure to this idea through language and putting the idea into a book of printed words, you can read what has been written in order to understand the thoughts produced. The words themselves don't matter; it is the meaning that is created when the words are pieced together that matters. This meaning comes from the fact that we have a shared social system of language in place, one that gives shape to and helps us express our intangible thoughts. The words "dog" and "god" are comprised of the exact same letters, but the order in which they are arranged produces vastly different meanings. Structuralism looks at the arrangement and sum of these parts, at how the pieces of the puzzle go together, to demonstrate how larger structures working together produce meaning from differences within this system. Linguistically, Saussure did not use the term "structure," but rather considered language as a system of *langue* (the overall system of language and rules)[6] and *parole* (the manifestation of the system as speech).[7]

With respect to our study of myth, French anthropologist Claude Lévi-Strauss borrowed from Saussure in developing a structural approach to the study of human cultures, arguing that myth is our way of making sense of the world. Comparing myths from different cultures across the globe, he recognized many common elements. Lévi-Strauss deemed these elements relational, meaning that they share similarities or relationships. He was especially interested in the ways in which myths were structured through binaries of opposition, particularly the ways in which the natural or biological world influences cultural production. An example he uses to demonstrate this is the Oedipus myth, which centers on the doomed hero Oedipus who cannot escape the prophecy that he is destined to kill his father and marry his mother. Lévi-Strauss considers this myth in terms of the natural binary of "overrating" and "underrating" blood relations. Oedipus's marriage to his mother is an example of overrating; this is considered a biological and cultural relationship that should not exist between family matters. The killing of his own father, on the other hand, is an example of underrating, and is also something biologically and culturally taboo. The former shows a closeness that should not exist and the latter a distance.[8] Myth, then, is a structural link between natural and cultural order.

Another way to consider the structural link between nature and culture is through food. In Lévi-Strauss's *The Raw and the Cooked*, first volume of his set *Mythologiques*, he opens with:

> The aim of this book is to show how empirical categories—such as the categories of the raw and the cooked, the fresh and the decayed, the moistened and the burned, etc., which can only be accurately defined by ethnographic observation and, in each instance, by adopting the standpoint of a particular culture—can nonetheless be used as conceptual tools with which to elaborate abstract ideas and combine them in the form of propositions.[9]

Using cooking as an example of the shift from natural to cultural, what Lévi-Strauss's work suggests is that meaning is created through society's mediation between these two worlds. People of all cultures have an understanding of the world, but that meaning is abstract. As with our discussion of language, society works to turn these abstractions into something more concrete. Along with words and languages standing for these ideas or abstract understandings, we also add the level of myth. Myths are the stories that we, as humankind, have told ourselves to make sense of the world and its abstract forces. One of the easiest ways for us to understand anything is to say what it is not. Structuralism helps with this distinction because it provides the structure for these dichotomies. If something isn't raw, it is cooked. If something isn't good, it is bad. If something isn't right, it is wrong. Myths play with this simple balance of opposite forces to explain the world. Over the course of time, people put these elements together in a way that creates a narrative.

Let's pause here to think about this a bit more. You're going to have to use your imagination, and if you're doing this imagination thing correctly and really get into the ideas of Lévi-Strauss, it might get a little wild and mess with how you see the world. Just go with it. Let's imagine we don't live in the twenty-first century. We don't have globalization or technology, and we aren't constantly consumed with mediated information. In this fantasy, we don't have society the way we imagine it today; there is no science and/or religion to explain the world around us. It is like we are the first people on Earth. If none of our conceptions of the world exist and there is no recorded history of ideas and facts, the world would appear extremely confusing. An easy way to make sense of the things you see, the water and land, the plants and animals, the colors, would be to point out differences. In pointing out differences, you begin to make categories. Eventually you can start explaining these differences and these observations. You begin to give words and language to this sense-making. You create an interesting story to explain how things got to where they are and why the world is the way it is. In creating this story, you are better able to understand the world and can begin to construct your reality. It isn't that the meaning of the world is in the story you create. It is that the stories you create give you a way to see the world.

This system of understanding the world based on difference is the basis of Lévi-Strauss's use of myth. What all myths have in common, Lévi-Strauss claims, is the creation of a culture. Through this system of meaning-making, humankind leaves the realm of nature and enters into one of organized structure. Much of what he is concerned with in his work is the understanding of the purpose of culture and society. By noticing differences, we enter culture and leave some of our nature behind. Cooking our food, placing rules on the relationships we can or cannot have with family members, are all ways in which we give meaning to the things we do, creating culture from nature.

Building on the structuralist approach, French cultural theorist Roland Barthes expanded on the ideas of Saussure and Lévi-Strauss. While Barthes still considered myth to be a system of meaning and a way of communication, he updated it to be more relevant to the time period in which he was writing: the mid-1950s. Rather than talking about cultures from an anthropological perspective in a distant place or a removed past, he drew inspiration from the mass culture of his present day and location and examined topics such as the striptease, professional wrestling, Gretta Garbo's face, and Einstein's brain in his work *Mythologies*. Embedded in these topics are messages, which Barthes refers to as myth.

The concept of signification is key to Barthes's study of myth. Barthes explains that a sign is made up of two things: a signifier and a signified. The signifier is what we would usually, in common everyday language, refer to as a sign. It is something that is standing for something else. The thing that it is standing for is the signified. To go back to an example used before, the word "book" means the actual object book you're holding in your hand. Therefore, the word "book" is the signifier and the object in your hand is the signified. Put together, these two things make a sign. This is where Barthes is influenced by Saussure and linguistics.

According to Barthes, though, signs have two levels of signification: denotative and connotative. The denotative is the first-order process of the semiological system and refers to the literal meaning of the sign. Barthes argues that the sign of the first-order is also the signifier of a second-order semiological system. The second-order system is the connotative and is where mythological meaning occurs. So, using our book example (the word "book" combined with the object in your hand), that sign becomes the signifier for the signified concepts of education, knowledge, earning a degree, achieving the American Dream, and being successful. This second-order semiological system more closely resembles the connotative meaning. Connotations are the added cultural meanings that objects and ideas carry. Myth resides in this connotative second-order process of signification.[10]

The famous example that Barthes uses to explain this process is a rose.[11] In the first-order process of signification, the word "rose" denotes a flower. However, when you give someone a rose, there is usually more meaning behind it than just the transmission of a flower. You give someone a red rose (or a lot of red roses) to show love and passion. You give yellow roses to denote friendship. Black roses probably mean you aren't too happy with a person if you're taking your time to send them. Again, the letters R-O-S-E combined to form the word "rose" in order to describe a specific flower is arbitrary. There is nothing natural about the combination of these letters that suggests a fragrant, perennial flowering plant. Our understanding of "rose" is dependent upon our culture and its rules, as is the belief and acceptance we have of different color roses meaning different things. If we think about nearly anything in our culture, we can see the ways that we add meaning to those signifiers. Over time, the meaning we ascribe to them may change. We then communicate in a new language of myth. There are the words we say that mean certain things, but how we say them adds more significance. We don't think about how we are using these added meanings when we communicate with one another. Barthes states, "myth is experienced as innocent speech: not because its intentions are hidden—if they were hidden, they could not be efficacious—but because they are naturalized."[12] According to him, we aren't purposefully hiding meaning. Rather, it is so ingrained in our daily life that we fail to take notice. Myth is something that is learned as we live in a certain culture. This emphasis on the naturalization of myth is very important and key to what we will be discussing in the specific examples of cultural myths that follow.

To recap, myth is a believed symbolic representation of a culture's mindset, identity, and way of life. It comes from a need to make sense of the world using sign systems, such as language, that a culture has in place. By analyzing this, we can get a better and deeper understanding of culture and a society's worldview.

Myth and cultural studies

The theories of myth we have been discussing thus far fall in the realm of structuralism, which influenced a great deal of social thought in the 1950s and 1960s. By the end of the 1960s, however, post-structuralism was on the rise. As you can deduce, post-structuralism implies that which came after structuralism. Many theorists who defined the post-structuralist movement recognized that the world and our reality are messier than structuralism allows. We don't always follow set rules and patterns laid out for us. In rejecting the notion of a preexisting structure, post-structuralists find the binary opposites we talked about before too set and definitive. Jacques Derrida, who is sometimes referred to as the father of post-structuralism, saw binaries as more arbitrary than Saussure or structuralism acknowledges. Rather than pointing to any inherent meaning, Derrida argued that binaries instead reveal power differentials between ideas or groups; they are set up in order to favor one concept over another (good/bad, black/white, reason/emotions). Derrida was also concerned with the ways in which meaning is not only structurally dependent, but also temporally. That means that when communicating, we don't break down our messages into separate parts. Instead, post-structuralism recognizes the need to look at the whole system of communication and acknowledges how what we say changes in different contexts. Post-structuralism also recognizes that there are variations in interpretation, not only that the world isn't so black-and-white, but that there is the possibility for never-ending signifying chains of meaning. Over time, Barthes, who started out as a structuralist, added to his analysis of signs and signification and became more of a post-structuralist by recognizing the inability of any one person to know definitively the meaning of any sign. Instead, there could be many meanings for a sign, as meaning is a continual process. He began to argue that signs are polysemic; they signify multiple things at once.

Another structuralist-turned-post-structuralist is Michel Foucault. He tackled similar topics but instead of referring to it all as myth, he used the word **discourse**. We'll use the term "discourse" frequently throughout this text to refer to the ways in which the relationship between knowledge and power circulates in culture through speech and thought in order to exert control

Important to this definition and Foucault's approach, as opposed to some of the pure structuralists, is the emphasis on the relationship of power. Many of the meanings ascribed to certain signs, words, and objects directly relate to power: who has more power, who has less power, and how specific meanings maintain or disrupt power dynamics. Since power is involved and can change hands over time, meanings will change accordingly. Acknowledging this is important to the move to post-structuralism as well as to our understanding of myth and its relationship to popular culture.

In order to understand the relationship between myth and popular culture, we need to explore how power manifests itself and works in culture and society. **Ideology** is a helpful concept here as it refers to the beliefs, practices, and principles that inscribe meaning, wield power, and shape society through a collective adherence of shared values. During the early part of the twentieth century, **Marxist** theorists, in particular, were interested in the concepts of discourse and ideology and their relationships to power. Marxism is concerned with labor and class differences in capitalist societies, particularly the disparities between the bourgeoisie (essentially the upper-class elites) and the proletariat (the lower class made of up of laborers). Between these two classes is the petite bourgeoisie (the middle class who had a little more independence but modeled themselves more like the upper class). In crude Marxist theory, the bourgeoisie have more power because they have more money, and the proletariat is at their mercy because they work for the bourgeoisie. When viewed through these simple economic terms, the bourgeoisie have a lot invested in keeping the status quo because they are the beneficiaries of the system. It works to even more of their advantage if they can keep workers, but pay them less, as there is greater potential for the bourgeoisie to increase their profits. Of course then, as now, "money talks," so those with money in the bourgeoisie would conceivably have more say when it comes to government and policy.

Antonio Gramsci, an Italian Marxist, wrote a great deal about ideology and its place in the political history of Italy and Europe while imprisoned during the fascist regime of Benito Mussolini. Gramsci is credited with the revival of the term **hegemony** to help explain his critique. Hegemony, from Gramsci's perspective, is a form of social control where those in power maintain their authority. While this is sometimes done forcefully, through military states, it is mostly achieved through consent and coercion. Ideology is key in this consent and coercion, and myths often work in tandem with ideology. Myth isn't just about meaning and understanding culture, but is, more importantly, about understanding culture in terms of power. Myth can be used as a tool of hegemony in support of the ideologies that continue the power and order of established institutions. Social **institutions**—such as the government, the military, education, marriage, and health care—are systems, organizations, or practices linked to established bodies of power. Taking into consideration the relationships of power, ideology, and social institutions gives us a different lens through which to study myth. Popular culture serves as a site of struggle between these different institutions and power dynamics. The myths that circulate as a part of popular culture, then, are tools for us to examine not only in terms of what they mean, but how they affect our mindset and reflect larger power structures. Through myth, popular culture becomes a staging ground for the constant battle to uphold and support these systems of power, while at the same time pointing out their weaknesses and inspiring in us a desire to change.

Deconstructing the American Dream

Let's return to the myth of the American Dream. Even if you're not convinced of its attainability, it is still an idea that as a nation we work to uphold. Perception of the vitality of the American Dream among Americans is popular fodder for polls and articles in mainstream news sources. Whichever way one wants to spin the strength of the American Dream, there is supporting data on both sides of the equation. For example, a 2015 poll conducted by CBS' *60 Minutes* and *Vanity Fair* shows that 44 percent (the highest of all categories given) of those polled say that "giving your kids a better life" best describes the American Dream. With this description in mind, 60 percent of those polled said they are living a better life than their parents' generation, while only 39 percent think that "today" is the closest the American Dream has come to its peak.[13] According to these numbers, we aren't doing too badly individually, even if less than half of those questioned think as a nation we have come close to achieving the American Dream. Another popular media source, Fox News, shows that many Americans (59 percent of those polled) believe they are better off than their parents' generation. Yet, if we're using the measure of leaving a better life for our children, then we are failing, with 61 percent of those polled stating we are *not* on track to giving a better life to the next generation.[14] Of course, polls like this are limited in what they tell us and are not representative of all people in the nation. The popularity of these types of polls, however, and the consistency of results among the various sources suggest a general trend about the American Dream. Overall, people think that as a nation we're on a path of decline in the likelihood of achieving what has been traditionally considered the American Dream. On an individual level, though, people are still hopeful and positive. Anecdotally, this might match the general consensus one encounters when having conversations about this with friends and family. There seems to be an understanding that as a nation we have many challenges today, particularly with respect to the lingering effects of the recession, rising income inequality, and the disappearing middle class, and that these challenges are making it so that the American Dream as we know it might truly become unobtainable. Even with an awareness of these trends, though, most of us think as long as we keep working hard enough, we'll be fine. Maybe this is how you feel. You're probably working toward an end goal of graduation, having been told that in order to get a good job, you need to go to college and get an education. Even though you might have said you didn't believe in the American Dream, your actions suggest that to a certain extent you subscribe to the conventions of it. And this, my friend, is because of myth. Whether we are buying it or not, the myth of the American Dream is sold to us again and again. Even if you understand on some level that movies with happy endings of love, family, and success in one's chosen occupation are designed as escapes in order to make us feel good, we still do experience that emotional rush. Feeling good is the reward that keeps taking us back to the cinema, Netflix, or our favorite television shows each week.

How does this connect to the rest of what we've been discussing in this chapter, though? The institutions in the United States that have been put in place all serve a very specific purpose. Social institutions maintain order and separate us from the disorganized chaos of nature. Through discourse, there are social messages about the government, economy, religion, education, and family, and much of these messages have to do with what we should and should not do: be productive, be nice, don't kill, and don't steal. These ideologies are directly connected to the myth of the American Dream and work in support of our social institutions. We must abide by laws, follow a moral code, learn what is deemed necessary in school in order to get jobs and pay taxes, and keep this dream alive by starting our own families. The narrative of this myth circulates throughout popular culture—with smaller cultural myths such as those of true love, the ideal of the nuclear family, the rise from rags to riches, and hard work equaling success—all working to uphold social institutions and moral order.

Take, for example, the institution of our government, which runs on the ideology of democracy. A democracy is a government of the people. Within a democratic state is the purported belief in equality and equal opportunity. As such, democracy stands for the greater good mounted on the belief that what is greatest for the greatest number of people is ideal. We strive for this in our government by splitting it up into local, state, and federal levels and having three separate branches: the executive, legislative, and judicial. The presumption is that this guarantees that no one person, or select people, holds too much power. Even though we don't all serve as government officials, we get to participate in democracy as voters. This is why state and local elections are so important; you are voting for the people who will best represent you and your interests and shape how the government works and the policies voted in place.

While democracy speaks to the greater good, our capitalist economic system correlates more to individual success. Capitalism is a system of free enterprise and private ownership, with a focus on private and individual profit rather than on the state and federal governments. So while our government is a democracy, capitalism is the ideology that influences the economic system of the United States. The emphasis on capitalism and the drive for wealth result in measuring success through accumulating money and acquiring goods. Success, then, is expressed through material possessions when the American Dream is understood as the promise of comfort and happiness achieved through profit and economic gains.

When viewed in this way, it is easier to see how the cultural myth of the American Dream supports national ideologies that justify and maintain established social institutions. The notion that "hard work equals success" supports and promotes capitalism when success is measured by what we own and how much money we have accrued. Using this logic on a national level, a robust capitalist economy is necessary for the United States to maintain its position as one of the strongest and richest nations in the world. Although not all countries are capitalist, the principles of capitalism drive the global economy, and therefore determine the measure by which nations stay competitive. This national imperative filters down into our everyday lives through our current cultural obsession with "busyness." We are "so busy" as a nation, even toddlers keep a tight schedule of play dates and structured activities. Busy-bragging (a close cousin to the equally odious humble-brag) promotes and upholds a culture of productivity and hard work. Our nation was founded on an ideology of the Protestant work ethic that, over time, has dropped the element of Protestant salvation in favor of the gods of capitalism. As *Wall Street*'s Gordon Gekko, played by Michael Douglas, famously said, "Greed, for lack of a better word, is good." And it is this greed that keeps us very busy working very hard.

Yet, even though we are working harder than ever, it seems that fewer and fewer of us have attained the American Dream. So, what gives? Here's where hegemony is useful to our analysis. Those who benefit most from our collective belief in the American Dream are those who are already in power. Since power is measured by wealth, the people in power in the United States are usually those with the most money and who run big business, control media, and form super PACs that sway government. A hegemonic criticism of the American Dream that correlates to the often-bemoaned "the rich get richer and the poor get poorer" could be that subordinate groups, in this case average American citizens, are controlled by the promise of the American Dream. Although individuals are working harder and harder for something that may or may not be attainable, the actual beneficiaries of that hard work are the government, economy, and corporations who profit from both our hard work and our spending. We may be working harder and harder, but we aren't necessarily getting more and more, though someone is.

Another way that dominant groups maintain their power over subordinate groups is through debt. In order to make money one needs to have a job, and in the United States today, the jobs that make the most money tend to require a college degree. According to the *60 Minutes* and *Vanity Fair* poll mentioned earlier, 47 percent of people polled responded that the best way to achieve the American Dream is to attend college.[15] One thing many of us know is that college is expensive and people go into significant debt in order to cover the cost of tuition. As more people earn college degrees, it is increasingly common for people to find it helpful to continue their education beyond the standard four-year bachelor's degree and pursue advanced professional or graduate degrees. Again, most often the drive for this education is not knowledge unto itself, but the desire to guarantee a higher level of income and standard of living. The accouterments of the American Dream such as a beautiful house, exotic vacations, and the latest electronics cost significant amounts of money. Rarely are these purchases paid for in cash. Instead, most often this lifestyle is financed through mortgages, car loans, and credit card debt. These finance options, as with student loans, all come with accompanying interest. The interest rates available not only depend on one's individual credit score, but also on financial institutions and banks such as the Federal Reserve, a system of the federal government. Individuals who carry debt are fiscally at the mercy of those to whom they owe money. This debt gives lending institutions a degree of power over the average American, adding to the institutional structures of power in place here in the United States.

In addition to the government and economy, there are other institutions that support the overarching myth of the American Dream. If we think back to the description of the American Dream that opened this chapter, you'll remember that family was key to this image. The picture of family that was presented— mother, father, and children—is the heteronormal ideal. **Heteronormativity** is discussed in detail in Chapter 7, but for the purposes of this chapter, we want to consider how this ideology works in support of the American Dream. Heteronormativity is the belief that sexual relations between men and women is the biological ideal as the two sexes serve to complement each other, and that marriage is the logical conclusion of this sexual pairing. Religion is often cited as the defense against same-sex couples and the strides taken and made for marriage equality. The protection of the institution of marriage and definitions of what constitutes a family tend to follow the standards of heteronormativity. A cultural myth in support of heteronormativity and the institutions of family and religion is the myth of true love. Starting with the fairy tales of childhood and their promise of one true love's kiss, this myth is presented to us from a very young age. We will be happy when we find our soul mate, the one person who completes us and makes us feel ways no one else ever has. This message of true love is sold over and over again in popular media, from romance novels to the music played on Top 40 radio. These narratives of "happily ever after" create the language that we use when we describe dating, marriage, and eternal happiness. We are sold this version of love over and over again, but why?

Monogamy is the practice of having only one mate at a time, preferably for life as solidified through marriage. While this type of mating does happen in nature, it isn't very common and there is no biological basis for it in human beings. Despite this lack of biological necessity, we have made monogamy very important to American culture. The myth of one true love supports monogamy and, along with the institutions of religion and family, helps maintain social order. Defining marriage as legitimate only when between a man and woman has the explicit purpose of privileging procreation as its primary purpose. Children, in turn, become the vehicle by which wealth and status are passed on from one generation to the next, upholding established power bases. Further, proclaiming through the institution of marriage that people are meant to be together until death do they part emphasizes the importance of small, independent groups of people (more commonly referred to as families) that support one another. Families, then, create stability in what could easily be seen as chaos and help maintain society through social order.

When viewed this way, we can see how myths work to create the current American society in which we live. Myth supports our institutions, ideologies, and ways of life and, in doing so, shapes our mindset. **Mindset** can be conceived of in two ways: it is the habits and beliefs that shape the way an individual sees the world, as well as the larger attitudes and behaviors of a culture. Each of us can have our own mindset, our personal way of seeing the world. It comes from how we were raised, what we experienced, and how these influences shape our own individual realities. Beyond our personal mindsets, there are also cultural mindsets made up of the myths and ideologies of a particular society in a particular place and time. The American mindset is different from the mindsets of other nations and oftentimes mindsets can lead to very serious conflict, even war. The American Dream as we often envision it today is modeled after the picture perfect 1950s Cold War–era United States. As the two super powers emerging from the Second World War, the United States and the Soviet Union were in a war of mindsets represented by the ideologies of democracy and capitalism in the United States and communism in the Soviet Union. At that time, people in the United States were being encouraged to get an education (with the G. I. Bill making it possible for many former servicemen); buy a new house (spurring the growth of suburban housing developments); furnish new households with modern appliances, home furnishings, and a car in the driveway (all available on credit); and start families (introducing the Baby Boomer generation). As opposed to the Soviet Union, the United States became more and more "American" and defined exactly what that meant— democratic and capitalist—as opposed to communist.

Our current War on Terror resulted in a reexamination of the American Dream in ways similar to the ideological schism of the Cold War. The tragic events of 9/11, the rise of ISIS, and the current unrest in the Middle East are extreme examples of the lengths individuals and groups will go to in defense of ideology. While religion is a key element in these conflicts, a number of other ideological factors, including democracy and capitalism, are also at play. It is not surprising, then, that one of the initial government responses after 9/11 was to ensure a "continued participation and confidence in the American economy."[16]

The comparison of the American mindset to that of our political enemies works to reinforce and further establish what being an American means. It is made up of our belief in the American Dream, romantic love, hard work as equal to success, and success measured through material gain. These beliefs support our ideologies of heteronormativity, democracy, and capitalism, and, therefore, strengthen our institutions in order to maintain the status quo. These beliefs are second nature and the process of naturalization of them begins at a very young age.

Child's play and the American Dream

We as citizens of the United States consent to this way of living because it is naturalized through the structures of "normal" life—the government, education system, our financial institutions—and is represented to us through popular media. Those who have power tend to maintain power, but rarely do we question this authority, in part due to our belief that we are living in the greatest nation in the world. This belief is not specific to the United States (no country's slogan is "We're Number Two!"), as **nationalism** is both pride in one's country and the ways in which nations work to achieve or maintain their national identity and status globally. Instilling a sense of national pride in citizens begins at an early age, from overt practices such as requiring students to recite the Pledge of Allegiance in school each morning, to the youthful pastimes of popular culture. Like apple pie or the Fourth of July, few things exemplify the wholesomeness of American values quite like the Boy Scouts of America. With their motto to "always be prepared," they appear to embody all that is good, moral, and decent in America's youth culture. Although not explicitly tied to these values, the Boy Scouts tend to represent the best and brightest of Christian, white, middle-class America.

The Boy Scouts began as a British youth movement in 1907. Although other youth-centered organizations for young males, such as the Boys Brigade, were already in existence, none equaled the quickly rising numbers or popularity of the Boys Scouts. Its founder, Lord Robert Baden-Powell, worried about the effects of increasing urbanization and industrialization, conceived of an organization that would bring boys back to the outdoors, while instilling in them a sense of duty and honor that would mold them into upstanding British citizens. The rise of the Boy Scouts in Britain coincided with the beginning of the end of the British Empire. As such, the early years of scouting were heavily influenced by imperialist ideals. In its formative years, scouting was very much tied up with British-ness, and was used as a way to instill British culture throughout the colonies.

As scouting spread, each nation adapted the model to its own culture and ideologies. The Boy Scouts of America was founded in 1910 with the Girl Scouts of America quickly following in 1912, along with the institution's growing importance to our nation's understanding of American values. In a radio address from 1935, US president Franklin Roosevelt spoke on the vital importance of the Boy Scouts to the nation, stating,

> The success of that Constitution is dependent on the attitude of mind and
> the degree of the spirit of unselfish cooperation that can be developed in

individuals. Scouting is essentially and clearly a program for the development of that unselfish, cooperative attitude of mind. Scouting revolves around, not the theory of service to others, but the habit of service to others. Scouting makes the individual boy conscious of his obligation to his patrol, to his troop, to his community, to his State and to his nation.[17]

As seen by Roosevelt's words, in just a little over twenty years of existence, this popular childhood activity was positioned as a vital organization in the molding of upstanding US citizens, with Roosevelt suggesting it almost unconstitutional to not be a scout. Through its laws, badges, and songs, scouting perpetuates a notion of tradition that infuses childhood activities with specific national values and ideals in ways that are fun for children.

The popular culture of a country's youth is more than just child's play. Consider, for example, the recent popularity of dystopian texts such as *The Hunger Games* and *Divergent*. For children born and coming of age in the twenty-first century, their youth and mindsets are informed by terrorism, ongoing war, domestic mass shootings, and a twenty-four-hour news cycle that provides them with unending coverage of these atrocities. Even those Americans born during the relative peace and prosperity of the 1990s entered adulthood during the worst recession in recent US history. Although not quite as bad as a zombie attack, college grads during this time faced a bleak job market with high levels of unemployment plaguing the nation. With such an uncertain future, it is no wonder dystopian fiction dominated popular culture during this time.

Take, for example, the case of Carl Grimes. He's the son of Rick Grimes, the main character on AMC's popular post-zombie apocalypse series *The Walking Dead*, which is based on the Image Comics series created by Robert Kirkman and Tony Moore. If you are not a fan of Carl, you are most definitely not alone. The character of Carl, especially during the early seasons of the series, was highly unpopular with viewers, so much so that there were social media sites dedicated to hating this character and wishing for his death. One of the very few children on the show, Carl's unpopularity stems from his weakness as a character. In early seasons he isn't as capable, strong, brave, or intelligent as the adults with whom he travels. As the weakest link, he often puts the rest of the group in unnecessary danger. He is, after all, just a kid. Before the world was taken over by zombies, his life mirrored that of an average American adolescent. An only child, he lives with his parents in rural, fictional King Country, Georgia. He goes to school every day, listens to his parents and follows their rules, abides by the law (his dad is sheriff, after all), and is at least culturally Christian following the tenets of morality and right and wrong. At the start of the series he exists as a normal pre-teen, adhering to society's guidelines and rules, having enjoyed a relatively carefree, happy, middle-class, wholesome childhood.

Up to this point, you may be able to identify with Carl. Until, of course, zombies are added into the mix, infecting most of the population of the United States, transitioning them into the flesh-eating eponymous "walking dead." Pandemonium is the obvious result, with everything that everyone thinks they know about the world and how it works no longer applying. Carl and the rest of the surviving children stop going to school, and many of them are orphaned. Nationally, the government and all law enforcing agencies disintegrate, and religious beliefs and faith in a higher power dissolve. Carl's world goes from one of order and rules to one of chaos and basic survival. The institutions put in place to maintain society crumble, forcing the survivors to re-learn how to live. During this transition, it quickly becomes apparent how easy it is for the children to begin killing in order to recalibrate right and wrong, something the adults don't get the hang of so quickly. The adults, who have lived far longer following the mindset of America as we know it, still have faith in the system of order to which we are accustomed. They work to institute rules and laws and try to impose a traditional education on the children. Many of them still also hold onto the religion and beliefs they had before the zombie attack.

While *The Walking Dead* follows the transition from order to chaos and attempts to rebuild the world before being completely devastated, other dystopian texts like *The Hunger Games* and *Divergent* focus on adolescents living in a post-apocalyptic world that has already regained some type of order, albeit an order that is highly restrictive and unjust. Katniss from *The Hunger Games* and Tris from *Divergent* differ from Carl in that they don't have to adjust to a changing world. They already exist in an altered society, one that is less than ideal and in need of a revolution. The ultimate promise of these texts is the triumph of democracy and return to the freedoms we value and enjoy today. It may seem odd to end a chapter on the American Dream with these dystopian nightmares, but these stories of survival not only offer hope to audiences—particularly those dealing with the anxieties of entering adulthood during troubled times—but also work to maintain the ideologies, myths, and mindset of our nation in the face of uncertainties.

Conclusion

The next chapter will go into greater detail into **genre**, and the ways in which it functions through popular culture to track and respond to shifts in cultural anxieties. In order to do this, though, it was first important to explore the concept of myth, not only in terms of its popular culture expressions, but also its broader relationship to the institutions, values, and beliefs that shape our nation. As we discussed, myths such as hard work equaling success and true love conquering all support the larger myth of the American Dream. These myths are circulated through popular culture and work to uphold and justify national values such as democracy and capitalism, while maintaining the order and structure of our society.

Notes

1   Ray B. Browne, "Myths," in *Profiles of Popular Culture: A Reader*, ed. Ray B. Browne (Madison: The University of Wisconsin Press, 2005), 13.

2   Trudier Harris-Lopez, "Genre," in *Eight Words for the Study of Expressive Culture*, ed. Burt Feintuch (Chicago: University of Illinois Press, 2003), 104.

3   Alan Dundes, "Folk Ideas as Units of Worldview," in *Toward New Perspectives in Folklore*, ed. Americo Paredes and Richard Bauman (1972; repr., Bloomington, IN: Trickster Press, 2000), 123.

4   Ferdinand de Saussure, *Course in General Linguistics*, ed. Charles Bally and Albert Sechehaye, trans. Wade Baskin (New York: The Philosophical Library, 1959), 15.

5   Ibid.

6   Ibid., 9.

7   Ibid., 13.

8   Claude Lévi-Strauss, "The Structural Study of Myth," *The Journal of American Folklore* 68, no. 270 (1955): 432–34.

9   Claude Lévi-Strauss, *The Raw and the Cooked: Mythologiques Volume 1*, trans. John and Doreen Weightman (1969; repr., Chicago: The University of Chicago Press, 1983), 1.

10 Roland Barthes, *Mythologies*, trans. Annette Lavers (New York: Hill and Wang, 1972), 114.

11 Ibid., 113.

12 Ibid., 131.

13 "60 Minutes/Vanity Fair Poll: The American Dream," *CBS News*, April 6, 2015, http://www.cbsnews.com/news/60-minutesvanity-fair-poll-the-american-dream/.

14 "Fox News Poll: The American Dream Is Alive—For Now," *Fox News*, October 23, 2014, http://www.foxnews.com/politics/2014/10/23/fox-news-poll-american-dream-is-alive-for-now.html?intcmp=latestnews.

15 "60 Minutes/Vanity Fair Poll."

16 George W. Bush, "Address to the Joint Session of the 107th Congress," *Selected Speeches of President George W. Bush*, https://georgewbush-whitehouse.archives.gov/infocus/bushrecord/documents/Selected_Speeches_George_W_Bush.pdf.

17 Franklin D. Roosevelt, "Address to the Boy Scouts of America and Some Observations on the Constitution," *National Public Radio*, August 21, 1935.

3

Genre

I try not to discriminate against genres.

—Ryan Gosling, Internet Meme

It's a Sunday night, and faced with the prospect of getting ahead on your homework for the week or catching up on the latest Netflix release, you grab your laptop and settle in. Maybe you're the kind of guy who's into "Critically-acclaimed Emotional Drug Movies," or a gal who is into "Raunchy TV Comedies Featuring a Strong Female Lead." Either way, you're in luck; both of these categories are included in the over 76,000 "micro-genres" offered by Netflix. Perhaps you're more studious than your Netflix-watching peers and instead grab your calculus textbook and pop on Pandora before settling in with some integrals. Rest assured, there are multiple stations for "Studying" available to help you get in the zone. Looking to do some reading for pleasure instead? Well, what's your fancy—mystery? Romance? Dystopian science fiction? Your Kindle app can quickly help you find what you are looking for. It seems that no matter what our pleasure, popular culture is there to offer us a variety of texts set to fulfill whichever emotional release we desire, as well as increasingly easier ways to find exactly the song/film/book we never even knew we needed. While the algorithms and "science" behind genre nowadays are often tied to marketing and the goal of delivering audiences for the highest profits, the study of genre and its role in society goes much farther back than this.

The earliest studies of genre date back to Ancient Greek poetry and drama. In *Poetics*, Aristotle sets off to conceptualize "Poetry in itself and of its various kinds, noting the essential quality of each; to inquire into the structure of the plot as requisite to a good poem; into the number and nature of the parts of which a poem is composed; and similarly into whatever else falls within the same inquiry."[1] While his use of the term "poetry" might throw you, it's helpful to consider that the origins of this word are "to make" or "create." With this in mind, we can see that Aristotle was concerned with the essential qualities of artistic creation and how, in turn, we might group different creative products. All of the "poems" or artistic creations in the same group would have common characteristics; they could follow the same type of plot, have the same types of heroes and characters, exhibit the same types of thoughts and emotions, and have the same style of diction. As the original genres of tragedy and comedy were developed, "the two classes of poets still followed their natural bent: the lampooners became writers of Comedy, and the Epic poets were succeeded by Tragedians, since the drama was a larger and higher form of art."[2] From these earliest distinctions it is apparent that genre carries with it not only a means to classify, but also serves as a measure of taste, with certain forms valued over others. Genre, then, not only helps to distinguish different cultural products from each other, but also feeds into other larger cultural categories of definition, success, and distinction.

While Netflix and Pandora certainly weren't what Aristotle had in mind in *Poetics*, the concept of genre is one that has existed for some time as a means to sort and categorize works of art and products of culture. For the purposes of our study, in this chapter we discuss **genre** as a contract between popular culture producers and consumers, with certain expectations on each side of the equation that adapt and shift in response to historical, ideological, and cultural contexts. Producers must think about what audiences want and expect, deliver on that, and in the process perpetuate cultural values or accommodate significant cultural shifts and changes. Much like the cultural myths discussed in the last chapter, in this chapter we will discuss different genre theories before exploring in detail some current genre trends. By the end of this chapter, you will be able to recognize the ways in which genres share thematic and stylish properties and their relationship to collective cultural expectations.

Genre theory

Despite literary theorist Northrop Frye's 1957 claim, "the critical theory of genre is stuck precisely where Aristotle left it," genres, and the theories behind their development, have gone in a number of directions.[3] The study of folklore, for example, depends heavily on the classification of creative output. Using what has been compared to "butterfly collecting," early folklore scholars set out to collect tales, traditions, folk art, and other forms of folklore expression. By pointing out the similarities in these types of expression, folklorists could trace similarities, beliefs, and even movements of people. Finnish folklorist Antii Aarne's work, added to by American folklorist Stith Thompson, led to the creation of the Aarne-Thompson Tale-Type Index and Thompson's *Motif-Index of Folk Literature*. These indexes have, and continue to serve, those interested in the study of folklore. By indexing all of the various tale types and motifs that occur in traditional folklore stories, from "witch as stepmother" to "slipper test," folklorists were able to point out similarities in tales all over the world. These similarities help to categorize folklore and connect various groups of people while teaching universal themes of right or wrong, the goal of early folklore studies. Russian folklorist Vladimir Propp also studied the structure and makeup of folk tales in his important work *Morphology of the Folk Tale*. In this work, Propp examined the structure of traditional folk tales pointing out the characteristics they all share. In this sense of early folklore scholarship, the importance of recognizing similarities was to classify all of the folklore texts collected. Once these could be categorized into various types, structures, and forms, patterns would emerge and help to point to deeper implications of the meaning buried in the texts and lives of the individuals sharing them.

In addition to the structuralist approach to genre used in folklore studies, early literary approaches to genre were rhetorical in the sense that "the genre is determined by the conditions established between the poet and his public."[4] In other words, this is the contract of shared expectations referred to in our definition of genre, and the purpose of exploring these expectations and conditions is "not so much to classify as to clarify such traditions and affinities," in order to expose relationships between textual elements that would not necessarily be noticed without the proper established context.[5]

The foundational literary criticisms of genre focused on what Frye referred to as traditional genres of epos, fiction, drama, and lyric. Most likely these are not the genres you immediately think of when browsing through Barnes & Nobel or Amazon.com. Increased literacy rates in the early twentieth century, along with technological developments in printing, led to mass-marketed pulp fiction, "dime novels," mysteries, and romances that paved the way for the contemporary literary genres with which you are most likely familiar. As with Aristotle's distinction of tragedy over comedy, these popular fictions are often considered inferior to Literature. Literature, in this elevated sense, fits the definition of elite culture in that it speaks to elevated social status and education. This distinction contributed to the inferior status of what was termed "popular culture," as it was more accessible to those with less education and status. This stigma of popular literature was, in part, because of their mass appeal and formulaic plots and constructions.

Distinguishing between genre and formula is a good starting point to our analysis of popular culture texts. While these two terms are often regarded as interchangeable, it is more appropriate to regard them as two distinct steps in a particular method of textual study. If, at its most basic, genre is a combination of conventions and inventions,[6] then formula is the structure of specific conventions and inventions utilized by a body of similar works. Genres are not static, but rather evolve over time. Conventions are the recurring elements that appear in the bodies of work that make up a genre, and are often referred to as the genre's semantics. The structures in which the semantics are arranged are the genre's syntax.[7] Character types and **icons** (settings, props, costumes) are the visible semantics that build genre as they acquire meaning through repeated use.

To explore these terms, consider *The Bachelor*. This show has been a popular ABC staple since its premier in 2002. Each season is the same in that there is an eligible bachelor, a variety of eligible bachelorettes, a series of humiliating competitions, and silly group dates. Each episode culminates in a rose ceremony where those women who receive roses get to remain for a chance at love, while those who don't are sent packing. Eventually through these eliminations, one woman remains. The icons that have become familiar for the show over the course of its many seasons are the house where they all live, the exotic locations they visit, the trips to visit the families of the finalists, the use of the rose to mean opportunity and love, and the bachelor character choosing between his many types of bachelorettes, who all fit different stereotypes. Putting all of these together makes up the syntax of each episode and the season as a whole while reinforcing the theme of romantic love between two people. As exhibited with *The Bachelor* example, the textual and symbolic meanings associated with generic conventions accumulate over time and repeated use. The rose, as a symbol of love, means another opportunity at love, while the visit with the parents represents a level of intimacy and connection between the individuals.

However, not everything stays the same. Inventions are added over time in order to keep the genre fresh and current within a contemporary context. As genres evolve, many inventions become formalized and incorporated into subsequent texts, becoming conventions themselves. For example, *The Bachelorette* began in 2003 as an attempt to challenge the forced patriarchy of the original show. Rather than showing a man dating multiple women, it showed a woman dating multiple men at the same time. Though reinforcing the image of ideal love as being between one man and one woman, it flipped the double standard on its head. Soon after, other networks picked up on the conventional formula of this dating reality television show and, using inventions, altered it to appeal to different audiences. VH1's several seasons of *Flavor of Love* featured Flavor Flav of the rap group Public Enemy as he dated multiple women. Rather than a rose, he presented them with an iconic large-faced clock on a chain (for which he was famous) if he wanted them to stay. Soon after, Bret Michaels of the rock band Poison got his own version of a dating reality show with multiple seasons of *Rock of Love*. Since roses were already taken, and he wasn't known for something as iconic as clock necklaces, Bret presented his would-be loves with backstage passes if he wanted them to continue on for a chance at being his one and only. Women from each of these shows also got their own spin-off shows. Not to be outdone, MTV further changed the genre with *A Shot at Love with Tila Tequila,* which featured a bisexual woman who had both men and women vying for her affection in order to receive a key at the elimination ceremony at the end of each episode.

Looking at the structure of formula, genres are interpreted not necessarily by what they say, but rather *how* they say it through repeated elements or conventions. John Cawelti, an early scholar who championed both the academic study of popular culture and the study of popular genre fiction, distinguished between genre and formula as follows:

> Genre can be defined as a structural pattern that embodies a universal life pattern or myth in the materials of language. Formula, on the other hand is cultural; it represents the way in which a culture has embodied both mythical archetypes and its own preoccupations in narrative form.[8]

Producers and audiences have shared expectations regarding genres, and genres evolve and emerge over time as a way for media industries to reach populations by producing texts that have, in a sense, already been proven to be successful (hence, the number of sequels, reboots, film adaptations of popular novels, and pretty much anything coming out of the Marvel Universe). Formulas tap into these expectations, drawing from previous archetypes or conventions while simultaneously confirming current beliefs. Shows like *The Bachelor, The Bachelorette,* and all other reality dating shows pick up on the larger theme of love. We are all told we need love and that finding it with "the one" is the mission on which we should dedicate our time and energy. Within this genre, that quest for love stands above all else; this quest is at the heart of the genre.

However, the fact that formula is more cultural rather than universal suggests that it succumbs to changes and fluctuations in culture. While love may be a universal concept, finding love in the United States today with high divorce rates, increased cynicism, and looking at it like a competition has changed that quest significantly. The formula of the genre has changed to accommodate that. By working within the bounds of formula, conventions provide the necessary structure, while inventions work to perpetuate the genre and are the basic differences required to make texts unique. In competitive dating reality television shows, through the many adaptations of the "date and eliminate" formula, semantics, such as the people, actual dates, and the icons given to stand for another opportunity at love, have to change. These minor inventions are vital to a show's success because they keep audiences interested and the show current. From changing the bachelor from a no-name "normal" person to a celebrity like Flavor Flav or Bret Michaels, producers can attract different audiences. Rather than watching the show really expecting to see two people fall in love, audiences can watch to laugh at the ridiculous antics of has-been celebrities.

In addition to their practical necessity, conventions and inventions also maintain a second level of significance with respect to culture. In their recognizability and persistence, conventions work to maintain and uphold values in society. Where conventions validate existing cultural beliefs, inventions provide new insight while allowing genres to conform and respond to ideological shifts. Formulas, then, become the way in which conventions and inventions are structured to fit cultural needs. Looking at the evolution of genres, therefore, is useful in tracking shifting cultural ideals from one time period to another. The dating shows switching to celebrities, particularly a bisexual woman, demonstrate cultural shifts. Rather than being asked to conceptualize love as being between a man and women, *A Shot at Love with Tila Tequila* says that love could actually be between two women. More and more reality television shows are switching from this more traditional sense of love and embracing the many ways love can look and be expressed between diverse individuals spanning from same-sex couples to polyamorous relationships.

Although formulas are instrumental in making a text popular, the reliance on formula is often one way in which critics denounce generic texts as artistically weak, unoriginal, and/or insignificant as compared to "high" art, which often maintains the unique view of its author while utilizing sophisticated stylized elements of production. A counterargument to this, of course, is an emphasis on how "genre creativity is defined by exactly that manipulation of past motifs to create new work."[9] Taking a stale and repeatable formula and updating it for new audiences, new times, cultural changes, and leaving viewers and consumers surprised is an art form itself. Weird Al Yankovic has been taking popular songs spanning four decades and parodying them. His genius isn't in creating a brand new song each time, but rather in taking an existing song structure and creatively changing the lyrics. It isn't brand new, but it is still creative, new, and serves a different purpose than the original song.

Rather than stress character development or overarching themes, motifs, and metaphors, formulaic works focus on a cyclic sense of excitement, suspense, and gratification. In this way, they encourage audiences to "participate ritualistically in the basic beliefs, fears, and anxieties of their age."[10] The sense of excitement and suspense is mediated by formulaic structures and conventions, and any anxiety felt is therefore not real; the reader/viewer is always confident there will be a resolution. Similarly, any sense of gratification felt through the enjoyment of these popular texts is in many ways false, since there is no actual apprehension. Therefore, by offering no genuine resolution to the real-life situations that provide the need for escapism in the first place, the need remains, perpetuating the genre cycle. For example, *The Bachelor* can exist for over twenty seasons because of the emotional roller-coaster that is each episode and season. While the audience will have favorites for the eligible bachelor to choose, his ultimate choice is unknown to the audience until the very end. That suspense, and the way the show is edited to build upon it, is what the audience wants. Even though most of the relationships celebrated in the confessions of undying love at the end of each season fail, audiences expect this and are not let down. Instead they watch again, taking that same roller-coaster ride, in the hope that the next season will turn out differently and someone will have a "happily ever after" kind of life.

As genres work to maintain a balance of the traditional, expected conventions and the new, exciting inventions, they inevitably do change and progress. Film critics and scholars take note of this and classify genres as having four main cycles: primitive, classical, revisionist, and parodic.[11] The primitive stage is the genre's origin. By its nature, texts in this period are more original than their successors, and many of the genre's conventions are established at this stage. With the dating reality show example, early examples might be dating game shows like *The Dating Game*, which has had many iterations since its premier in the 1960s. The revolutionary idea of taking the metaphorical dating game and turning it into a literal game, introducing strangers, and doing it for television audiences, was new and intriguing. As conventions are established and the genre is increasingly formalized, it enters the classical phase. Here the genre becomes more recognizable as its values, characters, and icons become shared and expected by audiences. Again, many different types of dating shows aired on a variety of networks throughout the 1980s, 1990s, and 2000s. However, the formula set by *The Bachelor* proved to be a winning one and helped to define many dating shows since. The classical period can last for some time before the revisionist period emerges. As the name suggests, it is here the genre's conventions are tested and revised in response to shifting cultural needs. At this point the genre can become experimental or even elegiac, looking back fondly to its origin phase. In doing so, it may turn inward, using the genre and its conventions to question popularly held values and beliefs. The various examples of *The Bachelor*–like shows (*The Bachelorette*, *A Shot at Love*, *Flavor of Love*, and *Rock of Love*), as well as the many other types of dating shows that emerged with the rising popularity of reality television programming of all kinds in the 2000s, speak to the different ways people were playing with the formula from the classical phase, revising it for new audiences with new twists and turns. The genre may also go in the opposite direction toward parody. In this instance, the genre mocks its own conventions, often becoming self-reflecting in spoofing the characters and icons. The reality dating shows have not escaped parody. From skits on *Saturday Night Live* to E!'s *Burning Love* to Lifetime's *UnREAL*, the formula is mocked. With over-the-top portrayals of dating contestants, these scripted shows carry a commentary about the belief love can be found on a reality TV series. *Burning Love* makes fun of the types of characters on each season: the dumb one, the smart one, the successful one, the weird one, the parent and many other more outlandish character types. *UnREAL*, however, takes a darker turn and, rather than pointing fingers at the contestants, instead points at the industry that willingly lies, ruins lives, manipulates, and endangers real people all in the name of good television. As the genre cycles through these phases, it eventually is "reborn," starting the process all over again. Who knows what types of dating shows we will see going forward from here?

From romance to bromance

It is important to remember that genre is an overall concept, and not a medium, or form of entertainment and communication. Therefore, genres cross the artistic media of literature, film, and television. In spite of standardization, false gratification, and their negative associations to relaxation and escapism, genres become "cultural products because they successfully articulate a pattern of fantasy that is at least acceptable to if not preferred by the cultural groups who enjoy them."[12] One way this is achieved is through the affirmation of existing beliefs through the presentation of them as the material that make up the interest and attitudes of characters and situations across forms of media. Genres can often also spawn "sub-genres" that offer further refined conventions and can be specifically adapted for different audiences. For example, "romance" serves a large genre classification, with a number of subgenres under its umbrella, such as the dating reality show example provided above. Other popular subgenres include romantic comedies, romance novels, chick lit, and love songs. Tracing developments in the romance genre over the past thirty or so years—with an emphasis on the cultural groups who consume these texts—can show us ways in which inventions in one area can influence genre production in a number of ways.

Janice Radway's 1984 book *Reading the Romance* is a seminal study in the reading practices of women, the target audience for romantic texts. As an ethnographic study, Radway's *Reading the Romance* focuses on the romance publishing industry of the late 1970s and early 1980s, the narrative style of romance novels, and Radway's interviews with romance novel readers. Romance novels are mass-produced texts that feature a romantic and sexual relationship. The setting, attractive characters, extremely dramatic plotline, and episodes of detailed romantic and sexual encounters contribute to the fantasy that stands in stark contrast to regular life. According to Radway, *Reading the Romance* "was designed initially to see whether it was possible to investigate reading empirically so as to make 'accurate' statements about the historical and cultural meaning of literary production and consumption."[13] Radway's work was groundbreaking in a number of ways: its attempt to legitimize the study of romance novels; its methodology, which involves women readers; and its ability to bridge together the disciplines of cultural studies and literary studies. In order to understand the relationship and possibility for agency that audiences demonstrate in their interaction with media messages, Radway examined the ways in which cultural texts and practices are a part of the larger social life of their consumers. To do this she looked at the social and material situations in which romance reading occurred and the conditions organizing women's private lives in relation to romance reading. What surprised Radway was that despite many of the negative stereotypes and representations found in the novels she studied, the women she interviewed constructed their act of reading as acts of independence in that their reading was a way of temporarily refusing the demands associated with the roles of being mothers and wives. As a result of this, Radway turned the focus of her study on attempting to locate what romance novels provide readers in terms of what they perceive as lack in their lives. As explained by Radway, "What the book [*Reading the Romance*] gradually became, then, was less an account of the way romances as texts were interpreted than of the way romance reading as a form of behavior operated as a complex intervention in the ongoing social life of actual social subjects, women who saw themselves first as wives and mothers."[14]

This statement speaks to the heart of the academic study of popular culture. Popular culture study is not only concerned with the texts we consider "popular," but with uncovering the deeper cultural and social meanings of these texts and how they are a part of the everyday lives of ordinary Americans. The importance is not to evaluate the literary merit of romance novels, but to consider *why* audiences are reading them and what purpose they serve in relation to larger cultural values and beliefs. In the case of Radway's readers, the reading of romance novels was something they did for themselves; reading created a space where husbands, children, and the demands of the home could not intrude. It did not necessarily matter that the stories were fantastical and predictable—in some ways these were the very qualities that made them successful. Time was limited, and readers wanted to be sure of what to expect. They also wanted plots and characters that involved different situations from their own, providing an escape from the reality of their everyday lives.

As women's roles began to change in the 1980s, with more young women entering college and more and more women working full-time as opposed to staying at home with children, popular romances began to lose their appeal. As the genre began to adapt and grow, a new subgenre emerged: chick lit. After the success of Helen Fielding's *Bridget Jones's Diary* (1996), and its subsequent film adaptation (2001), publishers began to actively seek texts along a similar vein in the hopes of replicating its success. Harlequin, the publisher of mass-market romance stories for women, recognizing a shift in interest from its primary demographic, also launched a new line of books along this same style.

This act at once not only positioned chick lit within the traditional model for women's fiction, but also recognized its thematic and stylistic divergences. However, chick lit's almost immediate association with a standardized product and mass marketing techniques further detracted from its potential literary merits. Chick lit's obsession with fashion and consumption, coupled with the form's commercial roots, relegated it quickly to a "women's genre," one that was subsequently deemed undeserving of widespread scholarly attention or critical discussion.

The term "chick lit" was first used in print in 1995, when editors Cris Mazza and Jeffrey DeShell titled their collection of women's fiction *Chick-Lit on the Edge: New Women's Fiction Anthology*. Although Mazza used the term "chick lit" to empower women writers and point out the ways in which women's fiction is often overlooked, within a very short time chick lit became known as trifling stories chronicling the escapades of single women.[15] With an apparent emphasis on the trivial, chick lit went from a broad, contested term to a generic marketing one that fit into preexisting stereotypes of women's writing. Despite Mazza's great pains in tracing and proving that the term originated with her anthology, no popular media or commercial outfit acknowledged this source. Rather, "chick lit" has become the label or name attached to the new genre of fiction that began in the mid-to-late 1990s that chronicles the exploits of women in their late twenties and early thirties.

The trend caught on so quickly that "in attempting to classify chick lit, we face the daunting prospect of determining what recent fiction by women featuring a female protagonist or a cast of characters is not chick lit."[16] Typically, the conventions of the chick lit genre include: a quirky heroine who is lovable despite, or perhaps because of, her imperfections; the romantic quest to find Mr. Right (one that leads to a relationship, but not necessarily marriage); sexual adventure in the romantic quest; the heroine's growth in self-knowledge; the heroine as a working girl, often in journalism, media, or the fashion industry; an emphasis on shopping and consumption; and "the privileging of entertainment value, particularly humor, over any challenging or experimental content or style."[17] Books such as *The Devil Wears Prada*, *Confessions of a Shopaholic*, and *The Nanny Diaries* are popular examples of this chick lit genre (and, not coincidentally, all were adapted into chick flicks).

Books falling within the genre are also easy to judge by their cover. Not only is the content the same but so are the outside identifiers. The colors of the books tend to be light and pretty pastel colors of turquoise, pink, and purple, and feature stereotypical womanly things such as shopping bags, jewelry, or even wedding imagery. Although there are slight variations between books, as well as subgenres such as "mommy lit" or "sistah lit," for the most part these stories fit the standardized mold of genre fiction.

Chick lit and its cinematic sister, the chick flick, are both part of a broader popular culture trend of "chick culture."[18] Again, when we study genres it is important to explore the ways in which they reflect larger cultural trends, ideologies, and attitudes. The rise of chick culture and its associated chick genres are related to the "girl power" movement of the 1990s and the broader cultural backlash of postfeminism, what media scholar Susan Douglas refers to as the media's brand of "enlightened sexism."[19] It is important, therefore, to consider the emergence of chick culture and its related genres alongside cultural attitudes related to **feminism**, the movement for social, political, and economic equality between men and women. Just as feminism is often distorted through media, the term "postfeminism" is a debated concept. If we take this term literally, it means "after feminism," which seems to be the interpretation most explored through popular culture. The implication of this interpretation suggests we have somehow achieved or moved past the goals of feminism, or that feminism is no longer relevant in contemporary society. It also presupposes that we have at some time experienced or lived in a feminist age, a point that few would debate actually occurred. Although postfeminism can also apply to the divergent theories associated with previous feminist movements, it should not be considered synonymous with third-wave feminism, as is sometimes erroneously suggested.

The popular depictions of women in chick lit and chick flicks are of women who are preoccupied with constructing their identities through consumerism, and the subsequent, albeit false, suggestion is that through this consumption one is empowered. Along with this questionable notion of empowerment is the genre's co-opting of feminism without any regard to the actual political and cultural concerns of the movement. Therefore, reading the genre through the lens of postfeminism, and in turn, reading postfeminism through the lens of genre, reveals deeper questions about the relationship between feminism and popular media, as postfeminism dangerously ignores many of the crucial founding principles of feminism. As such, the media's promotion of postfeminism privileges consumerism and capitalist structures as the remedy for gender, racial, and economic disparities in lieu of the political and activist strategies of traditional feminism. The effects are such that the chick genres serve to respond to anxieties related to these schisms, particularly with respect to women's advancement into the workforce, becoming a blend of feminism and antifeminism in their plots and characters. While these texts may be feminist in their outward appearance, they are sexist in their intent, insisting that "women have made plenty of progress because of feminism—indeed full equality has allegedly been achieved—so now it is okay, even amusing, to resurrect sexist stereotypes of girls and women."[20] By celebrating the stereotypical feminine activities of shopping for shoes and the pursuit of that sparkling diamond ring, the lives of women are trivialized. Though featuring women in the storylines and with the industry catering to mostly female audiences is a step in the right direction, the simplification of women to love-obsessed consumers takes away from the progress and equality feminism has brought.

A similar blend of feminism and antifeminism can be seen with the success of *Fifty Shades of Grey*. On the one hand, the books and film adaptations appear to be celebrating the sexual liberation of women and their freedom to explore their sexuality however they see fit. In many other ways, though, the trilogy falls back on many of the same tropes and fantasies that appear in the books discussed by Radway. Despite the supposedly scandalous, outrageous, and erotic elements of the relationship between Anastasia Steele and Christian Grey, all one really needs to know about *Fifty Shades of Grey* is contained on the first page of the first chapter. In fact, one need not read past the first line. Readers are introduced to the text and its protagonist Anastasia Steele with the opening sentence, "I scowl with frustration at myself in the mirror." Immediately the novel aligns itself with a tired stereotype of what it means to be a woman. Our heroine is yet another example of a girl who is frustrated with her image in the mirror. This motif is not new, and is continually recycled through a variety of narratives and genres where women are conditioned to believe that their worth and value as individuals are tied up with their appearance and image. "Scowling" in the mirror, Ana's frustration is about as conservative of a description of a women that there can be. The additional details that follow—that she is brilliant but shy, and that she is a virgin who has never been in love before—cast her in the mold of traditional fairy tale or romance novel heroines. Christian, the object of her affection, is a modern-day cross between Blue Beard and Heathcliff: a twenty-eight-year-old billionaire and former orphan, a gruff but handsome hero who happens to have a predilection for kinky sex.

Christian is immediately attracted to Ana, in large part due to her apparent resistance to his wealth, handsomeness, and seductive charms. The two soon find that they cannot resist their attraction to each other and before readers know it, Christian is introducing Ana to his "Red Room of Pain." The rest of the novel (and series) revolves around Anastasia's and Christian's evolving relationship, particularly his inability to engage in emotional intimacy, while simultaneously trying to control Ana's life, from what she wears to when she eats. While these elements of the text are eroticized through the lens of BDSM, they also conform to (and perhaps reinforce) much stricter stereotypes of gender and traditional sexuality scripts in Western, heterosexual couplings. The nature of Christian and Ana's relationship mimics what Radway noted about the traditional romance, which, as she describes, is

> never simply a love story, [but] is also an exploration of the meaning of patriarchy for women. As a result, it is concerned with the fact that men possess and regularly exercise power over them in all sorts of circumstances. By picturing the heroine in relative positions of weakness, romances are not necessarily endorsing her situation, but examining an all-too-common state of affairs in order to display possible strategies for coping with it.[21]

Fifty Shades of Grey mimics the romance's relationship with patriarchy, but puts it in a contemporary context that is grappling with the dynamics of equality between men and women. On the one hand, the text reinforces notions of patriarchal dominance, while on the other hand, it can be read as liberating for women because it allows them to be released from the supposed pressure and responsibility of equality and permits them to explore the fantasy of submission that patriarchy endorses.

To simply regard *Fifty Shades of Grey* as compensatory literature, though, ignores the complex social relations between, text, genre, and culture we have been discussing in this chapter. In addition to concerns regarding representation, as an artifact of popular culture, it is also necessary to consider *Fifty Shades of Grey* with respect to its production. Author E. L. James got her start writing under the alias "Snowqueens Icedragon," and what became *Fifty Shades of Grey* was originally posted as "Master of the Universe" on the website FanFiction.net. As fan fiction of Stephenie Meyer's young adult series *Twilight*, the intent was to appeal to more mature fans of *Twilight* by making the relationship between Bella and Edward more sexual. The popularity of the fan fiction led to *Fifty Shades of Grey, Fifty Shades Darker*, and *Fifty Shades Freed*, which were picked up by an Australian publisher who released them as e-books and print-on-demand paperbacks. The popularity of "Master of the Universe" is tied to the popularity of *Twilight* and speaks to some of the more traditional responses to romance fiction and the desire for readers to project themselves into the story. Fan fiction in general allows readers a great deal of agency in crafting their own narratives within already established worlds and structures. The success of the *Fifty Shades* trilogy, then, is in part due to an already established fan base and the success of the *Twilight* series. As a result, word of mouth, coupled with the forbidden or illicit elements of the text, created a buzz about the series making it a best seller.

The sexual nature of *Fifty Shades* not only speaks to its success, but also to the ways in which genre shifts respond to cultural anxieties. While sex is prevalent across media, there seems to be a national concern about the ways in which we as a country do and do not talk about sex. As a society there is a constant mixed-message regarding sex and sexuality in the sense that is it all around us in music, movies, television, and literature, and yet there is a large percentage of society that ignores and/or marginalizes any open and honest discussion of the subject. This is especially true when we consider the lack of comprehensive sex education in schools in connection with concerns over sexual consent, rising levels of low self-esteem in teens, and an unwillingness to regard relationship violence as a public health concern. The popularity of *Fifty Shades* and the debates it has sparked suggest that on some level there is a cultural desire to discuss society's changing relationship with the ways in which it understands and talks about sex.

If women are confused about their changing role in this cultural landscape, men are too. While chick lit and chick flicks have emerged as one response to shifting sexual politics, the bromance is another subset of romance and romantic comedies that has gained popularity in the twenty-first century. The development of the bromance reflects the history of romantic comedies which have chronicled shifting attitudes toward sex, dating, and relationships in the United States over the twentieth and twenty-first centuries. Screwball comedies and farces of the 1920s and 1930s such as *Bringing Up Baby* and *It Happened One Night* reflect the economic hardships of the Great Depression and center around class relations, with conflict arising from the mismatched couplings of the rich and poor, ultimately championing true love over class differences. Anxieties around women entering the workforce post–Second World War, resulting in laws such as the Equal Pay Act of 1963, were played out culturally in the sex farces of the 1960s. Made popular by stars such as Rock Hudson and Doris Day, these films featured characters such as the "cad" and "modern working gal," and centered around the sexual dynamics that resulted in women's increased presence in the professional workforce. The women's liberation movement of the 1960s and 1970s was in part fueled by the reproductive justice gains of *Eisenstadt v. Baird* (1972) and *Roe v. Wade* (1973) and made way for the "nervous romances" of the 1970s and early 1980s such as *Annie Hall*. Given the spike in divorce rates at this time, it is not surprising that these films were often pessimistic in tone and featured characters with multiple sex partners, suspicious of stereotypical notions of romance, and uninterested and/or unfulfilled by marriage. The conservative backlash to these trends, which resulted in a return to "family values" in the 1980s and early 1990s made way for romantic comedies such as *Pretty Woman* and *Sleepless in Seattle*, which featured the "meet cute" between the romantic leads and harkened back to a more old-fashioned theme of true love conquering all.

Love is increasingly becoming a four-letter word. As cynicism continues to grow as the quest for love becomes more complicated through dating sites and apps, people wait longer to get married, and more and more people continue to divorce, the die-hard believers in romantic love aren't necessarily winning the cultural battle. The genre of bromance is an effect of these changing perceptions of love. No longer concerned with the quest for love, it is the highlighting of friendships that we turn to. Though not bros, the women in HBO's *Sex and the City* (1998–2004) shared this. As the show chronicled their many relationships with men, which were mostly disastrous and embarrassing, the focus of the show was on the friendship of the women. Men came and went in and out of the lives of the four main characters, but the women were always there for one another. Their friendship took precedence over their romantic relationships. While films and tales of male best buds have existed for centuries, with their own dedicated genres, such as the buddy-cop film, the new millennium and our new cynicism about love have brought a new type of romance: the bromance. Films that look very much like they might be a traditional romantic comedy as they center around the events leading up to a wedding are not what they appear; the focus of the film is not on the groom and the love of his life, the bride, but instead focuses on the development and sustaining of his relationships with other men. *I Love You, Man* and *The Wedding Ringer* are both films about a couple preparing for their wedding. However, the men find themselves in a bind when coming up with groomsmen as they come to realize that they do not have male friends to make up their wedding party. Rather than trace the highs and lows of the romantic relationship of the bride and groom, these films trace the meeting, initial disdain, and ups and downs of the creation of male friendships.

Weddings are also the focus of the first two films in *The Hangover* series, focusing on the antics of a group of men at a bachelor party. Once again, the plot does not center around the betrothed couple, but instead a group of friends. *Bridesmaids*, also released in 2011, does something similar. Though the film is entirely about the events leading up to a wedding, it isn't about the bride and groom. In fact, the groom doesn't even speak in the film and is more of a prop than a character. At the end of all of these movies, the wedding inevitably takes place, but the celebration is of the friendships, not of the romantic relationship. In a culture where the odds that the happy couple getting married won't stay happy for long and that their marriage will end in divorce, friendship and the people who will get you through the tough times and the heartbreak become the most important relationship to build and foster. This noticeable shift in films about love suggests that our culture is becoming more aware of and accepting that some people may find it more worthwhile pursing and sustaining friendships than romantic relationships.

"I'm not going to write you a love song"

While Sara Bareilles may have declared she's not "gonna write you a love song" in her 2007 hit, romance is certainly a theme that carries over into the music we listen to. Bareilles's tongue-in-cheek tune is a nod to the commercial success of pop songs about love and romance, and speaks to the ways in which these topics cross music genres, inspiring musicians and songwriters as it has filmmakers and novelists. Take, for example, Taylor Swift's 2008 smash hit "Love Story." The song and its accompanying music video hit borrow from Shakespeare's *Romeo and Juliet* and feature a number of conventions and icons from the romance genre (white dress, prince/princess, marriage as the ultimate desire/conclusion). "Young love" and "love at first sight" are established in the opening lines of the song and first shot of its accompanying video as Swift sings, "We were both young when I first saw you" before chronicling the tale of two star-crossed lovers à la Romeo and Juliet. Featured on Swift's second album *Fearless*, the song's popularity helped establish Swift's crossover from country to pop stardom. Despite whatever qualms Kayne West may have about Swift's talent and appeal, her success is useful in our consideration of genre and popular music.

In addition to corresponding to audience tastes, genre also works as "a tool with which culture industries and national governments regulate the circulation of vast fields of music. It is a major force in canons of educational institutions, cultural hierarchies, and decisions about censorship and funding. The apparatus of the corporate music industry is thoroughly organized in generic and market categories."[22] Hence, when we consider Taylor Swift's rise in popularity and fame, it is not coincidental that this ascension occurred with the transition of her as a country music star to a crossover musician with a sound more in line with mainstream pop. With respect to music, genres and their affiliated artists are not only associated with certain sounds, but also communities of people, regional locations, and different time periods. As with the other media we have been discussing in this chapter, when we talk of genre and music, we are referring to a "distinctive cultural web of production, circulation, and signification. That is to say, genre is not only 'in the music,' but also in the minds and bodies of particular groups of people who share certain conventions. These conventions are created in relation to particular musical texts and artists and the contexts in which they are performed and experienced."[23] Music conventions function in ways similar to what we have been discussing, where expectations between performers and audiences are established through repetition as they become a type of communication of values and beliefs.

Country music is an example of a genre of music that, though polarizing, comes with a very clear set of conventions, values, and beliefs. Fans of country music love the genre and its authentic artists, while those who don't like country music *really* don't like it. Many people describe their musical taste, as "anything but country" when introducing themselves and their preferences to others. However, country music is undoubtedly a distinctly American genre of music and tied to many foundational American values. Developing particularly out of rural working-class lifestyles, themes such as hard work, farming, love, heartbreak, death, God, faith, patriotism, the hearth, country parties, and automobiles define the genre. Conventional sounds, such as a guitar and other stringed instruments, not always of the electric variety; rich singing voices with a twang; and two-stepping beats mark the sound of the music. Cowboy hats, boots, flannel, and rhinestones are conventional icons of adornment for the country star who works to convince their audiences of their simple country roots.

While all genres have their haters, country music has many critics who suggest that country music, like chick lit described above, is simple and trivial. The conventions of country music, such as its inherent twang, forced country accent, descriptions of hard work and poverty, and lyrics that purposefully manipulate emotions are not elite high culture. The themes of love, loss, and fun are easily accessible as they are spelled out very clearly. No one is perceived to be too rich or too educated. Country music can appeal to unrefined audiences with no knowledge of high culture. In fact, in country music, being simple and living a simple life are prized above most everything else. Country music never felt the need to subscribe to the traditional conventions or desires of popular music, and because of that developed its own way. Rather than aspiring to be included on popular radio stations, MTV, or featured more prominently in award shows, country music developed its own radio stations across the nation, television network (CMT—Country Music Television), and award shows (CMA—Country Music Awards). Though not fully mixing with other genres of music, it did go the way of them with the commercialization. As Bill C. Malone says it in *Don't Get Above Your Raisin': Country Music and the Southern Working Class*:

> In country music's subtext, one hears the hopes and fears of rural southerners struggling to balance the internalized values of a disappearing rural life with the external demands of an urban world into which they have been inexorably drawn.[24]

By being drawn into that world, the genre inevitably changed. It became influenced by sounds and themes of other genres and now country singers are often rebranded as "crossover artists" when they reach a certain level of commercial success, like America's sweetheart, Taylor Swift.

New forms of country music also emerge in response to larger musical trends and commercialization. In the 1960s and 1970s, as a backlash to the more commercialized and shiny version of country music coming out of Nashville, outlaw country emerged. As a way to hang on to the values of the old musical tradition in the face of the glitz of mainstream country, the more rugged cowboys continued to sing about heartbreak and rule-breaking while seeking answers at the bottom of a bottle. These outlaws found themselves becoming more popular with individuals who were part of the rock, psychedelic, blues, and folk scene, not just the mainstream country scene.

Though still a very popular musical genre, and quite formulaic in its releases, country music also continues to grow and expand. As rap music became increasingly popular around the country, country artists began to incorporate more rap conventions into their music. Country-rap, or "hick-hop," is a hybrid genre that takes country music themes and puts them to generic rap conventions. By rapping the lyrics rather than simply singing, incorporating heavier beats, and more electronically produced music, country artists are growing and expanding their musical repertoire and audiences. Though in the 1990s artists such as Bubba Sparxxx and the Nappy Roots, rap artists who happened to be from more rural southern parts of the United States, were gaining air time, they weren't necessarily popular with country music audiences. The rural themes were appealing, but the rap sound was too far off of the mainstream. However, with Colt Ford's "Dirt Road Anthem," made more popular by Jason Aldean's version, hick-hop began to take off. Though still using the themes of country music such as simple rural living, driving trucks off road, young love, and field parties and singing some of the lines of music, the lyrics are mostly rapped. More and more country artists are collaborating with rap artists. Ludacris joined Jason Aldean for a remix of "Dirt Road Anthem," Nelly collaborated with both Florida Georgia Line and Tim McGraw, and LL Cool J joined Brad Paisley for the song "Accidental Racist" talking about race, judgments, and stereotypes often not reconciled in rap or country music.

Music, like film, television, and literature, is an expression of society and culture. The types of music that people listen to reflect their lifestyles. Those economically disadvantaged rural people who have felt marginalized by the money and progress of industrialization put their sorrows and frustrations into song. As that became more popular, the genre developed and changed. It held onto the themes and conventions that defined it, but opened itself up to more opportunity and commercial success. As time goes on, all musical genres will continue to change and flourish. Examining those changes closely will provide useful insight into the cultural shifts that will ultimately define us.

Conclusion

This chapter outlined theories of genre, helping us to understand how as different forms of cultural production have been developed and refined, genres have adapted to various artistic media. Despite, or perhaps because of, these developments and refinements, the elusiveness of a singular genre theory remains consistent. As Rick Altman, a well-known scholar on film genres, admits,

It should be possible to outline the major principles of genre theory established by two millennia of genre theorists. Yet this is precisely what we cannot do. Even so simple a question as the meaning and extent of *genre* remains confusing, for the term inconsistently refers to distinctions derived from a wide variety of differences among texts.[25]

Therefore, our goal in this chapter was to introduce you to these differing uses of genre, as well as to establish the importance of genre to popular culture with respect to production, reception, and representation. Understanding that genres provide a set of guidelines for the producers of popular culture and an agreement between them and their audiences, locating the conventions provides insight into the stable values and beliefs that permeate our culture. Whether it's the concept of romantic love or the appreciation of the simple rural life, genres exist to reinforce these beliefs. However, the study of genre also points to important shifts. Through the examination of inventions, which ultimately change the way a genre looks and develops, the shifts in culture become evident.

Although we focused on a few specific genres for discussion, our purpose was to trace these genres to demonstrate broader concepts related to genre as a type of popular culture presentation that has historical, stylistic, and commercial implications. As a set of expectations between audiences and producers, genres work to create labels and categories integral to the decisions relating to the marketing of texts and the choices of artists and distributors. On a deeper level they function as a response to cultural concerns and as a tool for media industries, demonstrating the ways in which popular culture texts both respond to and shape larger national ideologies within certain cultural contexts and time periods. Lastly, as both a blueprint and a structure, genres help provide links to shared pasts while helping to carry on the traditions of various communities and cultural groups.

Notes

1   Aristotle, *Poetics*, ed. with critical notes by S. H. Butcher (New York: Macmillan, 1902), 7.
2   Ibid., 17.

3   Northrop Frye, *Anatomy of Criticism* (1957, repr., Princeton, NJ: Princeton University Press, 1990), 13.

4   Ibid., 246.

5   Ibid., 247.

6   Louis D. Giannetti, *Understanding Movies* (12th edn. 1972, repr., Englewood Cliffs, NJ: Prentice-Hall, 2011), 355.

7   Rick Altman, "A Semantic/Syntactic Approach to Film Genre," *Cinema Journal*, 23, no. 3 (1984): 10.

8   John Cawelti, *Mystery, Violence, and Popular Culture* (Madison: University of Wisconsin Press, 2004), 9.

9   Leo Braudy and Marshall Cohen, *Film Theory and Criticism* (5th edn. 1974. New York: Oxford University Press, 1999), 610.

10 Giannetti, *Understanding Movies*, 355.

11 Ibid., 359.

12 John Cawelti, *Adventure, Mystery, and Romance: Formula Stories as Art and Popular Culture* (Chicago: University of Chicago Press, 1976), 34.

13 Janice Radway, *Reading the Romance* (Chapel Hill: University of North Carolina Press, 1984), 65.

14 Ibid., 67.

15 Cris Mazza, "'Who's Laughing Now?' A Short History of Chick Lit and the Perversion of a Genre," in *Chick Lit: The New Woman's Fiction*, ed. Suzanne Ferriss and Mallory Young (New York: Routledge, 2006), 28.

16 Stephanie Harzewski, "Tradition and Displacement in the New Novel of Manners," in *Chick Lit: The New Woman's Fiction*, ed. Suzanne Ferriss and Mallory Young (New York: Routledge, 2006), 31.

17 Juliette Wells, "Mothers of Chick Lit? Women Writers, Readers, and Literary History," in *Chick Lit: The New Woman's Fiction*, ed. Suzanne Ferriss and Mallory Young (New York: Routledge, 2006), 49.

18 Suzanne Ferriss and Mallory Young, *Chick Flicks: Contemporary Women at the Movies* (New York: Routledge, 2008), 1.

19 Susan Douglas, *Enlightened Sexism: The Seductive Message That Feminism's Work Is Done* (New York: Henry Holt, 2010), 9.

20 Ibid., 9.

21 Radway, *Reading the Romance*, 75.

22 Fabian Holt, *Genre in Popular Music* (Chicago: University of Chicago Press, 2007), 3.

23 Ibid., 2.

24 Bill Malone, *Don't Get Above Your Raisin': Country Music and the Southern Working Class* (Chicago: University of Illinois Press, 2003), 28.

25 Rick Altman, *Film/Genre* (London: British Film Institute, 1999), 11.

4

The Culture Industries

I'm not a businessman, I'm a business, man.

—Jay Z

The death of Steve Jobs on October 5, 2011, prompted an outpouring of grief worldwide typical of what one might expect for the passing of a head of state, international superstar, or religious leader. Makeshift memorials cropped up at Apple stores, with post-it note condolences and apples carved with Jobs's quotations mixed in with the usual flowers and accoutrements of improvised shrines. Mourners, with their iPhones and iPads set to images of candles, came together to form technologically enhanced vigils. Old media announced his death with newspaper headlines across the globe, while Facebook, Twitter, and new media spread the word with the trending hashtags #isad and #ThankYouSteve. In the years since his passing, Jobs's permanence in our cultural landscape has been solidified not only through his innovations that changed the ways in which we communicate and experience the world, but also through the popular culture tributes his life has inspired including numerous biographies, a graphic novel, feature films, documentaries, a television miniseries, and even a mural by the elusive Banksy.

While the products he helped create—which include Apple personal computers, the iPod, iTunes, the iPhone, and the iPad—are an important part of Jobs's legacy, his true vision lay with his obsession on creating taste. Known for being meticulous with design, Jobs crafted an experience for consumers that went beyond merely purchasing a product. To be a "Mac person" during Jobs's heyday was to be associated with a certain type of consumer, one whose concern for design and detail were just as important as utility. From advertisements to the sparse aesthetics of Apple stores, Jobs fashioned a consumer experience that likened technology to art, shopping to curating. As such, his products were infused with meaning that went beyond function. When viewed this way, the cultural reach and ripple effects of Steve Jobs and Apple become an entry point to considering this chapter's focus on the **culture industries**: the individuals, companies, and institutions that shape and control the production of popular culture products and their associated cultural meanings.

At this point in our academic study of popular culture, a couple of things should now begin to become clear. One is that popular culture isn't simply something that is liked by a lot of people (although it can be), but it also includes any cultural text, product, or practice that plays an important role in our contemporary culture. This is what we mean when we describe popular culture as the activities, objects, distractions, and/or focus of daily life. This runs the gamut from film, television, and other forms of entertainment, to shopping, games, and holidays, to instant messages, emojis, and social media. Popular culture encompasses all of the things that we preoccupy ourselves with on a daily basis, whether we realize it or not. This is one reason why the study of popular culture can be difficult; these products and practices are so ingrained in our daily lives, they can be hard for us to even recognize, never mind analyze from an objective standpoint. Further complicating our study is the way that popular culture tends to be omnipresent, affecting the majority of us, while often representing the interests of certain groups and/ or a minority of people. Our chapter on cultural myths and the American Dream began to touch on this topic with its discussion of the way that discourse and certain ideologies work to reproduce power structures and uphold institutions in the United States. This chapter, with its focus on the culture industries, will build on our previous discussion in its exploration of the production of culture and the ways in which the culture industries help to shape the taste and preferences of members of society. After reading this chapter, you will have a greater awareness of the role popular culture plays in maintaining and resisting institutionalized power and you will further your ability to analyze popular culture texts in order to determine their larger significance in society.

Mass culture as popular culture

As stated, for the purposes of our study we are thinking about popular culture as the events, materials, practices, beliefs, people, and texts that make up and shape the daily life of a majority of people. When most individuals picture popular culture, however, their minds conjure images of the mass culture of popular media. Viewed from this lens, and at its most basic, mass culture tends to be accessible and affordable. Rather than being produced by a craftsman or artisan for a specific individual, mass culture gets its name in part from its mass production. The products of mass culture are produced by corporations for disparate and unknown audiences in order for them to appeal to the most people and make the highest profits. While our study of popular culture is much broader than this, in this chapter we want to be thinking about approaching popular culture in terms of its production—for whom and by whom.

Production refers to the creation of popular culture products and texts, as well as the media ownership, values, and processes that influence and contribute to their construction. Production, along with representation and consumption, is a component of a tripart approach to the study of popular culture. In this chapter, we will consider these as three distinct processes, but we also will want to make sure to pay attention to how they flow into one another and how production and consumption are always tied to representation, and how representation is always influenced by production and consumption. **Representation** relates back to the previous chapter on myth and its discussion of semiotics and the ways meaning is produced through sign systems. As noted, representation helps to construct the world in particular ways that have direct correlation to how society is structured and organized. Representation also refers to the ideas, beliefs, and values that are supported, promoted, and perpetuated through popular culture texts and practices. In short, it is what audiences "see" when they interact with popular culture. **Consumption** has to do with the ways that audiences purchase, borrow from, use, consume, and make meaning from the popular culture that surrounds them. Later chapters will discuss in more detail the ways in which groups and communities have different processes and understandings of cultural products, but when we think of consumption, it is important to pay attention to the various institutional structures and processes involved in the use and practice of popular culture.

Our starting point, then, is on the production of popular culture. This involves understanding the design, making, and selling of products, with respect to advances in technology and the corporations and businesses involved with these processes. The mode of production and the associated roles that corporations play in this process help distinguish these forms of popular culture, often referred to as "mass media" or "mass culture," to folk culture or high or elite culture, which tends to be produced individually by a single creator. Mass culture as popular culture, however, is a big business today, and the corporations and partnerships behind its production are referred to as the **culture industries**.

The concept of culture industries was introduced briefly in the chapter on genre, with respect to the ways in which genre films, music, and literature tend to be formulaic in response to the demand for a guaranteed audience. Film companies, recording studios, and publishers make up the culture industries and are in the business of selling products. With a focus on profit, it is in the interest of the culture industries to create products and texts that will appeal to ready-made audiences. Imagining what we know of our culture as something that is willingly and purposefully produced rather than something that develops naturally on its own can be jarring. To imagine that there are businesses and industries producing our culture for profit, affecting not only how we amuse ourselves, but how we think and feel, takes away from our autonomy, our agency, and our sense of self. While the notion of us as complete cultural dupes, pawns not living our own life, but rather doing the bidding of someone else, is not really true, it does motivate us to think deeper about the production of the popular culture texts we consume.

In order to fully understand the rise of mass culture as popular culture, it is important to pay attention to the role of industrialization to the process. Industrialization changed many things, from production to daily life. When things change, those who are slow to take up the change fear that it will bring the downfall of society, and this fear drove many early cultural theorists and critics writing at the time. For them, industrialization and the move to mass production were seen as nothing short of a threat to civilization itself. This school of thought was particularly popular in Europe and Great Britain, and was rooted in the fear that a rise of the working class threatened the way of life that had sustained social and economic systems for centuries. Cultural critics like Matthew Arnold worried that new forms of mass media, fueled by industrialization in the mid-nineteenth century, led to a weakening of the social and moral order of society. The rationale of Arnold and his contemporaries was the moral concern that as people moved into cities as a result of urbanization and industrialization, fewer people were going to church and its role as the center of community was losing its stronghold. The fear was that this would result in a lack of religion or moral values in people's lives, and that this spiritual vacuum would be filled through popular culture and the values of consumerism. This concern corresponded to the rise of a middle class—fueled in part by the economic shifts in production, a rise in political democracy, and greater rates of free public education—which was developing its own set of values and morals that seemed to be at odds with prevailing notions of high Culture. Rather than individualized and single-authored artistic texts prized by the bourgeois, there was a shift toward mass-produced commodities like pulp fiction and popular music that reflected not only this new class and their lifestyles, but also seem to be aimed at escapism and instant gratification at the expense of "true" or cultured art. This resulted in criticisms of the working class, and more broadly the masses of the general population, as childlike, morally corrupt, and/or easily distracted and pacified. By the early twentieth century, critics like F. R. and Queenie Leavis argued that "In any period it is upon a very small minority that the discerning appreciation of art and literature depends: it is (apart from cases of the simple and familiar) only a few who are capable of unprompted, first-hand judgement."[1] These concerns over the perceived debasement of culture not only fueled class divides, but also laid the groundwork for the academic discrimination against popular culture for decades to come.

The Frankfurt School: Not really a school or in Frankfurt

While British cultural studies in the early half of the twentieth century were concerned about the rise of mass culture with respect to social classes, another school of thought was influenced by the rise of fascism in Europe. The

Frankfurt School was a group of German intellectuals and scholars loosely affiliated with the Institute for Social Research (Institut für Sozialforschung) who witnessed the Nazis' use of mass culture to control society. Fleeing persecution, many of these scholars resettled in the United States where they continued to be skeptical of both capitalism and Soviet socialism and the ways in which political ideology is disseminated through culture. The Frankfurt School was influenced by **Marxist** thought and the belief that "the ideas of the ruling class are in every epoch the ruling ideas, i.e. the class which is the ruling *material* force of society, is at the same time its ruling *intellectual* force."[2] Focusing on the ways US culture tends to work as an ideological tool for capitalism and as a way to maintain social authority, the Frankfurt School became critical opponents to the rise of mass and popular culture in the mid-twentieth century.

Theodor Adorno and Max Horkheimer, two theorists associated with the Frankfurt School, coined the term "culture industry" in their chapter "The Culture Industry: Enlightenment as Mass Deception" in *Dialectic of Enlightenment* to describe the ways in which mass production and the institutions and structures of production create a commercial and commodified culture that promotes, embeds, and supports the products, lifestyles, and institutions of American capitalism. The result, according to this line of thought, is that the culture industry depoliticizes those in the working class through distraction and by discouraging the public from engaging in thought outside of their present and immediate gratification. Instead, the culture industry organizes leisure time along the same lines of industrialization and the then-new workday. What's at stake with this shift, according to Adorno and Horkheimer, is the artistic integrity of "authentic" cultural products, with the unfortunate result being, "Films and radio no longer need to present themselves as art. The truth that they are nothing but business is used as an ideology to legitimize the trash they intentionally produce."[3] Their argument centers on their belief that art for art's sake, or for some higher purpose or truth (like a critique of life itself), has been sacrificed for profit and other means of social control. According to fellow Frankfurt School theorist Herbert Marcuse, authentic culture displays "the defeated possibilities, the hopes unfulfilled, and the promises betrayed," and contains the power of opposition and possibility to be a subversive force.[4]

Mass culture, however, fueled by the culture industry, robs the individual and culture of any greater good or autonomy. More contemporary critics are quick to note, though, that this version of authentic culture as more original or revolutionary is often infused with a false nostalgia and tends to rely on its own ideological assumptions and biases.

The Frankfurt School tends to take a very negative view of the products, activities, and media often deemed popular culture. These objects are seen as a purposeful distraction from more important quests for truth and understanding. An example of contemporary criticism borrowing from the Frankfurt School of thought would be concerns surrounding cell phone usage among Millennials. The argument goes that young people are too concerned with social media than actual socializing, would rather text than talk, and are more interested in consuming television, film, and music than in creating their own works or expressing themselves. As a result, critics worry that rather than engaging politically and intellectually in the development of the country, the majority of citizens instead turn selfishly inward, prioritizing their own lives and comfort levels and preoccupying themselves with the products of popular culture. This has negative impacts on the culture at large, it is assumed, because it reduces the level of art and creativity and also makes it so that people are more easily manipulated and tricked into falling in line. If you're too busy with your phone and posting photos of your breakfast, or interested in celebrity gossip, then you're not going to really pay attention to the ways that you might be taken advantage of by the government, corporations, or other groups who wield power over you.

The election cycle of 2016 saw an outrage against "fake news" and the rise of "post-truth." Imagining journalism as something to be sold, as opposed to objective facts and reporting of actual events, stories that resembled "news" had no intention of reporting the truth, but instead promoted headlines to appeal to readers on all sides of the political spectrum. Often referred to as "clickbait," these stories were nothing more than juicy headlines spread on the Internet. Once clicked, a flood of advertisements pop up before, in the middle of, and after the "news" report. The sites which host these stories and produce these headlines receive income from the advertisements, and the more people who see the advertisements and click on their page, the more money they get. These sites aren't producing anything with real political or intellectual merit, just something that appears to be of importance. Rather than actually learning anything, people consume "news" that support their already held beliefs, whether or not those beliefs are correct or have any basis whatsoever in fact. When viewed this way, through the lens of the Frankfurt School, news becomes a commodity produced by an industry. Rather than inform to better the social good, news is sold with the intention of confirming people's preconceived (and often false) beliefs and to distract them from real political, economic, and social awareness.

Of course, not all of the Internet is an intellectual wasteland, nor are smartphones the harbingers of the end of civilization as we know it. While many of the Frankfort School's ideas tended to the extreme in their negative views of popular culture, a more generally agreed-upon effect of the culture industry is standardization, or the ways in which they argue "culture today is infecting everything with sameness."[5] Although it may appear that there are a vast number of products being produced for consumers, these products all tend to be incredibly similar, with a limited number of businesses in control of their production. Standardization refers to both production and consumption, influencing which products get made and how they are used. The Frankfurt School argues standardization results in a collective model of consumption that is stripped of agency and political action. The individual, transformed into consumer, is "absorbed" into the culture industry through a process of **pseudo-individualization**, where individuals assert false displays of individual identity through the consumption of products altered in a way to appear unique, but are at their core identical. This can be seen anywhere from fashion to tech products to home décor. Additionally, marketers are increasingly branding "lifestyles"—ways of living and consuming—as a means to connect consumerism to identity formation. As a result, **market segmentation** has gained traction as a process for shifting the production of goods and culture to specific groups and lifestyles in order to target distinct cultural tastes and specialized audiences. Corporations argue that market segmentation exposes them to more potential consumers for companies while making individuals and target groups feel important and that their needs are being met. Conversely, this practice lends itself to pseudo-individualization, and rarely takes the individual into actual account. Further, some people are resistant to being categorized in this way, while others say that it is difficult to reduce people down to one specific lifestyle, product, or identity.

To understand this, let's return to Steve Jobs and his revolutionary mobile device, the iPhone. Though handheld devices with Internet and computing capabilities existed before the iPhone, Jobs reimagined the product, introducing touch screens, simple app interfaces, improved video and photo capabilities, and expanded computing power. Recognizing the potential of his design, in 2007 Jobs filed patents for the shape and design of the phone before its release. Soon, however, other companies were making and selling very similar products: gone were keyboards, slides, and flip covers; instead they were abandoned for thin rectangles with touchscreen interfaces. Apple swiftly retaliated in the courts, with *Apple Inc. v. Samsung Electronics Co., Ltd.* being the most famous of cases in the smartphone patent wars. While these legal battles continue, through standardization virtually all brands of smartphones (Apple, Samsung, Google, LG, HTC, etc.) have adopted the same basic look while performing the same basic functions. This makes each individual phone at least on par with the rest by providing consumers with what they have come to understand a smartphone to be. Regardless of the pixels of the camera, the processing power, and all of the voice-activated bells and whistles, the differences in the phones are not significant, but our impulse to argue they are and to define ourselves by which product we inevitably purchase is.

While the Frankfurt School was very critical of mass production and its effects on the individual and the cultural products of popular culture, their writings on this topic are influential and significant nonetheless. Their emphasis on the importance of studying popular culture in terms of production is still relevant today, as it stressed the need to take into account the larger economic context in which culture circulates. Our understanding of popular culture, however, will look at production, representation, and consumption as a whole—shifting the emphasis of study away from just audiences or textual analysis—in order to consider the ways societal institutions work in conjunction with these elements.

Mass culture and culturalisms

During the second half of the twentieth century, critics in the United States, such as Dwight Macdonald, began to explore the ways popular culture began to dominate life in the post–Second World War period of the Cold War. Macdonald preferred the term "mass culture," reasoning, "its distinctive mark is that it is solely and directly an article for mass consumption, like chewing gum."[6] Macdonald's work focuses on the rise of "kitsch" (the German word for mass culture, derived from the German word *verkitschen*, to "sell," "sentimentalize," or "cheapen") and how its overwhelming quantity gives it dominance over artistic production associated with high or folk culture. In doing so, it "destroys all values, since value judgments imply discriminations."[7] In this way, Macdonald sees mass culture as "democratic" in the negative sense that it refuses to discriminate or be ruled by matters of taste. The downside is that the elimination of aesthetic quality often results in a dumbing-down of culture to the lowest common denominator, and the products that result are mass marketed to lowbrow taste. This, along with the fact that "mass" implies a loss of individual, human identity, leads Macdonald to conclude that kitsch and the products of mass culture "is not and can never be any good."[8]

We still hear these types of criticisms of popular texts regularly, such as with the work of popular recording artists, with their digitally created background music and auto-tuned voices. Purists argue this isn't real art, but rather music manufactured to appeal to people with no sense of artistry or discriminating tastes. These critics fear that if we continue on this path, "real" music will cease to be made and culture will suffer as a result. This type of criticism is not restricted to music, as any new artistic fad, whether of music, fashion, television, film, or toys, tends to be criticized at the height of its popularity due to its appeal to large groups of people. The argument follows that these products must lack any real substance if the masses can access, understand, and enjoy them. This is a snobbish approach, and one that the study of popular culture has been struggling with since its inception.

Other schools of thought, however, refuse to take such a negative or restrictive view of the production of popular culture. Richard Johnson, Raymond Williams, Stuart Hall, and other scholars associated with the Centre for Contemporary Cultural Studies (CCCS) at the University of Birmingham took a less deterministic view of production, arguing that the Frankfurt School of thought failed to take into account that individuals or groups may have their own reasons for consuming products outside those set by producers, as well as that cultural products and texts take on new meanings through the process of consumption. Instead, thinkers associated with the CCCS stressed a certain amount of agency on the part of the average consumer and were interested in the ways in which the study of these cultural products and practices could lead to insights on the ways in which the individual is involved in his or her own social practices, relationships, and navigation of the world, and, in turn, the ways in which these factors blur the lines of production, text, and consumption.

French scholar Michel de Certeau also saw more hope for consumers than the Frankfurt School would have allowed. In *The Practice of Everyday Life*, Certeau's goal is to "indicate pathways for further research" into the "continuing investigation of the ways in which users—commonly assumed to be passive and guided by established rules—operate."[9] Taking on the Frankfurt School's position that audiences and consumers are passive, weak, and eager to gobble up any message being sent to them, Certeau opened the doors for exploration into a number of different ways that audiences, consumers, and normal everyday people actually maintain their freewill when faced with the products and environment shaped by the culture industries. Using terminology introduced by Certeau, we can think of the ways in which the culture industries and other institutions that hold power in our culture and society act, perform, or operate as "strategies." Consumers, however, do more than passively receive these messages; they actively respond and add to them. These reactions are referred to as "tactics."[10] Though the powers that be have some control over us and dictate how daily life goes, ultimately, as individuals, we control our responses to the texts and practices of the culture industries. We aren't helpless dupes, but instead autonomous thinkers that can accept or reject what comes our way. One way in which Certeau sees this happening is through the practice of "poaching," where, "everyday life invents itself by *poaching* in countless ways on the property of others."[11] If we consider the culture industries as "others" and their products as their property, then how we choose to use, respond to, change, or manipulate those products can be seen as an act of poaching. Just because something is intended for a particular use or purpose doesn't mean that is how it will ultimately be used. Henry Jenkins elaborated on Certeau's theory of poaching in his book *Textual Poachers: Television Fans and Participatory Culture* to describe the far from passive reception of popular culture in fan communities, which will be elaborated on in later chapters. For now, though, it is important to remember that rather than consuming and leaving products as is, fans and consumers actively engage, respond to, create, alter, and enrich the texts they consume.

Scholars like those from the CCCS, Certeau, and Jenkins contribute to the understanding of popular culture as more than a passive reception of mainstream beliefs and values, but as a site of struggle where those who do not have power in the traditional sense, and may not appear to be any formidable match or opponent to the culture industries, can still exert their individual sense of agency when it comes to what they think and create. Products of popular culture aren't necessarily a death knell for creativity, but an opportunity for new forms of expression.

Culture industries 2.0

A lot has changed since the Frankfurt School of thought dominated social theories with respect to the culture industry. Globalization, along with new forms of technology and media platforms, have helped increase the global reach of popular culture texts. Instead of a singular "culture industry," a broader understanding of culture industries allows us to consider the ways in which cultural texts take multiple forms and play an increasingly vital role in shaping all aspects of contemporary society. Similarly, instead of being focused on one cultural product (for example, film, music, or television), we can consider the ways in which media conglomerates work across sectors and have a hand in a number of modes of cultural production, are involved in cross-promotion of cultural products and practices, and, as a result, reach diverse audience sets. The culture industries of today not only include the music and film industries, but expanded broadcasting (radio, television, and streaming services), print and electronic publishing, the Internet, video and computer gaming, and cross-platform advertising and marketing. While for-profit corporations make up the core of the culture industries, it is also important to take into account the role of governments in legislating, regulating, and subsidizing the culture industries.

Globalization has transformed our contemporary landscape as technological advances have allowed for greater movement of peoples and goods across borders, alongside increased modes of communication. Economically, the impacts of globalization include the expansion of capitalism globally and the integration of economies across sectors of trade and production. Culturally the effects of globalization can be seen through the dissemination and influence of cultural products, foodways, rituals and ceremonies, and more general ways of living. While the positive aspects of globalization should not be overlooked, it is important to understand the ways in which globalization capitalizes on preexisting global inequalities related to nation, class, race, and gender. With respect to the culture industries, these inequalities are seen with those who do and do not have access to consumer goods, the disparity between those in control of the means of production versus those working on the factory floor producing goods, and inequalities with respect to which stories, goods, and practices circulate within a global marketplace. These types of disparities are being exposed through the use of personal narratives in books such as Kelsey Timmerman's *Where Am I Wearing: A Global Tour to the Countries, Factories, and People That Make Our Clothes* and *Where Am I Eating: An Adventure Through the Global Food Economy,* which shed light on the impact our lifestyles in the United States have on people across the globe in an effort to humanize on the other side of the production. Global humanitarian groups, such as Students and Scholars Against Corporate Misbehavior, report and serve as watchdogs on global companies such as Disney, Zara fashions, and Foxconn, the Taiwanese contract manufacturing company that produces the iPhone and other electronic goods. Foxconn, in particular, has come under fire for labor violations, including child labor and poor working conditions that have led a number of employees to commit suicide. These types of accounts, along with an increasing awareness on the various forms of human trafficking and the knowledge of forced labor for various industries, have led activists to call on people to consciously change their consumption habits. Slaveryfootpring.org hosts a survey asking questions about one's home, automobile, food, toiletries, clothing, electronics, and even sporting goods to determine the number of slaves working to sustain that individual's lifestyle. Though raising awareness, these efforts have not yet proven to be an effective match against the culture industries' drive for cheap labor and higher profits.

One way cheap labor and increased profit margins are abetted is through **neoliberal** policies associated with globalization such as deregulation, privatization, and a de-emphasis on public or community services, practices which are also closely tied to the culture industries. The Federal Communication Commission (FCC) was founded in 1934 and functions as an independent US government agency tasked with regulating communication by "radio, television, wire, satellite, and cable in all 50 states, the District of Columbia and US territories."[12] In its early years, the FCC licensed stations locally (as opposed to nationally) in order to promote local content, set aside stations for educational use (making way for public broadcasting systems), and regulated ownership in an attempt to prevent media monopolies. During the 1980s, though, neoliberal policies were adopted by the FCC, including increasing the number of radio and television stations permitted to be owned by an individual entity and removing guidelines for minimal amounts of noneducational programming (allowing the marketplace to determine what's best for public interest). In 1987 the Fairness Doctrine, which required broadcasters to devote airtime to providing contrasting views of matters of public interest, was eliminated, paving the way for the rise of polarizing cable news programming. Throughout all of this, the effects of deregulation are apparent. Fewer companies own more networks, which are in charge of disseminating information to the public across media platforms. Less and less of what is broadcasted is aired for educational purpose or vetted for accuracy; instead, our media purposefully caters to audiences without any sense of responsibility other than making a profit, opening the door for the clickbait and "fake news" discussed above.

Congress passed the Telecommunications Act of 1996, which amended the Communications Act of 1934. The 1996 Act was the first to include the Internet, and further relaxed standards with respect to broadcasting and telecommunication markets, including offering provisions for media cross-ownership. This set the stage for Internet service provider America Online's (AOL) purchase of Time Warner in 2000, the largest business merger—and subsequently, biggest business flop—in America's history. While the intent was to allow content developed in one communication medium to be reused, recycled, and reinforced in another, the execution was never successfully managed, and the companies eventually split in 2009. Despite the failure of the AOL-Time Warner deal to successfully integrate media brands across multiple platforms, mergers and acquisitions, especially those involving Internet start-ups, persist. Multi-sector and multimedia integration, along with horizontal and vertical integration, have helped reduce competition, increase profits through the ownership of various stages of production and distribution, and support the integration of the culture industries. These practices make corporations more self-reliant and self-sustaining therefore creating more profits while at the same time reducing their overall costs. While this benefits corporations, the savings in cost is not necessarily passed on to the average American consumer, and often these practices cause the closing of small business that cannot compete on this level, limiting the diversity of products and number of consumer choices available overall.

The result of these practices has led to the use of the term military-industrial media complex to describe the belief that there is a small group of corporations that control the means of production not only of media, but are also heavily tied to industrial and military holdings, and therefore promote messages and content increasing support of military endeavors that drive profit. The term "military-industrial complex" was first used by Dwight Eisenhower in his farewell presidential address, where he warned:

> In the councils of government, we must guard against the acquisition of unwarranted influence, whether sought or unsought, by the military-industrial complex. The potential for the disastrous rise of misplaced power exists, and will persist. We must never let the weight of this combination endanger our liberties or democratic processes.[13]

Eisenhower, recognizing the rise of America's global military dominance, warned against the use of American "defense" as a pretense for corporation and industry influence in matters of public policy. This critique has since been expanded to include the entertainment industry broadly, and the power of its relationship to other industries and government politics. For example, General Electric (GE) has business divisions in power, oil, gas, renewable energy, health care, transportation, as well as the entertainment industry through its NBCUniversal and Comcast holdings. As with earlier critiques of the culture industry, the concern of a so-called military-industrial entertainment complex is largely to preserve economic class interests while manufacturing specific desires that uphold dominant ideologies. Companies like GE—with assets across energy, entertainment, and consumer product sectors—have the ability to control the supply of the commodities, can influence prices, limit the number of competitors, and control perception through the production of information culture across media platforms. Not only can these varied interests by one corporation influence government and public policy through lobbying, but with respect to the media, have the possibility to control public discourse, leading to limited viewpoints. This argument is continually expressed by both liberal and conservative parties, such as when both Bernie Sanders and Donald Trump complained about the media's role in the 2016 presidential election. More broadly, we can see this narrowing of perspective manifest as the infotainment that often passes for news media today. Closer examination of the narratives expressed through the media reveals the ways discourse is shaped by various news outlets, and how certain information or viewpoints get more discussion than others, while those outside of the mainstream are ignored or negatively and/or erroneously portrayed through the media.

I shop, therefore I am

So far, the majority of this chapter has been focused on production. But where does that leave us, as the average American, navigating the landscape of the culture industries? Given Chapter 2's discussion of the myth of the American Dream and its basis in consumerism, we can begin to see the connection between production, mindset, and the individual. If we follow the logic of Marxist thought adopted by the Frankfurt School, our role in this system of capitalist production is that of consumer. Technology, outsourcing, and a shift toward a service economy means fewer and fewer Americans are employed in careers that engage the economic **base** or modes of production such as mining, farming, or factory work. Instead, more and more individuals are employed in service sectors and jobs that see them disconnected from the actual fruits of their labor or tangible products. This disconnect bleeds into a commodity culture that, from a Marxist perspective, values objects and things that are bought and sold, at the expense of valuing human connection or the products of one's labor. This shift is supported by the **superstructure**, the cultural and ideological manifestations of the economic base, the actual means and process of production. As a result, value relates not only to an object's worth in terms of its actual use, but its broader worth in terms of exchange and circulation. Use value, then, refers to the value attached to a commodity in terms of its utility, while **exchange value** refers to the value placed on goods in comparison to other products in the financial market. Borrowing from anthropologic notions of "totem" and "fetish," Marx used the term **commodity fetishism** to describe the "mystical character of commodities" where, in capitalist economies, value is not determined by the work related to an object's production, nor for its utility, but dictated by the market based on its perceived social value.

While there are trends which advocate for minimalism and tiny houses, for the better part of the twentieth and now twenty-first century, America has organized life through the lens of commodity fetishism, with retail therapy and the acquisition of goods as the remedy for all personal and social ills. In 2011, the television series *Parks and Recreation* gave us both a mantra and unofficial holiday dedicated to this notion when characters Tom Haverford and Donna Meagle introduced the concept of "Treat Yo Self Day." Dubbed "the best day of the year," and now unofficially celebrated annually on October 13 (the day in which the episode that introduced it first aired), "Treat Yo Self Day" is devoted to treating oneself to clothes, fragrances, massages, mimosas, fine leather goods, and whatever else our little hearts desire. Those fly sunglasses you've been eyeing? Treat yo self. A new pair of kicks? Treat yo self. A fancy dinner with apps and zerts? Treat. Yo. Self. You're worth it, and happiness is only one "buy now" click or swipe of the credit card away.

While the question as to whether or not we can buy happiness is certainly debatable, the acquisition of goods does afford individuals with status in our contemporary society. In *The Theory of the Leisure Class: An Economic Study of Institutions*, Thorstein Veblen coined the term **conspicuous consumption** to refer to the visible social and class markers associated with the purchase and use of specific goods and services, often in excess of what is necessary, as a means to indicate and represent an elevated social status. A Timex watch will tell you that you are late for class just as readily as a Rolex, and a used Honda Civic can get you to the same destination as a Ferrari can. The difference, though, between the products in these two examples is more than just their respective price tags. This is where conspicuous consumption becomes apparent: it is the acquisition of certain products in order to live, and let others know you are living, a particular lifestyle. Having a Rolex or a Ferrari signifies distinguishing taste, a certain amount of wealth, and access to upper socioeconomic levels of social class. On the other hand, anyone can have a Timex or used economy sedan and, therefore, no specific status is associated with these items. By flaunting expensive and sought-after possessions, individuals make their position in our society's social hierarchy apparent. This concept relates back to the second chapter's discussion of the American Dream and its structuring around the goal of achieving wealth and status through the purchase of specific, identifiable consumer goods. This practice also relates back to commodity fetishism, as certain objects and goods take on symbolic value outside of their intended use.

Conspicuous consumption can also relate to one's identity, where in a consumer society, we are what we own. More than just objects, certain products project ideas about who we are as individuals, such as proudly buying goods "Made in America," or being a Mac versus a PC person. This can be seen when we wear the jersey displaying the logo of our favorite sports team just as much as when our bags display the logos of our favorite designers. Even without literal labels, the acquisition and display of certain goods categorizes individuals. For example, those who tend to follow the latest fashion trends without any personal or independent style often fall victim to the pejorative label "basic" for their seemingly blind devotion to mainstream styles. Young, white women are particularly susceptible to the "basic" label, and can be easily identified by their uniform of leggings, Uggs, and accompanying Pumpkin Spiced latte, appearing on Instagram under #blessed. Consumption, then, is more than just the acquisition of goods, but a means of distinguishing individuals between different social groups. Tied to this effect is the practice of **branding**, the image cultivated in order to project a company, product, or individual's "essence" and associated values, skills, or qualities. Branding can be achieved through a symbol, such as the Nike swoosh, or a slogan, such as "Just Do It," and is designed to make products and companies stand out, on their own, and even reach an iconic status. Increasingly college students are encouraged to craft their own brand before heading off into the job market, and celebrity brands now span across markets from screen to stage to department store, whether it be clothing, kitchenware, perfume, or makeup line.

The consequences of all this consumption and the turning of material goods into icons of the gods of consumerism have led some critics to diagnose the United States with a serious case of "affluenza." The term, coined at the end of the twentieth century, mockingly refers to "a painful, contagious, socially transmitted condition of overload, debt, anxiety, and waste resulting from the dogged pursuit of more."[14] Although the condition, itself, is made up, the consequences have been all too real, the most extreme being the case of Ethan Couch. Couch, referred to by the news media as the "affluenza teen," made national headlines in 2013 when he used affluenza as part of his legal defense after killing four people in a drunk driving incident. Only seventeen years old at the time of the accident, Couch's lawyers argued for leniency given that Couch's parents spoiled him and, therefore, argued he was unable to accurately tell right from wrong due to being raised to believe that his family's wealth afforded him certain privileges. Since Couch's trial, affluenza has been used more broadly as a term to describe the general malaise or feelings of depression despite material wealth and comfort, as well as for the spoiled behavior of the wealthy. Although affluenza itself is not a medically diagnosable condition, it has been increasingly used in popular culture to consider the effects of consumerism on the American psyche and individual identity.

The production of consumer goods plays into this condition, always ready with something newer, faster, sleeker, or better to replace the previous good that failed to provide you with lasting happiness and contentment. Industry designers refer to **planned obsolescence** as a strategy of production where products are purposefully designed in such a way that they will become out-of-date and in need of replacement in a short, predetermined time period and/

or before the actual need for a new replacement product. This can be seen from fashion (goodbye skinny jeans, hello wide-leg cuts) to electronics (how many phone chargers are taking up space in your junk drawer right now?) even to software updates (so that's why my iPhone runs slower now than before I updated!). While some of us may grumble at having to shell out for yet another cell phone or laptop, there are just as many others willing to camp out all night outside of their local Apple store to be the first in line for the next generation of iWhatever. In part, this has to do with our own relationship to consumer goods and the needs —physical and emotional—that they fulfill for us.

Key to this process is the role of advertising and the way it hails individuals, turning them into consumers. According to Adorno and Horkheimer, advertising is the "elixir of life" for the culture industry.[15] Taking a decidedly negative view of advertising and advertising practices as they relate to and represent social power, they argue that, ultimately, the "triumph of advertising in the culture industry: [is] the compulsive imitation by consumers of cultural commodities which, at the same time, they recognize as false."[16] The goal of advertising is to influence individuals into buying one good or service over another, and, if you have ever watched an episode of *Mad Men* or paid attention to the obscene amounts of money spent to buy commercial airtime during the Super Bowl, you know that advertising is an art unto itself. To Adorno's and Horkheimer's point, we buy the latest Jordans knowing that wearing them won't really turn us into the next Michael Jordan or LeBron James, any more than we really think that the newest mascara will give us clump-free lashes for miles like those Photoshopped on the models gracing the pages of *Cosmopolitan*. Despite our awareness of advertising's overall goal and purpose, effective marketing taps into our individual desires, plays upon our insecurities, and promises us more than just the good or service being offered. It's the peace of mind provided by our security system (*ATD, they're home even when we're not*) or insurance company (*we're in good hands with All State*) and the promise of adventure (*Built Ford tough!*) or romance (*every kiss begins with Kay*) possible through the acquisition of the right consumer good. Thus, more than just selling a product, advertising becomes a means of transmitting cultural meaning through material objects.

With the rise of new media, new possibilities have emerged for advertising, consumption, and the culture industries as a whole. Convergence, or the "flow of content across multiple media platforms, the cooperation between multiple media industries, and the migratory behavior of media audiences,"[17] has changed how and by whom media is produced and consumed. Advertising has become more sophisticated, following our "clicks" and Internet searches; we now get targeted ads on our Facebook walls and our Twitter feeds. Amazon knows what we like and what we search for, and, like Netflix and other streaming services and online marketplaces, offers us options based on our past purchases, viewings, and browsing history. Taking a positive view of the participatory culture of new media, theorists such as Henry Jenkins see convergence culture like Yelp, product reviews, and YouTube product vloggers turning consumption into a "collective process," where "None of us can know everything; each of us knows something; and we can put the pieces together if we pool our resources and combine our skills."[18]

With the increase in online activity, people are able to meet and interact through different social networking tools. Although these platforms are part of the culture industries, through consumption, they allow for the individual to assert identity and create new cultural productions. Recalling the theories of Certeau presented above, poaching can explain how the products of the culture industries present new opportunity for creation and meaning-making. He writes, "By challenging 'consumption' as it is conceived and (of course) confirmed by these 'authorial' enterprises, we may be able to discover creative activity where it has been denied that any exists."[19] The rise of emojis and memes are two such examples. Memes are pictures with accompanying words that relay some current trend, whether it be a news story or reference to popular media. Named after Richard Dawkins's adoption of the term used by geneticists to explain how ideas get passed around and evolved, the term "meme" now refers to the evolution and sharing of these Internet images. Many of the early memes used the same image over and over (the Goosebumps "Ermahgerd" Girl, Scumbag Steve, Kermit the Frog, and Dos Equis's "Most Interesting Man in the World" are just a few examples) with different messages, though they follow the same sentence structure but pick up on a different common frustrations or current events. Altering and sharing these memes is a form of artful communication, using the Internet as a space to create, share, and communicate one's own meanings.

Along with the popularity of Internet memes, emojis have also become common and prevalent, particularly with the rise of smartphones and tablets and increases in applications (apps) for these technologies. Stemming from a Japanese trend in having small cartoon images stand in for emotions, the trend of emojis soon infiltrated many different platforms. Stickers became available on sites such as Facebook and soon downloadable keyboards were offered in app stores for various smartphone devices. More and more emojis have been added over the years, with the greatest popularity surging in the 2010s. Beyond the original emoji set, other companies and franchises are getting on board with creating them. In 2015 Kim Kardashian's Kimoji app "broke the Internet" when a rush of buyers crashed Apple's App Store upon the emoji's release.[20] Other media crossovers include Comedy Central's *Broad City* emoji keyboard, featuring characters and jokes from the show, and Bravo's stickers and emoji keyboards featuring some of the women and more outrageous moments captured from *The Real Housewives* franchise. While these tools are produced by the culture industries, the communications that result through consumption become their own art forms. Text conversations are not simply typed words, but can become creative forms of expression. Having these various icons assist in communication, often encouraging shared knowledge and codes of inside jokes or interest, is an entertaining and highly complex communication context.

Our smartphones themselves are perhaps one of the most significant cultural products of the twenty-first century. Emblematic of our constant need to be communicating and interacting with the mediated world, they are also highly personalized. From phone covers to the background photos and aesthetic settings on the screen, phones offer options for pseudo-individuality within the context of the culture industries. For example, the arrangement of applications speaks to one's priorities. Most of us will put the apps we need most frequently on the first page or where we can easily access them. For people who use their phones for work, their phones may include work applications and access to multiple e-mail accounts. For those who are more interested in communicating with friends, their first page may have apps for social media such as Twitter, Instagram, and Snapchat. For others, it can be a mix. Looking at my smart phone, I take the mullet approach. The hair style made famous for the "business in the front, party in the back" style works for my phone needs. My e-mail, messages, phone, news applications, maps, weather, calendar, alarm, and camera are on my home screen, but swiping one more page takes me to photos, music, games, social media, meme generators, and fantasy football applications. I try to use my phone for work without getting too distracted, but in my downtime, I can give it a swipe and have hours of entertainment at my fingertips. Through my familiarity with my phone, I can look quickly at the apps on my screen and, based on color and image, know exactly which app is which, allowing me to interact with the products and platforms of the culture industries on my own terms.

Conclusion

While the Internet has helped to democratize a number of practices, it is also important to remember that factors such as education level, age, race, gender, and socioeconomic class impact the degree to which individuals have access to—and agency within—Internet cultures, and that these practices reflect larger disparities in capitalist consumer societies. For example, "haul" videos began cropping up on YouTube in the late 2000s, where teenaged girls and young women share videos of themselves detailing and reviewing their purchases from shopping trips. On the one hand, this practice highlights the heights of materialism and consumerist identity, particularly as they relate to stereotypes of gender and class with respect to white women. On the other hand, many of these women have turned this practice into personal businesses and, like other bloggers, are paid for their reviews and/or make money from embedded advertisements and corporate commissions on associated sales. In this way, these women are using systems designed by the culture industries and where they are traditionally seen at a disadvantage, and instead taking culture typically associated with a certain type of femininity and using it for their own gains. Further, their input not only has the possibility of affecting the direction other consumers take with their purchases, but also has the possibility of influencing the direction of future corporate production and marketing practices.

As such, this is just one way in which we can see how production, goods, and consumption are involved in a messy interchange dependent on a number of factors and variables that are constantly shifting. Therefore, the culture industries not only help shape the tastes and preferences of individuals and groups in society, but in turn, these individuals and groups constantly keep the culture industries in a perpetual state of reinvention. This struggle reflects larger power dynamics in society involving individual consumers, popular culture, and institutionalized power. As we continue our study of popular culture as everyday life, we will look not only at the effects of popular culture on the individual, but also consider other ways in which popular culture texts are used in society for alternate means in addition to corporate control and profits.

Notes

1   F. R. Leavis, *Mass Civilization and Minority Culture* (Cambridge: Minority Press, 1930), 3.

2   Karl Marx and Friedrich Engels, *The German Ideology* (London: Lawrence & Wishart, 1970), 64.

3   Max Horkheimer and Theodor Adorno, "The Culture Industry: Enlightenment as Mass Deception," in *Media and Cultural Studies: Key Works (Revised Edition)*, ed. Meenakshi Gigi Durham and Douglas M. Kellner (Oxford: Blackwell, 2006), 42.

4   Herbert Marcuse, *One-Dimensional Man: Studies in the Ideology of Advanced Society* (Boston, MA: Beacon Press, 1964), 61.

5   Horkheimer and Adorno, "The Culture Industry: Enlightenment as Mass Deception," 41.

6   Dwight Macdonald, "A Theory of Mass Culture," in *Mass Culture: The Popular Arts in America*, ed. Bernard Rosenberg and David Manning White (New York: The Free Press, 1957), 59.

7   Ibid., 62.

8   Ibid., 69.

9   Michel de Certeau, *The Practice of Everyday Life*, trans. Stephen Rendall (Berkeley: University of California Press, 1984), xi.

10   Ibid., xix.

11   Ibid., xii.

12   Federal Communications Commission, "About the FCC," fcc.gov.

13   Dwight D. Eisenhower, "Farewell Address," January 17, 1961, https://www. eisenhower.archives.gov/research/online_documents/farewell_address/Reading_ Copy.pdf.

14   John DeGraaf, David Wann, and Thomas Naylor, *Affluenza: The All-Consuming Epidemic* (2nd edn. San Francisco, CA: Berrett-Koehler, 2005), 2.

15   Horkheimer and Adorno, "The Culture Industry: Enlightenment as Mass Deception," 68.

16   Ibid., 71.

17   Henry Jenkins, *Convergence Culture: Where Old and New Media Collide* (New York: NYU Press, 2005), 2.

18   Ibid., 4.

19   Certeau, *The Practice of Everyday Life*, 167.

20   Luke Dormehl, "Forget Breaking the Internet, Kim Kardashian Broke the App Store," *Cult of Mac*, December 22, 2015, http://www.cultofmac.com/403244/ forget-breaking-the-internet-kim-kardashian-broke-the-app-store/.

5

Heroes and Celebrities

Show me a hero and I will write you a tragedy.

—F. Scott Fitzgerald

In the future, everyone will be world-famous for 15 minutes.

—Andy Warhol

The Internet let out a collective "Holy Heck No Batman!" when Warner Bros. announced in August 2013 that Ben Affleck would be next in line to don the latex suit of the Dark Knight in the much-anticipated *Batman v. Superman: Dawn of Justice*. From comic books, to television series, to feature films, Batman is one of the most enduring superheroes in both the DC Universe and our popular culture landscape. Affleck, an actor whose popularity and respect has seen a number of highs and lows throughout his career, upset a large majority of die-hard Batman fans, triggering a backlash that included the hashtag #Batfleck, Internet memes poking fun at the casting, and Change.org and White House petitions. The latter, taken down by the Obama administration, hoped to "make it illegal for Ben Affleck to portray Batman (or any superhero) on film for the next 200 years." Arguing that concerned Americans "care about our fictional heroes, often more than ones that actually existed," the petition holds nothing against Affleck per se, but points to his "history of ruining films that he doesn't star, direct, produce, and cater all by himself."[1] While *Batman v. Superman*, with its pairing of perhaps the most famous of DC's superheroes, had a premise with the potential for huge success, in many ways the film could not overcome its earlier unenthusiastic publicity. Although it opened strong, setting box office records in its first weekend, negative reviews and audience disappointment made the film a flop despite making a profit for Warner Bros.

Instead, more people seemed to enjoy a viral video associated with the film, which prompted the trending hashtag #SadAffleck. Uploaded by a YouTube user, the video shows an interview with Affleck and Henry Cavill, who plays Superman in the film. The sound of the interview, where Cavill attempts to spin the film's bad reviews, slowly fades out as Simon and Garfunkel's "The Sound of Silence" begins to play. All the while, the camera zooms in on Affleck sadly staring off into space. Given the actor's separation from his wife, actress Jennifer Garner, and other recent bad press surrounding his personal life (rumors of infidelity and problems with gambling and alcohol), it was hard for even the greatest of haters to not feel a little bad for Affleck. Still, in true celebrity form, and like the phoenix of his questionable back tattoo, Affleck's star will rise again.

Fictional heroes, like Batman in the example above, and their real-life counterparts, are characters and individuals who embody the values and ideals of their culture. While heroes may become celebrities in today's day and age, most celebrities, such as our example of Ben Affleck, are not considered to be heroes. This chapter parses out the differences between and blurring of hero and celebrity in popular culture today, discussing the role of heroes in contemporary society, our cultural fixation on celebrities, and the values associated with different types of heroes and celebrities and their various roles in popular culture. By the end of the chapter, you will be able to recognize the relationship between heroes and celebrity with respect to your own life and identity, as well as see their role in the creation of community and culture at large.

And then a hero comes along …

Whether they be family members, religious deities, or historical figures, most people can recognize individuals they consider to be heroes. For some, their heroes are people who have directly impacted their life and/or community. Others look up to prominent individuals who engaged in heroic acts of great leadership or self-sacrifice. The hero is someone we model ourselves after and hope to be, despite knowing (and possibly hoping) we may never find ourselves in situations where extreme acts of heroism are necessary. Instead, the attributes of our heroes that we most admire become the attitudes, values, and actions we try to infuse in our own everyday life. Heroes in our own lives can include single moms who work more than one job to best provide for their children, local teachers who go above and beyond in their mentoring and coaching of local youth, or friends and family members who have recovered from horrific accidents or courageously battled life-threatening illnesses. Alongside the heroes of our local communities are the national heroes in the military and law enforcement, individuals who bravely put their lives on the line every day so that American citizens can live in relative safety. At times when our country has been most vulnerable and under threat, heroes take on amplified importance in the popular culture landscape, such as servicemen and women during times of war, or the increased respect for firefighters and police officers in the immediate wake of 9/11.

Although these examples are all contemporary, heroes have been a mainstay of culture since the earliest days of mythology. While the details of their adventures and heroic acts may evolve over time to reflect shifts and trends in culture, the basic formula of the hero's narrative is relatively stable. As articulated by Joseph Campbell in his influential work *The Hero with a Thousand Faces*, "whether presented in the vast, almost oceanic images of the Orient, in the vigorous narratives of the Greeks, or in the majestic legends of the Bible, the adventure of the hero normally follows a pattern of the nuclear unit [...]: a separation from the world, a penetration to some source of power, and a life-enhancing return."[2] The stages of separation, initiation, and return of Campbell's heroic monomyth each contain a number of steps, with some narratives highlighting particular aspects and others eliminating certain elements all together. Most frequently these include: the call to adventure, refusal of the call, supernatural aid, crossing of the threshold, the road of trials, meeting with the goddess, atonement with the father, the ultimate boon, refusal of return, the crossing of the return threshold, master of the two worlds, and the freedom to live. Regardless of the emphasis on individual stages, the basic formula mimics the **rites of passage** discussed in our chapter on ritual and ceremony, with the outline of the hero transformed through an epic journey that concludes with a homecoming and the expectation that the hero will return to bestow his/her newfound knowledge to the community. Ultimately, Campbell argues, "The goal of the myth is to dispel the need for such life ignorance by effecting a reconciliation of the individual consciousness with the universal will. And this is effected through a realization of the true relationship of the passing phenomena of time to the imperishable life that lives and dies in all."[3] The purpose of the journey is a reconciliation between the material and spiritual worlds, an understanding between the inner and outer selves, and the transformation of growing up and making one's own way in the world.

Examples of the monomyth function in religious stories from the Buddha, to Moses, to Jesus Christ, and have been adapted through popular culture through tales such as *Star Wars*, *Harry Potter*, and *The Lord of the Rings*. Given the nature of the myth, many of its tellings are magical and fantastic in nature. The myth has been adapted for audiences of all ages, with versions for children less complicated than something like *The Matrix*, which is intended for adults. Although not a requirement, as a rite of passage, many stories that adapt the heroic monomyth are "coming of age" tales, with absent or deceased parents integral to the plot. An example you are likely familiar with is Disney's *The Lion King*. In the film, the death of Simba's father, Mufasa, sets Simba off on his journey away from the Pride Lands. Simba mistakenly believes he is responsible for his father's death, and his uncle Scar, the true murderer, convinces him to flee. This is Simba's separation, the first phase in the monomyth described by Campbell. He is removed from the only life that he has ever known and thrust into a world very different, one that will test him. The first step in his phase of initiation, Simba is tested by hyenas Scar sends after him. After managing to escape, he wanders scared and alone in the desert. For a brief moment, it looks as if our hero will not make it. Fortunately, Simba is found by Timon and Pumba, the meerkat and warthog who become his mentors, teaching him the problem-free philosophy of "hakuna matata." Simba grows from a child to young adult, happily passing his time with Timon and Pumba until he encounters Nala, his old friend from the Pride Lands. Nala tells Simba how the Pride Lands have suffered under Scar's rule and encourages him to return. Feeling guilty about his father's death, Simba initially *refuses to return*. After an encounter with the mystical Rafiki where Simba is reminded that his father lives on inside of him, Simba is visited by the ghost of Mufasa. This *atonement with the father* convinces Simba to return to the Pride Lands where he must face his uncle Scar. The two battle, with Simba ultimately prevailing. With Scar eliminated, Simba takes over as rightful heir to the kingdom. The Pride Lands bloom with life once again, and the film ends with Simba and Nala welcoming their own son, thus completing "the circle of life."

The Lion King, which, incidentally, also models itself off the plot of Shakespeare's *Hamlet,* can be read through the lens of the heroic monomyth. *The call to adventure* occurs when Simba is banished from the Pride Lands. His initial wanderings represent Campbell's *belly of the whale,* where the "idea that the passage of the magical threshold is a transit into a sphere of rebirth is symbolized in the worldwide womb image of the belly of the whale. The hero, instead of conquering or conciliating the power of the threshold, is swallowed into the unknown, and would appear to have died."[4] After rescuing Simba, Timon and Pumba initiate him to hakuna matata, and Simba grows into a carefree adolescent. It is the encounter with Nala that forces Simba to remember his past and decide if he will continue to live with no worries for the rest of his days or return to the Pride Lands to assume his responsibilities. The visit from Mufasa's ghost, touchingly depicted in the film, has Mufasa intone, "Look inside yourself Simba, you are more than what you have become. You must take your place in the circle of life [...] Remember who you are, you are my son and the one true king." This encounter mirrors Campbell's description of the atonement with the father, where, "The problem of the hero going to meet the father is to open his soul beyond terror to such a degree that he will be ripe to understand how sickening and insane tragedies of this vast and ruthless cosmos are completely validated in the majesty of Being. The hero transcends life with its peculiar blind spot and for a moment rises to a glimpse of the source. He beholds the face of the father, understands—and the two are atoned."[5] Having come to terms with his father's death, Simba finally realizes and embraces his destiny and completes the monomyth with his "return and reintegration with society, which is indispensable to the continuous circulation of spiritual energy into the world, and which, from the standpoint of the community, is the justification of the long retreat."[6]

Heroes embody characteristics most valued in a culture: they are brave, handsome/beautiful, intelligent, self-sacrificing, kind, resilient, and successful. The supermen and -women who are our fictional heroes may have self-doubt and be reluctant to accept their role as hero, but inevitably step up to the challenge and succeed, championing for the rest of us. When looking up to our heroes, though, it is important that we also recognize their shortcomings. These make the heroes more "real" since, after all, no one is perfect. Having flaws also makes heroes more relatable; we all make mistakes and can be self-conscious about our weaknesses, but if our heroes share these types of self-doubt, then they are easier to connect with. Harry Potter, for example, has many shortcomings. Throughout the books and movies, tracing the time from when he is an eleven-year-old to his transition into adulthood at seventeen, audiences watch as Harry completes the hero's journey as he finds out he is a wizard, matures, and grows into his destiny to fight the evil Voldemort. Like many of our heroes, Harry's start is rough; as a baby he witnesses the murder of his parents, and as a child suffers under the mistreatment and abuse of his muggle (non-magic) maternal aunt and uncle, the Dursleys. His call to action begins when he discovers he is a wizard and is whisked off to Hogwarts, the magical wizarding school. There the trauma intensifies year after year as attempts are made on Harry's life and he witnesses the death of his mentors and friends. At times Harry gets depressed, moody, dramatic, whiny, angst-ridden, abusive, frustrated, and frustrating. He isn't the best student, doesn't always do his work, isn't as competent as he is lucky in his near-death experiences, and his temper not only endangers his life, but also the lives of others. Yet for readers and audiences of all ages, these shortcomings are humanizing. If Harry were perfect, he wouldn't be relatable to audiences reading and watching his journey. Though he manages to triumph time and again, maintain his bravery, work for the benefit of others, and embody characteristics we value highly, his flaws make him more like us.

However, sometimes the characters we root for aren't just flawed, they're horrible. Many of our cultural heroes are actually **anti-heroes**: the protagonists who fail to possess traditional heroic and admirable qualities, often embodying the opposite. Instead of being brave and exceptionally good, working for the interest of others, anti-heroes are borderline villains who often lack courage and/or primarily look out for their self-interest. They are more selfish, work outside of the restrictions of laws, and don't subscribe to a particular moral code. Their flaws aren't just minor weaknesses, but dangerous. As a result, these characters can be more interesting than the straightforward and simple heroes. Their major flaws work to reinforce those values that we look for in a hero. A quintessential anti-hero is Walter While of AMC's hit series *Breaking Bad*, which ran from 2008 until 2013. Walter starts off as a struggling chemistry teacher diagnosed with cancer. Concerned for the future well-being of his family, Walter turns to cooking meth to make extra money for them. After a miraculous recovery from his illness, though, Walter doesn't stop his drug-making and dealing, but goes deeper and deeper into the world of drugs and crime. A murdering, drug-making criminal is by no means a hero, yet week after week, audiences tuned in to watch Walter's exploits, and despite their moral conscious, rooted for his success. Anti-heroes populate the fictional worlds of *The Walking Dead, Dexter, Sons of Anarchy, Mad Men, Game of Thrones, The Blacklist, Pirates of the Caribbean, Revenge, House of Cards*, and many other films, television series, literature, and comic books. While they may not be the epitome of all that is right with the world, they do embody something that audiences are feeling they need at the moment. In a time of constant news of political turmoil, war, mass murder, and other atrocities, coupled with a decline in trust for our government and law enforcement to look out for us and our best interests, new heroes are needed. If going by the book is failing to protect us, then radical action must be taken. Anti-heroes are the outlaw figures that just might bring about the change people feel is needed, and nothing as trivial as laws or morals can stand in their way.

Popular culture narratives of the monomyth, the hero's journey, and even the tales of our anti-heroes work to inspire us to live our life's purpose. While often clichéd, they serve as points of encouragement during times of heartache or despair, instilling a sense of faith, whether it be in a higher power or in oneself. They help teach us to embrace struggle and adversity, seek help from others, and encourage us to become ordinary heroes by giving back to our communities. Although popular culture can provide us with fictionalized accounts of heroes, it is important to remember that "we can make a celebrity, but we can never make a hero."[7] While professional athletes, actors, and other celebrities are often looked up to in society, they should not be confused with heroes. As historian Daniel Boorstin warned in the 1960s, "Celebrity-worship and hero-worship should not be confused. Yet we confuse them every day, and by doing so we come dangerously close to depriving ourselves of real role models. We lose sight of the men and women who do not simply seem great because they are famous but who are famous because they are great."[8] A **hero** is an individual who achieves greatness through some form of achievement, action, or deed. A **celebrity**, on the other hand, is an individual who achieves fame not for any specific action or accomplishment, but through their repeated exposure by and through the media. Boorstin's critique of celebrity was housed within a larger dismissiveness of popular culture and, therefore, should be taken with a grain of salt. Still, it is important to our study of popular culture to consider the ways in which celebrities have taken on the role of heroes in contemporary society and what this suggests about larger societal shifts with respect to role models, the power of the media, values, beliefs, and broader understandings of the individual within community.

A star is born

Early studies of celebrity point to the rise of the film industry and the role of Hollywood studios in the manufacture of stardom. As with our previous chapter's discussion of the culture industries, reading stardom and celebrity through this lens relies heavily on thinking about the individual's relationship to capitalism and the role of labor in the creation of celebrity. This not only involves the individual—in this case, the Hollywood star—but also all of the work involved in the creation of celebrity: film studios, agents, publicists, hair and makeup artists, photographers, trainers, paparazzi, and those of us that consume the resultant image. In the early days of the studio system, where stars signed exclusive contracts, Hollywood "controlled not only the stars' films but their promotion, the pin-ups and glamour portraits, press releases and to a large extent the fan clubs. In turn, Hollywood's connections with other media industries meant that what got into the press, who got to interview a star, what clips were released to television was to a large extent decided by Hollywood."[9]

While we will want to pay attention to the ways in which social media and Internet technology have altered this system, it is important to understand the origins of celebrity and the control and influence of the culture industries in shaping our perceptions of stardom. The earliest function of the star was to sell the film in which they appeared. While the

> development of celebrity in fields other than cinema has its own histories of course and, in some cases, the cultural content they carry is significantly different [...] the influence now exerted by the representation of celebrities from a range of industrial locations—sport, popular music, television—in the print media and on television, the development of the film star is perhaps the most elaborate and socially grounded instance of the broad phenomenon of modern celebrity.[10]

Therefore, although each industry has its own nuances associated with fame and stardom, our discussion of celebrity will look at the elements that are most consistent across artistic media. As their potential to become marketers for a host of other products and lifestyles became apparent, the star's position in society became one where they represented not only their films, music, or television series, but a whole host of other ideologies on the individual and his/her role in society. Myths of meritocracy and that anyone can be a success if they worked hard enough became a part of the narrative of the star. Further, in selling their image, the star system helped justify capitalist aims of making money and then using that money to acquire status through material goods. The blurring of the public and private lives of the star both made them accessible and out of reach for the average individual. Their lives became something to admire and attempt to emulate, an impossible mix of both availability and always just being out of reach.

The role of the celebrity in the popular culture landscape is one that touches on the many arms of the culture industries. Media outlets such as TMZ.com, *Access Hollywood*, *On Air with Ryan Seacrest*, and *US Weekly* all play into the creation of the celebrity, helping to cultivate and craft the celebrity image that blends the presentation of their public and personal lives. Graeme Turner, cultural theorist from Australia who has written extensively on celebrity and popular culture, sees this system of celebrity as "a genre of representation and a discursive effect; it is a commodity traded by the promotions, publicity, and media industries that produce these representations and their effects; and it is a cultural formation that has a social function we can better understand."[11] The celebrity, thus, is known for more than their acting or musical abilities, with the tipping point into celebrity occurring when public interest moves past their art or performance and extends to their personal life. Turner's use of genre to describe celebrity is instructive and can help us understand the celebrity lifecycle. As with our previous discussion of genre, there are certain repeated elements needed in the celebrity formula, with variations on the formula to create variety. P. K. Nayar coined the term "celebrity ecology" to refer to the environment of the celebrity as a whole, which includes the celebrity as spectacle, the media construction and audience interest in celebrity; the connection between consumerism, fashion, and celebrity culture; celebrity scandal; and the ways in which celebrities are a social process of power and identity.[12] We can regard these elements as part of the celebrity genre formula, with variations on the elements of identity, scandal, and presentation not only differentiating celebrities, but also shifting with the times to reflect larger cultural preoccupations.

To examine the elements of celebrity ecology, let's view them through the lens of *US Weekly*, a popular US weekly celebrity and entertainment magazine, with accompanying website and social media platforms. In an effort to attract readers at grocery store checkout lines, the front page most often contains a large celebrity photograph to accompany the weekly cover story, with smaller photos pointing to additional coverage one can find inside. Typical cover stories center on celebrity relationships, with headlines such as "Crazy Love" (Mylie Cyrus and Liam Hemsworth), "Surprise Wedding!" (Ryan Reynolds and Blake Lively), "At Home with Baby" (Jessica Simpson, Kate Middleton, Kourtney Kardashian, Kim Kardashian), and "It's Over!" (Taylor Swift and Tom Hiddleston, Owen Wilson and Kate Hudson, Bruce and Kris Jenner). In addition to Hollywood hookups and breakups, other headlines focus on the "private" lives of stars, celebrity workouts, and various scandals. Smaller cover stories point to diet trends, awards show coverage, and "behind the scenes" looks at popular television series or upcoming films. A great deal of coverage is devoted weekly to fashion, with the opening "Red Carpet" spread featuring a different designer each week, with various stars wearing his/her creations; "Who Wore It Best?", which pits celebrities in the same outfit or article of clothing against each other, along with a tally of votes from average people polled in NYC's Rockefeller Center; and "Fashion Police," which mocks stars and their fashion faux pas. A large portion of the magazine is devoted to "Hot Pics," pages of photographs of celebrities working, on the red carpet, and hanging out ("Stars, They're Just Like Us"). Other sections include "Loose Talk," notable weekly quips of stars; "Love Lives," photos of celebrity couples; and "What's in My Bag?" where stars detail the contents of their purse. "Breaking news" is updated on the publication's website and advertised through its various social media, all with the goal of keeping the public informed of the who, what, and where of celebrity culture. The staple features of the magazine are a micro-ecology of celebrity, with its focus on the supposedly private details of celebrity lives, the clothes they wear, the products they consume, and details on the latest celebrity scandals. Only a small portion of the magazine is devoted to the films, music, and television series that serve as the official vehicles for stardom.

The attention on celebrity fashion, the products they consume, and the brands with which they are associated are part of the larger system of celebrity as commodity. Along with this, celebrity also functions as popular culture as everyday life, as celebrities "circulate as images in everyday life and public spaces [...] and thrive on the response these images invoke and circulate even more as a result."[13] Through their image, celebrities help set trends, driving consumers toward certain products and practices in a desire to be like their favorite star. The relationship between celebrity and audience, as well as the control of the circulation of their image, has evolved in the twenty-first century, with reality television and social media inviting us into stars' lives to a greater degree than ever before, as well as giving stars' greater control of their image and access to it.

Reality television tends to highlight either the ordinary lives of (somewhat) extraordinary people or the extraordinary lives of seemingly ordinary people. Many celebrities have offered their lives up for scrutiny in the hopes of recharging their careers or to normalize them for the general public. *MTV Cribs*, beginning in 2000, allowed audiences a peek into the lives of celebrities as they opened the doors of their homes to cameras.

Famous people, including the members of Destiny's Child, Mariah Carey, Snoop Dog, Lil Jon, Tony Hawk, Kanye West, and Ashton Kutcher, all invited people to peek inside of their refrigerators, their bathrooms, their bedrooms, and their many amenities (tennis courts, basketball courts, swimming pools, golf courses, automobiles, and gyms) as a way to gain intimacy with that celebrity, as well as see how the other half lives. *The Surreal Life*, which ran for six seasons on VH1 from 2003 to 2006, took celebrities who were somewhat removed from the limelight and put them in a house to live together, *Real World* style, to see how they managed to get along. Featuring former stars of *The Brady Bunch*, pop star Vanilla Ice, porn star Ron Jeremy, actor Gary Coleman, model Janice Dickinson, professional wrestler Chyna, and many more, it showed washed-up celebrities as real people as opposed to their fictional or stage personas. In the heyday of new types of reality television, other shows featuring celebrities were born. MTV had *The Osbournes*, which ran from 2002 to 2005 featuring rock star Ozzy Osbourne, his family, and their antics, as well as *Newlyweds: Nick and Jessica*, showcasing the short-lived marriage of pop stars Nick Lachey and Jessica Simpson from 2003 to 2005. The inside look at these celebrities, their personal lives, and relationships was an entryway into the transparency necessary to turn an individual from just a famous person into a brand.

While the Kardashian clan had mild fame from their (deceased) father's role in the O. J. Simpson trial in the 1990s and Kim's catapult to fame with an intimate video of her with then-boyfriend and actor/singer Ray J, it wasn't until the premier of their show *Keeping Up with the Kardashians* on E! in 2007 that they became the celebrity powerhouse that they are today. Now the Kardashians and Jenners are household names and brands with the power to make or break others. Some people know more about the inner workings of this family than they do their own family due to the level of exposure the Kardashians have cultivated. A great deal of their success can be attributed to their use of social media. Social media platforms such as websites, blogs, Facebook, Twitter, and Instagram allow celebrities to cultivate their own images through a mix of professional posts and photos, alongside those that are of the mundane and unremarkable, reminding audiences of both the extraordinary elements of their lives (lavish homes, exotic trips, expensive products) and those that make them like any other human (celebrating holidays with family, taking their dogs for a walk, pictures of the bowl of cereal they ate for breakfast). Not only does this help us identify with celebrities and make us feel like we know them on a personal level, but it also demonstrates the ways in which celebrities help set the standards of what is trendy and cool, while driving business toward certain products, practices, and goods. In this way, while the celebrity is still a commodity him-/herself, something for audiences to consume, they also possess their own power, as social media allows the celebrity to cultivate their own image within the system of the culture industries and create a brand outside of studio control. Characteristics and qualities of both products and celebrity are blurred, conferring meaning on to each other, with the goal of increasing the marketability and profitability of both.

The rise of social media also means that fame and celebrity is in greater reach for more individuals. While perhaps not achieving the same levels as the Hollywood star, YouTube vloggers, web series stars, and reality TV contestants have opened the field for our understanding of the contemporary celebrity. They, along with celebrity "D-listers," minor Hollywood stars, have less social influence but still serve the celebrity function of social identifier. Known less for any particular achievement but typically for a specific event that leads to their hyper-visibility and a fleeting amount of fame, Chris Rojek refers to these individuals as "celetoids," individuals known for "any form of compressed, concentrated, attributed celebrity."[14] These can include individuals known for having an affair with someone famous, viral video stars, or short-lived reality TV contestants. Take, for example, William Hung. Hung's infamous off-key rendition of Ricky Martin's "She Bangs" for season three of *American Idol* catapulted him to brief celebrity as fans were attracted to his mix of enthusiasm, confidence, and lack of musical talent. His experience contrasts those of Kelly Clarkson, Carrie Underwood, or Jennifer Hudson, who managed to use their talents to parlay their status to celebrity. This not only involved their music abilities, though, but a transformation of their image (weight loss, makeovers, wardrobe updates) and shift into other music and television genres as well as film. Celebrity vehicles such as contest reality programming are successful in their promotion of the ideology of meritocracy and the belief that any average Jane or Joe has the chance for stardom. All of these various levels of exposure, from reality television to social media, give the appearance of democratizing celebrity. This desire for and belief in the possibility of reaching fame are necessary in perpetuating the celebrity culture.

I'm your biggest fan

Also necessary to the continuation of celebrity culture is the role of audiences and fans. Whether it is the active participation of audience viewers, as was the case with *American Idol* and similar shows, or fans who "follow" celebrities on Instagram, Twitter, Snapchat, and other social media, or just the more passive consumption of media images, audiences are vital to the maintenance of the celebrity system. As an increasing presence in popular culture, celebrities influence the construction of both cultural and personal identities. While the version of celebrity put forth on social media is certainly staged, this presentation and the awareness of it is part of the celebrity persona and the larger celebrity culture that has made the achievement of fame a goal or end unto itself for many young adults in America today. That is, achievement of celebrity status is not only seen as desirable, but as an increasingly possible outcome, regardless of how viable this attainment actually is. Culturally the celebrity works as an embodiment of society's values, even if those values are often contradictory or at odds with each other. On a personal level, celebrities can serve as models for individuals, shaping the process of cultural identity as we buy products endorsed by celebrities or emulate our behavior, speech, and practices based on those modeled by our favorite celebrities. While at times this process is explicit, such as Kylie Jenner's Snapchat tutorials that detail how her line of lip kits can help young women across America score the perfect pout, celebrity culture often has implicit influence over attitudes toward a number of social issues such as mental health, politics, divorce, or sexual identity. These positions and ideas are internalized by individuals not necessarily intentionally mimicking a specific celebrity, but rather our thoughts, responses, and beliefs as they relate to social issues are affected by lives of celebrities that play out in the media. Admiration of the Kardashians and Jenners might alter public opinion on the transgender community. Demi

Lovato's openness on her mental illness could assist those struggling or help those who aren't to better understand. *Celebrity Rehab* and the various celebrities who openly discuss their struggles with addiction might provide hope to others who find themselves in the same situation. What we choose to pay attention to in the lives of celebrities creates a cultural dialogue where people across the nation focus their attention on particular stories or topics. As these topics get discussed and dissected, with everyone feeling comfortable weighing in with their opinion, social anxieties and personal fears rise to the surface and are exposed. Beliefs can be fortified by the action of celebrities or minds can be changed as people gain insight into what it might be like to be someone else. With enough exposure, the lives and opinions of celebrities have the power to change the lives and opinions of all of us.

Early criticism of celebrity culture with respect to audiences stressed a negative "para-social" or second-order relationships, with fans investing time, energy, and attention to the lives of celebrities who they will never know and who will never reciprocate interest. This critique, which took a negative view of celebrity and fan culture, stressed an abnormal surrogate relationship between fan and star, with fans considered socially maladjusted in their obsession with their favorite celebrity. While this type of fan, made notorious in Stephen King's *Misery*, is often parodied or highlighted in popular culture, the majority of folks are fans of someone or something and do not fall into this unhealthy stereotype. The dominance of media across platforms in people's lives, the deliberate interaction of audience and text through shows like *The Voice*, and the changing nature of celebrity in culture has led to a more nuanced understanding of the relationship between celebrity and audience. More commonly, the fascination with celebrity culture suggests "a far more fundamental—be it social, cultural or even religious—function being served than is consistent with descriptions that see it as a merely compensatory, second-order practice."[15]

In *Claims to Fame: Celebrity in Contemporary America*, Joshua Gamson lays out classifications for audiences and their interpretive strategies: traditional, second-order traditional, postmodernist, game player: gossiper, and game player: detective. The audience types are classified based on their level of awareness of the production of celebrity, their mode of engagement, and their understanding of the nature of celebrity and celebrity text.[16] The different levels of audience engagement point to the understanding that one does not have to actively believe individual narratives of celebrity or be an avid consumer of celebrity culture in order for it to influence one's engagement with popular culture. Traditional and second-order traditional audiences tend to regard celebrity narratives as occurring "naturally," that is, not generated and staged through the media machines of public relations and entertainment news. Gamson sees their mode of engagement as one of modeling, fantasy, and identification with the celebrity. This is in contrast to the postmodernist audience type, who is highly aware of the production of celebrity and sees a deconstruction of the technique of celebrity, a "behind the scenes" look of the manufacture of celebrity, so to speak, as the primary mode of engagement. The game players have a medium to high level of awareness of the production of celebrity and use the celebrity narrative for their own social (gossiper) and discursive (detective) purposes. This is not the same as fandom, which will be discussed in more detail in our chapter on community, but for now, we can understand audience engagement with celebrity culture as more layered than passive reception.

Enjoyment of and participation in celebrity gossip falls into this category of engaged behavior. Gossip, in general, works in culture as an activity for circulating, examining, and assessing social norms and behavior as well as for the organization of identities and relationships. As a platform for celebrity gossip and scandal, popular culture becomes a staging ground for testing and evaluating culturally sanctioned behavior and is another way in which celebrity functions in the establishment of cultural identity. In a globalized society where individuals are both connected via the Internet but also geographically dispersed, celebrity also functions as a compensation for the loss of community, with "an avid attention to the figure of the celebrity and a greater investment in our relations with specific versions of this figure. In effect, we are using celebrity as a means of constructing a new dimension of community through the media."[17] Unlike the negative critique of the pathologized para-social engagement with celebrity, this view is a more nuanced understanding of how celebrity functions in larger social engagements between the individual and an increasingly mediated world. This approach also speaks to the way in which celebrities' lives are discussed and shared by individuals in the same way that classmates, coworkers, or family members are discussed. This is not to suggest that celebrities are on the same level of relations as our friends, loved ones, or even enemies, but rather that the circulation of knowledge of celebrity has a discursive function; the shared information base can unite individuals around a common source of public knowledge, such as the use of celebrities throughout this book to illustrate various theories and concepts.

Scandal

Celebrity scandal, in particular, has a way of mobilizing public interest, even in those who typically do not engage in celebrity gossip. Scandal, a key element in our contemporary US news machine in general, is particularly appealing when it involves those individuals whom we have placed on high pedestals. In many ways, it seems that the only thing we love more than a celebrity is a fallen one. "Bad boys" and "good girls gone bad" play into larger cultural narratives of sin and redemption, making the details of scandalous events just as important as the celebrities which they involve. Transgressive, immoral, and illegal behavior involving celebrity often highlights taboo elements of society related to sex, criminality, and/or deviancy. The scandalous behavior not only humanizes the celebrity to the level of the mere mortal, but often also points to larger failings in society related to greed, wealth, and overconsumption. This can take the form of excessive drug and alcohol use, adultery, tax evasion, or bankruptcy from overspending on lavish lifestyles. The average American can, on some level, identify with the transgressive act or, at the very least, its impetus. Coupled with this are the ways in which celebrities often come to see themselves as above the law and, therefore, their transgressions represent larger notions of American exceptionalism. The pattern of celebrity scandal fits that of larger narratives of sin and redemption. Part of the celebrity scandal narrative, then, is the ritual of the public apology. This involves an acknowledgment of the violation of cultural norms, which is necessary for the celebrity to be forgiven and taken back into our collective good graces. At this point, the contrite celebrity becomes more "human" and identifiable, and, as long as the transgression was not too egregious, can find his/her fame restored to previous, and at times even elevated, levels. Our willingness to forgive becomes a litmus test of acceptable behavior in society, and thus "scandals are not only about entertainment and titillation, they also serve another purpose—debate in the public sphere."[18]

Celebrity's sinister cousin—notoriety—operates along a similar vein. The cult of serial killers such as Charles Manson, the Zodiac Killer, or the Son of Sam (perpetuated through fictionalized popular culture narratives of their lives and deeds), as well as the manifestos of school shooters, terrorists, and other perpetrators of mass killings, reflects a dark side of fame in contemporary US culture. Those who commit such atrocious acts of violence often remark that part of the impetus for their behavior is the desire for infamy. Society's fascination with the macabre, both in its real and fictional manifestations, similarly speaks to both the attraction and revulsion to the most taboo of acts. Cultural fascination with murder (particularly among family members), cannibalism, necrophilia, and other sex crimes become a means of processing abhorrent acts of human behavior, acts that seem impossible and yet are committed in our communities by individuals who, on the surface, look and act just like us. Our captivation with the perpetrators of this behavior is not a sanction of these acts nor a public desire for them, but rather an attempt to try and understand the psychology behind individuals who engage in behaviors that are socially ingrained as amoral and unacceptable. Their "celebrity," thus, is less about emulation and more about public discourse and understanding.

Conclusion

Returning to Boorstin's warning that we should not confuse celebrity-worship with hero-worship is an interesting caution to consider in the wake of the 2016 US presidential election. Shortly after Boorstin's writings, Francesco Alberoni distinguished between individuals who possess "political, economic or religious power," and those "whose institutional power is very limited or non-existent, but whose doings and way of life arouse a considerable and sometimes even a maximum degree of interest."[19] Celebrities tend to fall in the latter category, while politicians are those who "have an influence on the present and future fortunes of the society which they direct."[20] The rise of media and the advent of televised debates (the famous Nixon and Kennedy debate demonstrated the power of image as it relates to political candidates), campaign commercials, and politicians appearing on late night talk shows and a host of other media outlets began to blur some of the lines between politician and celebrity. This was only intensified with the election of Ronal Reagan, a former actor, to our nation's highest office, as well as with other celebrities elected to public office, such as professional wrestler Jesse "The Body" Ventura serving as the 38th governor of Minnesota, Arnold Schwarzenegger serving as the 38th governor of California, and former *Saturday Night Live* writer and comedian Al Franken serving as a US Senator. Further, shows like Comedy Central's *The Daily Show* and *The Colbert Report*, with their mix of comedy and serious news reporting and political interviews, made politics mainstream in popular culture. On the flip side, there has been a history of celebrities endearing themselves to political causes, from Leonardo DiCaprio's work with respect to climate change awareness to Shailene Woodley's "stand" with Standing Rock in protest of the Dakota Access Pipeline on sacred Sioux land. This, of course, not only raises awareness of their social issue of choice, but also increases the visibility of the celebrity, extending a certain gravitas to their image.

Philosopher and early sociologist Max Weber's writing on charisma is often cited in theories of heroes and celebrities with respect to the way that leaders seem to possess a special quality that is almost supernatural or godly in its ability to transcend the situation at hand and take charge. While celebrities are not leaders in the same way as politicians, they share the charismatic ability to make individuals feel special, important, and unique while holding a form of power over others. Like the celebrity that seems both like us and other-worldly, politicians often deploy charisma in an effort to appear like the "common" or "working" man. Politicians will often tell of their "humble" beginnings or stage photos holding babies, wearing hard hats, or eating local delicacies, all in an effort to seem more identifiable to average American voters. In this way, folk culture and the popular culture of everyday life are instrumental in the celebrity formula of the politician. With the ebb and flow of popular culture currents, different political figures, like celebrities, come to prominence. Since charisma is tied to cultural anxiety or social tension, charismatic leaders tend to arise as a response to specific political or cultural fears or perceived threats.

In the 2016 election, Donald J. Trump, sensing an undercurrent of mistrust in the government, ran as a political outsider with the promise to "drain the swamp" of Washington. A businessman and real estate developer, Trump's rise to fame in the 1980s relied on his self-purported wealth, extravagant lifestyle, model wives, and glamorous associations. He parlayed this image and persona to mainstream celebrity through the television series *The Apprentice* and *The Celebrity Apprentice*, tapping into the consumer desire of everyday Americans coveting a chance for wealth and power (with *The Apprentice*) and fascination with celebrity (*The Celebrity Apprentice*). His use of Twitter and awareness of the conventions of celebrity allowed Trump to extend his performance from the small screen onto the political stage, paving the way for his stunning victory. While his win may have been shocking to some, in many ways his success is the epitome of the blurring of hero and celebrity in twenty-first-century American culture, a reflection of capitalist and consumer desire at the expense of other democratic ideals. Whether or not you agree with his politics and policies, his candidacy and victory solidify the importance of the study of celebrity and popular culture and the ways in which popular culture is a driving force in understanding identity, community, and culture at large.

Notes

1   Rachel Abrams and Marc Graser, "Fans Petition Warner Bros. to Remove Ben Affleck as Batman," *Variety*, August 23, 2015, http://variety.com/2013/film/news/fans-petition-warner-bros-to-remove-ben-affleck-as-batman-1200587228/.

2   Joseph Campbell, *The Hero with a Thousand Faces* (Princeton, NJ: Princeton University Press, 1972), 35.

3   Ibid., 238.

4   Ibid., 90.

5   Ibid., 147.

6   Ibid., 36.

7   Daniel Boorstin, "From Hero to Celebrity: The Human Pseudo-Event," in *The Celebrity Culture Reader*, ed. P. D. Marshall (New York: Routledge, 2006), 74.

8   Ibid., 74.

9   Richard Dyer, *Heavenly Bodies: Film Stars and Society* (2nd edn. 1986; repr., New York: Routledge, 2004), 4.

10 Graham Turner, *Understanding Celebrity* (London: SAGE Publications, 2004), 14.

11 Ibid., 8.

12 P. K. Nayar, *Seeing Stars: Spectacle, Society and Celebrity Culture* (New Delhi: Sage Publications Pvt. Ltd, 2009), 22–3.

13 Ibid., 2.

14 Chris Rojek, *Celebrity* (London: Reaktion Books, 2001), 20.

15 Turner, *Understanding Celebrity*, 94.

16 Joshua Gamson, *Claims to Fame: Celebrity in Contemporary America* (Berkeley: University of California Press, 1994), 146.

17 Turner, *Understanding Celebrity*, 6.

18 Nayar, *Seeing Stars: Spectacle, Society and Celebrity Culture*, 116.

19 Francisco Alberoni, "The Powerless 'Elite': Theory and Sociological Research on the Phenomenon of Stars," trans. Dennis McQuail in *The Celebrity Culture Reader*, ed. P. D. Marshall (New York: Routledge, 2006), 108.

20 Ibid.

6

Theories of Identity

Americans may have no identity, but they do have wonderful teeth.
—Jean Baudrillard, *America*

The 86th Academy Awards was in many ways like most other Hollywood award ceremonies. An annual celebration of "who's who" on the silver screen, the red carpet was once again rolled out as all of Hollywood's biggest stars gathered to honor the year's finest achievements in film given by the Academy of Motion Picture Arts and Sciences. It was the year of *Frozen* and *Twelve Years a Slave*, as well as the year that solidified "The McConaissance" of Matthew McConaughey with his Best Actor win for *The Dallas Buyer's Club*. Arguably, though, the night's biggest moment had little to do with Oscar at all. Halfway during the telecast, host Ellen DeGeneres huddled some of her "friends" together to take what has since been dubbed the "selfie of the century."[1] The picture included stars such as Meryl Streep and Brad Pitt, with Bradley Cooper actually taking the photo, inspiring DeGeneres to write: "If only Bradley's arm was longer. Best photo ever. #oscars." DeGeneres tweeted the photo during the ceremony, and within two hours the photo was "favorited" and "re-Tweeted" more than two million times, making history and "breaking" Twitter, as it disrupted the site's service for nearly twenty minutes due to user activity surrounding the image.

The selfie certainly had been having a moment well before DeGeneres's photo went viral. *Time* magazine listed "selfie" as one of its top ten buzzwords of 2012, and in 2013 the *Oxford English Dictionary* (*OED*) declared "selfie" the word of the year. The *OED* fittingly traces the etymology of selfie to a 2002 Australian Internet forum, and by 2005 the word was included in the photography inspiration and how-to book the *Photo Idea Index*, with author Jim Krause urging users, "Go ahead, point that lens right at your face and take a flash photo from point-blank range. Bend the rules of photography to the breaking point when you are both the shooter and the subject!."[2] Early selfies were either taken with a digital camera or camera phone held at arm's length or with the camera pointed at a mirror (a popular method for photos on the early social media network MySpace). With the iPhone 4s's introduction of the front-facing camera in 2010, however, along with the growing popularity of sites such as Instagram, the selfie genre has both refined and exploded in popularity. In June of 2015 Taiwanese company ASUS debuted its new phone the "Selfie," complete with a "selfie button," "selfie mode," and "beautification mode," designed to optimize an individual's selfie appearance. While the introduction of the Selfie phone is extreme, it is undeniable that everyone from the president to the pope has embraced the selfie, with the Kardashians solidifying the rules for putting one's best face forward: hold your phone high, know your angle, know your lighting, and know your duck face![3]

If we consider the selfie as a genre, a number of conventions appear: selfies are spontaneous, yet never accidental; casual; amateur; quickly disseminated; and often include a caption and/or hashtag for context. Meant to be shared, the selfie provides individuals the opportunity to shape and disseminate their own image, offering insight not only into who we are, but also "where we are, what we're doing, who we think we are, and who we think is watching."[4] Given the ease, speed, and preponderance of selfies, they have become a record of everyday life in the twenty-first century; not only a product of popular culture, but a tool with which to explore both the understanding and presentation of the self. This notion of the self, and more specifically its social markers, our identity, is the focus of this chapter. On the following pages, you will be introduced to different theories of identity and will begin to see the role of popular culture in shaping an individual's conception of his/her self and identity.

Born identity?

Selfies aside, questions of identity surround us daily. ID cards—whether issued by the government, employers, or other institutions—purport to detail who we are, while providing and/or limiting access to a variety of services. Passports, driver's licenses, and student IDs all fall into this category and signify our entrance and belonging to a number of locations. Increasingly, there are also our online identities, the avatars and profiles we send off into virtual space, which may or may not correspond to the identities we inhabit in the physical world. This very notion of "online" versus "offline" identity demonstrates the variable ways in which we think of identity, as well as the precarity associated with it, ranging from unstable identities to identity complexes to identity theft. *Catfish: The TV Show*, which centers on false identity and online dating, is a perfect example of the ambiguities associated with identity and the ways in which the Internet has opened up a world of possibilities of reconceiving and manipulating identity, whether it be for innocent or malicious intent. As it relates to popular culture, then, identity can mean a number of things on both an individual and collective level. It can refer to how we think of ourselves (either as individuals or as a group), a means of representation (how identity is presented in and by popular culture), or as a means of self-expression (how we use popular culture to present ourselves to others). Popular culture, therefore, provides a means of both shaping our perceptions of our identities and the identities of others, as well as a way to express these different identities. The presentation of identity is necessary, as identity is culturally recognizable and is a way in which we order and make sense of the world.

The notion of "difference" is also important, as identity is often defined through what it is not, or as cultural theorist Stuart Hall (1996) notes, "Above all, and directly contrary to the form in which they are constantly invoked, identities are constructed through, not outside, difference."[5] Thinking back to our chapter on genre, an example of this would be someone who, when talking about music preference, says, "I listen to everything, except country." In constructing our identities through difference ("I like music that is *not* country"), we not only distinguish ourselves (i.e., someone with "good" taste in music), but also solidify our unity with others (people who share our music preferences and dislike of country music), forming various communities. Community and group identity will be explored in greater detail in subsequent chapters, but for now it is necessary to note that popular culture is influential on both levels of identity, and has increasingly been a force that simultaneously disrupts and stabilizes conceptions of identity.

Understandings of the self and identity have shifted as a response to social, cultural, and political change over the twentieth and twenty-first centuries. Our earliest notions of the self came from the Enlightenment, where the individual was seen as fully formed and individualized from birth, retaining a consistent identity throughout his life. The use of the word "his" here is purposeful, as these early understandings of the self were rooted in white, European, and masculine thought, where considerations of common factors of identity today, such as gender, race, or ethnicity, were at best ignored, and at worse seen as less than, defective, or aberrations from the norm. Broad in scope, the Enlightenment dominated intellectual thought during the late seventeenth and early eighteenth centuries. Focused on reason and individualism, the Enlightenment as a movement gave birth to a variety of theories that influenced the sciences, religious thought, and political order. Although the French Revolution and other upheavals in Europe would signal the end of the Enlightenment period, one of its lasting legacies is the individual's notion of self-awareness.

Analyze this

While the industrial revolution, urbanization, and the First World War brought forth a great deal of social and political global change leading up to and into the early part of the twentieth century, perhaps the greatest influence on shifting notions of the self can be traced to a single individual: Sigmund Freud. If you've ever tried to analyze one of your own dreams, accused someone of being anal, or caught yourself in a Freudian slip, you have the theories and legacy of Sigmund Freud to thank. Much of this legacy has to do with the **Frankfurt School**, a group of social and cultural theorists influential in founding the field of critical theory during the interwar period of the First World War and the Second World War. The work of the Frankfurt School is diverse and wide-ranging (and is referred to in a number of chapters throughout this book), and many of the thinkers associated with this movement applied Freudian psychoanalysis to social theory and to our understanding of the relationship of identity to society. Therefore, a basic understanding of Freudian psychology is useful in considering the formation of identity and its relation to popular culture.

Psychoanalysis is the term used to refer to the theories and practices associated with Freud's understanding of human development, which largely rests on his notion of the "psyche," the way in which the mind functions at the center of thought, emotion, and behavior. According to Freud, the psyche is divided into the "conscious" (that which exists in the external world) and the "unconscious" (our internal world), which is made up of our instinctual desires and drives, as well as our repressed thoughts and emotions. The psyche is responsible, consciously or unconsciously, for adjusting and mediating the body's responses to its social and physical environments.

Freud's structure of the psyche is divided into three parts: the id, ego, and superego. The id is our unconscious; we are born with it, and the id is solely about fulfilling desire. As such, it is the unconscious force that serves as the source of instinctual impulses and demands (think a mob of shoppers when the doors open at Walmart on Black Friday). Working somewhat in opposition to the id is the ego. The ego resides in the realm of the conscious, and most immediately controls our thoughts and behavior. Developed through cultural contact, the ego is most in touch with external reality. According to Freud, the ego controls our behavior based on the cultural codes of our society. In describing these two elements of personality, Freud wrote, "the ego represents what may be called reason and common sense, in contrast to the id, which contains the passions."[6] The third element of the psyche, the superego, is the division of the unconscious that is formed through the internalization of the ethical standards of society. It sensors and restrains the ego through an understanding of morals and values. Produced by the ego, Freud describes the relationship between the two as, "whereas the ego is essentially the representation of the external world, of reality, the superego stands in contrast to it as the representative of the internal world, of the id."[7] In many ways the superego is our quest for perfection, our philosophical and spiritual ideals.

While few today practice psychoanalysis as a therapeutic model, or rely heavily on Freudian theory for psychiatric work on an individual, the persistence of Freud's influence is still readily seen through popular culture. Freud's ideas have been referenced, adapted, and portrayed in literature, film, and television as a way to structure plot, character, and conflict in a number of popular culture texts. For the purposes of our study, then, we are more concerned with the impact of Freudian theory as it relates to popular culture's relationship to identity formation, as opposed to thinking of it in terms of medical diagnosis. For example, Freud's work on dreams has been linked with film theory, where the film is seen as a type of "fantasyscape." Author-centered analysis approaches films and media texts as projections of an author's dream, the manifest content of his/her latent or hidden desires. Or, in other cases, such as the filmography of director Alfred Hitchcock, films can be read as analysis and interpretation of Freudian theory (i.e., the Oedipus Complex in *Psycho*, trauma and repression in *Marnie*, scopophilia in *Vertigo*, etc.). Audience-centered analysis, which will be discussed in greater detail in the next chapter, at times relies on psychoanalytic theory to consider the ways in which audiences symbolically play out desires and fantasies through the texts they consume.

The mirror has two faces

Along with Freud, one of the most influential twentieth-century thinkers in the field of psychoanalysis is Jacques Lacan. Like Freud, Lacan's writing and theories influenced a number of disciplines and fields in the twentieth century, ranging from the humanities, cultural studies, and the social sciences. Lacanian psychoanalysis is structured around the notion of "lack." For Lacan, the separation one experiences from his/her mother is foundational in the development of the psyche. Lack refers to this separation from the union with the mother, and it drives subjects to overcome this supposed "lack" in an endless quest in search of an imagined moment of plenitude. Lacan referred to this imagined moment as '*l'objet petit a*'. Since we can never achieve reunion with the mother/lack, we use substitutes and symbolic strategies as a means of displacement for our unattainable objects of desire. As discussed in Chapter 4, this is why we believe our life will be "complete" when we get the newest cell phone, gadget, or latest pair of sneakers, only to find that in a few months, or sometimes even weeks, something else has come along that we absolutely cannot live without.

With respect to our current discussion of identity, Lacan's "mirror stage" refers to the child's desire to construct a sense of self. Lacan postulates that this significant moment in identity development occurs somewhere between the ages of fifteen and eighteen months when a child looks in a mirror (real or metaphorical) and begins to recognize him/herself as a separate individual. That is, the recognition of the self as a subject that looks and an object that is looked at. The child's recognition, however, is "fictional"[8] according to Lacan, as it only offers an image of completeness of the child. Lacan uses the term "imago" to refer to the image of a complete ideal self, which is a creation of the external world. This is in opposition to the "ego," by which Lacan means the internal self. With respect to identity, Lacanian psychoanalysis is a negotiation between the image of an ideal self and the ego, which takes place through imaginary and symbolic processes.

The film *Divergent* (based off of the Veronica Roth novel) demonstrates this concept and its relationship to identity well. Set in a dystopian future, society is divided into "factions," which individuals are placed into based on personality and psychological aptitude testing. The film's protagonist, Beatrice, is a "divergent," meaning that she is capable of independent thought and, therefore, is less likely to be susceptible to social control. Early in the film, audiences learn that Beatrice's birth faction, "Abnegation," is raised to be selfless. They eschew vanity, and Beatrice only gets to see her own image (from the chest up) for a few minutes a few times each year. When she enters the room for her aptitude test, however, she glances at herself in a mirror, and sees her full body—her full "self"—for the first time. Although she is much older than a baby, the film alludes to the "mirror stage" during this and the subsequent test scene, where Beatrice must "choose" who she will become. After her testing, Beatrice returns home, where she sneaks glances at her image in household objects such as her spoon. These acts foreshadow Beatrice's ultimate decision to leave her family and "Abnegation" to become a "Dauntless," where she renames herself "Tris" and claims her new identity.

Marxism reloaded

In addition to engaging theories of psychoanalysis, many contemporary cultural theorists also respond to and borrow from another influential figure—albeit a very different kind—from the twentieth century: Karl Marx. Just as Freud and Lacan were concerned with identity formation in relation to the psyche and its negotiation with the outside world, Marx was interested in the ways in which identity is formed in response to outside forces. His concern, however, was more related to economic and social structures, most notably the response of class to capitalism, and their effects on identity formation. As discussed in the previous chapters on cultural myths and icons and consumption, **ideology** refers to the beliefs, practices, and principles that inscribe meaning, wield power, and shape society through a collective adherence of shared values. For Marx and for many influenced by his work, ideology is one of the driving forces behind identity formation, particularly as it relates to labor and social class.

Influenced by both Lacan and Marx, Louis Althusser defined ideology as "an imaginary relation to real relations."[9] By this he means that ideology is an understanding or representation of the world created through the existence of actual structures, events, and systems. The concept of ideology was important to Althusser, as he saw it as key to an individual's identity formation in relation to society and the state. Specifically, Althusser argued that this formation occurred through a process of interpellation, where "all ideology hails or interpellates concrete individuals as concrete subjects."[10] That is, society and culture call upon individuals to act in certain ways; therefore, our identity both responds to and shapes ideology. According to Althusser, this is carried out through the "Repressive State Apparatus" (RSAs) and "Ideological State Apparatuses" (ISAs). The RSAs reside in the public domain and include official offices such as the government, military, and the justice system. ISAs, on the other hand, function in the private domain and include the family, the media, religion, and popular culture. Unlike the RSAs, which alter and shape our behavior by violence or force, ISAs are subtler in their ability to coerce individuals into specific behaviors and identities. From religious tenets ("Thou shalt not steal") to product slogans ("Choosy moms chose Jif!"), we are constantly bombarded by messages on who we should be and what we should do. Though these messages come at us from all directions, we do not necessarily pick up and respond to them all. Those that we do answer the call of are the ones that we then internalize and use to form our identities.

The ways in which ideology and ISAs operate in culture are through means of **discourse**. Michel Foucault, influenced by Althusser and his work, used this term to describe the ways in which the relationship between knowledge and power circulates in culture through speech and thought in order to exert control. An understanding of discourse is important to contemporary discussions of identity, as an individual's perception of him-/herself is shaped by a variety of discourses in modern society, many of which are circulated through popular culture. This theory of discourse's influence on identity will be explored more fully in the next chapter, where we will consider the discourses that surround specific identity markers, such as gender, race, and class. Before focusing on these specific identities, though, we want to consider the ways in which various political shifts, industrial advances, and economic powers have shaped our understanding of identity in the second half of the twentieth century into the twenty-first century. Advertising, consumer culture, and the rise of the media coalesced in the second half of the twentieth century to offer up a number of possible different avenues for identification. This proliferation of discourse and influences results in what some refer to as a "crisis of identity," creating a "postmodern subject." This development, as described by Stuart Hall, is one where, "as the systems of meaning and cultural representation multiply, we are confronted by a bewildering, fleeting multiplicity of possible identities, any one of which we could identify with—at least temporarily."[11] It is from this process that many argue that identity is not fixed or permanent, but rather a fluid negotiation between an individual and the changing world around him/her. Whereas as identity was previously conditioned by traditions and customs dictated by institutions such as religion, community, and the nation-state, political, technological, and ideological shifts in the second half of the twentieth century offered new avenues for self-expression and modes of identification.

Performing me

As all of these theories work to explain the way that the self is conceived and created internally, sociologist Erving Goffman describes how that identity is outwardly expressed and shared with others. The title of his famous book *The*

Presentation of Self in Everyday Life suggests that who we are, the self that we create from past experiences and imposed ideologies, is then channeled into a performance in one's everyday dealings and interactions. Goffman says that the understanding of this presentation begins with the recognition that people read one another, looking upon other individuals for markers of identity that might point to characteristics such as occupation, interests, socioeconomic class, and any number of things. Understanding something about another person or persons helps us to approach and successfully engage unknown individuals, situations, and contexts. What people read, though, in a person is actually a performance. Using the analogy of drama and acting throughout his book, Goffman compares everyday life to a stage performance where individuals are actors who perform the character of self to audiences of other people. He defines performance in this way, as "all the activity of a given participant on a given occasion which serves to influence in any way any of the other participants."[12] Our understanding of **performance**, then, is the stylized, repetitive acts that communicate the expression of self or the enactment of beliefs to audiences. In these daily performances, the individual is the performer, or the "harried fabricator of impressions involved in the all-too-human task of staging a performance" acting out and performing their fabricated character, "a figure, typically a fine one, whose spirit, strength, and other sterling qualities the performance was designed to evoke."[13] Therefore, individuals put on their best face and highlight their best or desired characteristics to portray a character to their audience, the others they interact with in their daily lives. This performance of self is also dependent on outside factors such as the setting, props, and other individuals present. Combined, these elements compose the "front region," while the "back region" is where the full performance is constructed and the props are stored. That is, the back region is the place where individuals can drop all of the details of the performance and instead work on its creation. When applying this to our daily lives, there are elements of our routine that we all want to hide from others. The act of "getting ready" to go to school, work, or out for the night is typically private. No one wants an audience for the struggle to pick out clothing, put on makeup, fix hair, and other forms of primping, because this shows the effort and preparation for the performance, and part of the performance of self is that who we are is effortless. As we will explore in the next chapter, this act of performance influences how we express the socially constructed characteristics of our gender, racial, and even socioeconomic identities. Not only does this occur in face-to-face contact, but in how we carefully craft and present ourselves through various social media platforms by posting thoughts, images, and shared links to portray who we are. This presentation relates to Goffman's assertion that "[i]ndividuals will be concerned with maintaining the impression that they are living up to the many standards by which they and their products are judged," and, therefore, work to "give off" that impression.[14] Our selves are therefore not just the internalizations of outside influence, but the carefully crafted, though partially unconscious, efforts of outward expression to an audience to impress upon them an image of who we are.

The effects of globalization and neoliberal practices on identity have created a "do-it-yourself society, [where] we are now all entrepreneurs of our own lives."[15] This mentality is reflected in popular culture through Pinterest boards devoted to inspirational quotations, exercise routines, and the latest makeup trends; magazines which offer "25 Successful Men Whose Life Stories You Should Hack" and promise a "New Year, New Booty"; television series aiming to reshape and re-clothe our bodies (*The Biggest Loser*, *What Not to Wear*); and wearables such as Fitbit and Apple Watch, which can tell us everything from how many steps we have taken in a day to how good of a night's sleep we've had, all in effort to help us transform into the best possible versions of ourselves. These latest technological aids are part of the "quantified self movement," which uses technology and Web apps to track personal data in an attempt to gain "self knowledge through numbers."[16] The advent of such technology and its fusion with our bodies and selves have led some to argue that we are now in an age of "posthuman" identities, which are fluid in their location and representations of expression, and are not fixed to a singular notion of self or body. Instead, identity is understood as a shift "away from notions of the long-term and emotional depth and towards identity-practices based on plasticity, flexibility, and adaptability."[17] As individuals and cultural forms become more portable in the twenty-first century, so, too, do our identities find new forms of mutability and mobility.

Our bodies, our selfies

So far, a great deal of our discussion has centered on notions of the "self." So, what then, does any of this have to do with identity, or our example of the selfie from the beginning of the chapter? To begin with, while there are similarities between the concepts of personality and identity, identity suggests a more active engagement with a specific trait or characteristic than personality. Much of this engagement is reflective of cultural ideology and heavily shaped by discourse. Popular culture, then, becomes both the means and the stage for this engagement, a site of struggle for power relations embodied on an individual level. As defined by Stuart Hall, identity is, "the meeting point, the point of *suture*, between on the one hand the discourses and practices which attempt to 'interpellate,' speak to us or hail us into place as the social subjects of particular discourses, and on the other hand, the processes which produce subjectivities, which construct us as subjects which can be 'spoken.'"[18] Theorized in this way, identity is not fixed, but is rather a negotiation of the self within a number of cultural and political contexts. Rather than a stable constant, identity is in a state of flux.

This idea, which we will refer to as a **social construction theory**, is in contrast to earlier, essentialist notions of identity. Enlightenment notions of the self fall into the category of essentialism. Essentialism, as its name suggests, hinges on the notion that there is something "essential," or fundamental, about an individual that shapes his/her identity (or "essence"). As such, essentialism relies on a false belief that individuals are categorized based on inborn, central features exclusive to their grouping. Essentialist ideas often rest on stereotypes related to a number of identity markers, including race, gender, sexuality, and religion. Those who take an essentialist perspective on identity see identity as a basic element within an individual, an element that is inherited, and therefore uninfluenced by outside factors such as culture, politics, or historical context. In the "nature versus nurture" debate, essentialism aligns itself on the side of nature. It is in this way that essentialist notions of identity are perpetuated through deceptive beliefs in biology, progress, and history that see these concepts as stable, fixed, and unchanging over time.

One of the criticisms of this approach to identity is that essentialism tends to rely on binaries. A binary is a way of arranging the world in terms of ideas, structures, and/or individuals seen as two factors defined in opposition to each other (male/female, black/white, thought/feeling, etc.). In defining two objects or traits in opposition to each other, a hierarchy is created, leading to power struggles (which will be elaborated on in much greater detail in the next chapter). That is, when you define two things in opposition to each other, one is seen as "good" and the other seen as "bad" (or, at the very least, as "not good"), which is, in itself, a binary. This is a very "black and white" way of thinking, which rarely represents the reality and complexity of the world and its inhabitants. In addition to establishing a false hierarchy, another criticism of binaries is that defining terms in opposition to each other doesn't really tell you anything specific about the individual elements being compared. For example, if I say I am a female because I am not a male, that doesn't really tell you what a male *or* female is. Binaries are rooted in notions of essentialism, where identity is fixed, and in creating this one versus the other, a power structure is always in place. This is due to the oppositional nature of definition with binaries, where meaning is generated through difference. Structuring identities through binaries is troublesome because it suggests a simplistic relationship between seemingly (though rarely) opposite terms, when in actuality difference is neither inherent nor as clear cut as the oppositional relationship suggests.

While social and physical scientists continue to debate "nature versus nurture," most contemporary discussions of identity use a social constructionist approach. As its name suggests, the **social construction** theory is an active approach to identity that considers the ways in which identity is constructed through social structures and culture. To examine this idea more fully, let's return to the selfie. Grab your phone and take a quick photo of yourself. Now take a few moments and jot down what you see. In mine, I see a female, one who is white, young*ish* (at least I think so), and appears to be "healthy." My immediate observations relate to the body: the physical presentation of my self. In contemporary culture, identity and the body are intimately related. It may seem that these observations related to my sex and race are "natural." These assumptions will be questioned more fully in the next chapter. For the moment, though, it is enough to say that, as with identity, the body both inscribes meaning and has meaning inscribed upon it through popular culture. For example, in my selfie, one might notice that I am wearing casual clothing and small, somewhat conservative jewelry. Although these are not observations about my body specifically, they are examples of how I present myself through material goods and my body in order to project a certain image to the world. I am wearing makeup and my newly cut hair is styled. These are some of the quickest ways in which one might identify me as female. In terms of my own engagement with my body and identity, although elements of my appearance are casual, I actually made a number of choices and put a fair amount of effort into shaping and clothing my body. These choices are very much influenced by popular culture, both by what I consider to be "in style," as well as what I consider "appropriate" for my social location (class, education level, profession, etc.). There are a number of ways in which the body can be modified (tattoos, piercings, makeup, etc.) in order to project identity, and these constructions and their associated values and meanings are the focus of the following chapter.

As philosopher and cultural critic Susan Bordo notes,

> When we admire an image, a kind of recognition beyond a more passive imprinting takes place. We recognize, consciously or unconsciously, that the image carries values and qualities that 'hit a nerve' and are not easy to resist. Their power, however, derives from the culture that has generated them and resides not merely 'in' the image but in the psyche of the viewer too.[19]

While Bordo is referring to the media images we see through popular culture, we can apply this same reasoning to selfies—both our own and those we see of our family, friends, and celebrities shared through social media. If you scroll through your Instagram feed or Facebook, you can begin to see the values and qualities presented by these images and the ways in which we as viewers identify with them. They are not only projections of an individual's identity, but carry with them meaning and ideology circulated through popular culture. The images themselves become a kind of discourse, not only presenting the identity of one individual, but also serving as a tool by which others can shape their own identities. As the distinction between public and private life continues to blur in the twenty-first century, the selfie, along with social network photo sharing, becomes an increasingly important way for individuals to negotiate their own place within a globalized and mediated world. Certainly, tools such as image filters and Photoshop offer the option of putting one's "best face forward," and there is a conscious choice as to how we frame these images and what aspects of our life we choose to share. While not always a true representation of our reality, however, these images do offer a glimpse into both who we are collectively as a society and how we wish the world appeared to us.

Conclusion

As you consider your selfie, we can think back to our goals of the chapter, which were to become familiar with theories of identity and to use those theories to begin to make connections to our own identity constructions. With this in mind, we can begin to see, with the very concept of the selfie itself, that popular culture is a defining factor in the formation of our identities. As discussed, our understanding of identity has developed over the course of the twentieth and twenty-first centuries. Rather than seeing our identities through an essentialist view, where identity is a fixed element of our selfhood that remains unchanging, contemporary theories of identity are rooted in the notion of social construction. Although some have argued that this resultant "crisis of identity" is detrimental to the individual and society as a whole, others advocate for a more positive appreciation of the multiple ways in which one can identify with other individuals and groups, and advocate for a more fluid understanding of identity. Our next chapter will continue this exploration of the social construction of identity, paying particular attention to specific identity markers, and locating them within larger discourses of power within popular culture and society.

Notes

1   Lillian Min, "Oscars 2014: Ellen's #Selfie Wins Internet. Breaks Twitter," *Yahoo Movies*, March 2, 2014, https://www.yahoo.com/movies/bp/oscars-2014–ellen-s–selfie-wins-internet–breaks-twitter-034518537.html.

2   Jim Krause, *Photo Idea Index* (Cincinnati, OH: HOW Books, 2005), 148.

3   Huffington Post, "Kim Kardashian's Rules on How to Take the Perfect Selfie," *Huffingtonpost.com*, December 2, 2013, http://www.huffingtonpost.com/2013/12/02/kim-kardashian-selfie-rules_n_4372892.html.

4   Jerry Saltz, "Art at Arm's Length: A History of the Selfie," *Vulture*, January 26, 2014, http://www.vulture.com/2014/01/history-of-the-selfie.html.

5   Paul Du Gay and Stuart Hall, *Questions of Cultural Identity* (2nd edn. 1996. Los Angeles: Sage, 2011), 4.

6   Sigmund Freud, *On Metapsychology: The Theory of Psychoanalysis* (1914; repr., Harmondsworth: Pelican, 1984), 364.

7   Ibid., 366.

8   Jacques Lacan, "The Mirror Stage as Formative of the Function of the I," in *Ecrits: A Selection*, 1949, trans. Alan Sheriden (New York: Norton, 1977), 2.

9   Althusser, "Ideology and Ideological State Apparatuses (Notes Toward an Investigation)," 82.

10   Ibid., 85.

11   Stuart Hall, "The Question of Cultural Identity," in *Modernity: An Introduction to Modern Societies*, ed. Stuart Hall, David Held, Don Hubert, and Kenneth Thompson (Malden, MA: Blackwell, 1996), 598.

12   Erving Goffman, *The Presentation of Self in Everyday Life* (New York: Anchor Books, 1959), 15.

13   Ibid., 252.

14   Ibid., 251.

15   Anthony Elliott and Charles Lemert, *The New Individualism: The Emotional Costs of Globalization* (New York: Routledge, 2016), 3.

16   Gary Wolf, "Homepage," *Quantifiedself.com*, http://quantifiedself.com/.

17   Anthony Elliot, *Identity Troubles: An Introduction* (Abingdon: Routledge, 2015), 9.

18   Du Gay and Hall, *Questions of Cultural Identity*, 5–6.

19   Susan Bordo, *Twilight Zones: The Hidden Life of Cultural Images from Plato to OJ* (Berkeley: University of California Press, 1997), 127.

7

Social Constructions of Identity

Now every girl is expected to have Caucasian blue eyes, full Spanish lips,
a classic button nose, hairless Asian skin with a California tan, a Jamaican
dance hall ass, long Swedish legs, small Japanese feet, the abs of a lesbian
gym owner, the hips of a nine-year-old boy, the arms of Michelle Obama,
and doll tits.

The person closest to actually achieving this look is Kim Kardashian, who, as
we know, was made by Russian scientists to sabotage our athletes.

—Tina Fey, *Bossypants*

As discussed in the previous chapter, identity has personal and public dimensions; it is both how we see ourselves and how others see us. But what happens when a disconnect occurs between the two? In 2015 America grappled with this question when Ruthanne and Lawrence Dolezal reported that their daughter, Rachel, who had recently filed hate-crime complaints, had been erroneously presenting herself as black to authorities and the media. Ruthanne and Lawrence, both Caucasian of European descent (with traces of Native American heritage), are Rachel's biological parents. Dolezal, who was then-president of the Spokane, Washington, chapter of the National Association for the Advancement of Colored People (NAACP), self-identifies as a black woman and altered her outward appearance more in accordance with how she sees herself. Questions surrounding Dolezal's identity—and racial identity more broadly—quickly made national news, with numerous media outlets reporting on the story, becoming a Twitter trending topic, and with Dolezal ultimately giving "exclusive" interviews with NBC's *Today* show and on MSNBC.

The Dolezal story broke shortly after Bruce Jenner's April 24, 2015, interview with Diane Sawyer, where he declared, "I'm a woman," before revealing Caitlyn

Jenner to the world via her July 2015 *Vanity Fair* cover. Jenner's transition was chronicled on the E! reality TV series *I Am Cait*, which introduced America not only to Caitlyn Jenner, but also to the vocabulary and world of the transgender community. TLC's *I Am Jazz* and ABC Family's *Becoming Us* were two other reality television series that premiered in the summer of 2015 with a focus on transgender individuals and their families. That same year Jeffrey Tambor won both a Primetime Emmy and Golden Globe award for his portrayal of the transgender character Maura Pfefferman on the Amazon original series *Transparent*. Tambor's wins came a year after trans-woman Laverne Cox was nominated for a Primetime Emmy for her work on the Netflix original series *Orange Is the New Black*.

These stories, as well as the racial tensions resulting in the Black Lives Matter movement, concerns over immigration and refugees, and other identity-based conversations led *New York Times* writer Wesley Morris to declare 2015 as the "Year We Obsessed Over Identity."[1] Similar to our discussion in Chapter 6 on the malleability and contemporary D.I.Y. ethos of identity, Morris argues, "Our reinventions feel gleeful and liberating—and tied to an essentially American optimism." This "optimism" comes at a time of political unrest, an uptick in mass shootings in the United States, global tensions, and acts of terrorism. In a way, control over our own identities becomes even more potent when the outside world seems less stable and less knowable than ever before. As a distraction from the less than ideal day-to-day, a turn inward to focus and dwell on the ins and outs of one's self allows for an escape from negative outside events. In June 2014, Gallup polls revealed that Americans are increasingly losing confidence in all branches of the US government.[2] At the same time, the government, under the auspices of the National Security Agency (NSA), continues to collect data on US citizens in an effort to thwart terrorism here and abroad. The relationship between identity and the government takes place through forms of **biopower**, a term used by French philosopher Michel Foucault to describe the power of the state over individuals via the body. The body is key in this system, where "power relations have an immediate hold upon it [the body]: they invest it, mark it, train it, torture it, force it to carry out task, to perform ceremonies, to emit signs."[3] Increasingly, though, our bodies also become sites to work against these forms of power. It is not "just a physical entity which we 'possess,' it is an action-system, a mode of praxis, and its practical immersion in the interactions of day-to-day life is an essential part of the sustaining of a coherent sense of self-identity."[4] It is in this way that we will consider the body's relationship to identity and popular culture.

On the following pages we will be discussing different identity markers, and you will deepen your understanding of the role of popular culture in shaping one's self-conception and identity. As you will see, the relationship between identity and popular culture largely takes place through the process of **social construction**. As discussed in Chapter 6, social constructivist theories of identity work against fixed, essentialist notions. Unlike essentialism, theories of social construction are based on the idea that identity is largely a creation of societal institutions. This idea challenges the essentialist belief that identity is something that is "natural" or grounded in biology, instead focusing on how our identities are created by social interactions and where those identities place us within larger power structures. Social institutions such as the family, religion, school, the judicial system, and the media all have a role in shaping our evolving sense of identity, whether it be about our gender, race, class, or sexuality. When defining identity, these institutions also work to normalize some, suggesting that "normal" people are a certain way and that everyone who falls outside of that "norm" is Other. This balance of norm over Other affords certain individuals more power over others as culture sets up to better accommodate them. This is **privilege**, an advantage one has based on the circumstances of their birth and factors to which the individual has no control. Those who conform to the norm along lines of race, gender, and class, for example, are then said to have "white privilege," "male privilege," or "class privilege." At the same time we use the popular culture practices, texts, and expressions of these social institutions to actively shape our understanding and presentation of identity, we are also forming our ideas about the identity of others through popular culture.

The results of these impressions often form the foundation for stereotypes. **Stereotypes** are preconceived ideas or notions related to the perceived characteristics of a group of people, the result of which indicate larger power relations in society. The role of power is an important, but often overlooked, aspect of stereotypes. The influence a stereotype has, and its ramifications on an individual or group, is directly related to the power dynamic between the parties involved. In this chapter we will also explore the identity markers of gender, sexuality, class, race, and ability and their associated stereotypes in order to demonstrate popular culture's role in the social construction of identity, and the ways in which identity, in turn, responds to and shapes popular culture.

Doing gender

It used to be when an individual was born, the doctor would announce, "It's a boy!" or "It's a girl!" and our life as a gendered individual would begin. As ultrasound technology became less expensive and more widely available for all pregnancies in the late 1980s and early 1990s, more and more couples had the option of finding out the sex of their baby before birth. While exact figures on the number of couples who find out the sex of their unborn child are unavailable, the last Gallup poll to survey this information suggests that "sixty-six percent of Americans between the ages of 18 and 34 say they would like to know whether they are having a boy or a girl before the baby is born."[5] Couples often state that it helps them to "prepare" to know the sex of the child, but prepare what, exactly? The basic needs of an infant—diapers, clothes, car seat, a place to sleep, etc.—have nothing to do with a baby's sex. The type of items, their style and associated characteristics, however, have quite a bit to do with an individual's first understandings of gender.

It is important at this point to note the difference between sex and gender. **Sex** is the biological identity assigned to an individual based on physiological factors such as reproductive organs and hormones. **Gender**, on the other hand, is the social construction of our sex, based on physical and behavioral representations of the self, attitudes, power differentials, and the ways in which males and females are conceptualized in society through culture. One of the key theories of social construction that relates to gender is Judith Butler's notion of performativity. In her book *Gender Trouble*, Butler writes, "There is no gender identity behind the expressions of gender; [...] identity is performatively constituted by the very 'expressions' that are said to be its results."[6] What Butler suggests here is that the way we think of gender as something that is inherent or "natural" is erroneous; in reality, gender is a performance. It is part of the self that we curate and perform to audiences in our daily life, similar to Goffman's theories explained in the previous chapter. When Butler states there is "no gender identity," she is not suggesting that gender, as a concept, in nonexistent; rather, her theory is a way of understanding our practice of gender as a staged display of culturally dependent variables, rather than biological mandate; there is nothing beyond gender's presentation of itself. In this way, we can see gender as a set of stylized and repeated acts that include physical presentation, clothing, speech patterns, physical movement, and the ways in which we think about ourselves as gendered individuals in the world. We "perform" our genders, and these performances are so ingrained in society that the process becomes *naturalized*. This process of naturalization is important, as it is the way in which we begin to internalize and believe the gender scripts presented to us by society.

When we begin to understand gender as a learned practice, something we "do," we can see how the social construction of our gendered identities begins to take place before we are even born. For example, recently there has been a trend of "gender reveal parties" where couples and families learn of the sex of their baby before it is even born. These couples are given a sealed envelope with the results of their sonogram, which is then given to a baker who will bake a cake or cupcakes that has blue or pink cream filling (or cake) depending on the sex of the baby. At the party, the couple cuts into the cake (or bites into a cupcake), and when they see the colored filling, the sex of their child is "revealed": blue for a boy and pink for a girl.

It is at this moment that the social construction of gender begins. While the trend of the "gender reveal" party is relatively new, since the 1990s baby showers have been themed around the sex of the unborn baby, with blue and pink being the quickest and most identifiable example, not only for the shower invitations and decorations, but for clothes, blankets, toys, and baby gear bought for the unborn guest of honor (yellow, green, and increasingly gray serve as the colors of choice for "gender neutral" showers where the baby's sex is unknown and/or kept secret by the parents-to-be).

This gendering often continues in the clothing that couples buy for their unborn child, the ways in which they decorate their nurseries, and even the ways they discuss their baby. Parents hoping to opt out of the gendering of their baby may find it difficult, as consumer choices and variety are often limited. As stated earlier, when a child is born, the first thing the doctor announces is the child's sex. This announcement is so we can immediately begin to understand how we are going to treat the individual. The language we use to describe babies demonstrates this early process of the social construction of gender. We have "bouncing baby boys," which connotes ideas of activity, vitality, and sport. On the other hand, we have "sweet, precious baby girls," which shapes our early impressions of the female sex as kind, passive objects valued for their gentility and appearance. In a study of the visual images and messages found on cards congratulating couples on the birth of a child, these gendered constructions are repeated, with "visual images indicative of physical activity" more prominent on boy cards, and "verbal messages of expressiveness, including sweetness and sharing" appearing more on cards for girls.[7] Perhaps more shocking, though, is the finding that more cards for boys expressed congratulations and sentiments of happiness for parents than for those congratulating the birth of a daughter. In terms of how this might translate to behavior, studies have shown that fathers handle male infants more physically[8] and mothers, similarly, have more physical interactions with their sons while preferring more gentle methods of bonding with daughters.[9]

It is not surprising, then, that the toys children are given also reflect this notion of social construction and play heavily into the types of activities these young individuals will begin to be socialized toward. This gender divide can be seen in the marketing of toys and the ways in which stores typically have aisles for "boy toys" and "girl toys," where the toys specified for boys include action figures, bikes, building sets, and electronics. The toys for girls, however, tend to include arts and crafts items, bath and beauty accessories, and dolls. If bikes and sporting equipment are included, they tend to be pink or purple, as opposed to the blue and green boy versions. As a part of popular culture, games and toys are some of the primary vehicles for the social construction of gender for children. Boys are taught to play with active toys such as sporting equipment, trucks, and toy guns, which at best encourage physical fitness, dexterity, and activity, and at worse endorse violence as a means of conflict resolution. Girls, on the other hand, are given toy vacuums and kitchens to prepare them to be wives and homemakers, dolls to practice and model motherhood, and makeup and beauty accessories to help solidify the importance of their physical appearance to their identity and worth.

Given the overreliance and emphasis on women's appearance in contemporary society, Naomi Wolf articulated the theory of the "beauty myth" to discuss the way that the beauty industry and image culture of contemporary US society has used the concept of women's beauty as a means of control. She argues "we are in the midst of a violent backlash against feminism that uses images of female beauty as a political weapon against women's advancement: the beauty myth."[10] She outlines the following stipulations of the beauty myths in society: beauty objectively and universally exists; women want beauty, men want women who possess it; beauty is a part of natural selection and evolution; beauty is an element of godliness; aging is not beautiful; and above all else, to be thin is to be beautiful. They key thing to remember here is that Wolf is pointing out that these are *myths*—there is nothing biologically or historically true about these common stereotypes and assumptions. In reality, Wolf argues, "the beauty myth is always actually prescribing behavior and not appearance."[11] That is, the beauty myth is not about beauty at all, but rather women's autonomy and empowerment in contemporary society. Wolf argues that the beauty myth becomes more powerful in times when economic and political freedoms are more liberal toward women, and serve as a "checkmate" on women's empowerment. This works by creating and maintaining feminine insecurities related to appearance and body image. This distraction of how one looks keeps women under the control of what Wolf refers to as "male institutions" and from achieving full equality in society and the workforce. Rather than supporting each other, women are often portrayed as "catty" and placed in competition with each other (seen on reality TV, for example, with shows such as *The Bachelor*), with the focus on women's appearance as their primary asset.

This emphasis on women's beauty begins at a young age. In 2012 Lego brand found itself embroiled in controversy when it introduced its "Lego Friends" line. While the line has since expanded its offering to include pieces such as a news van and a skate park, the original line included sets for a hair salon and a shopping mall. The line features female characters and is specifically marketed toward young girls, with accompanying advertising awash in pink and pastels with a strong emphasis on friendship. Associated materials such as activity books and quizzes on the Lego Friends website can help you determine your fashion style, how you "juice" (as in smoothies, because every eight-year-old juices, right?), and how to plan a dance party. While some of the activities are geared toward vacation adventures and "dream jobs," there is little emphasis on construction or creativity, the building blocks of Lego, so to speak. This "girlification" of Legos, at the expense of the toy's intended purpose and mission, upset a number of parents and individuals who did not see the need to gender a toy that had been enjoyed by boys and girls for years, and were particularly upset by the way the gendering worked against the toy's very purpose to encourage building and active play.

It should be noted that there is nothing necessarily wrong with friendship, the color pink, or some of the aforementioned activities associated with the social construction of girlhood. The stereotypes surrounding these constructions, and the power differentials they perpetuate, however, create a troubling imbalance in society. To stick with our Lego example for a moment longer, it is socially acceptable for a girl to play with a Lego Friends set as well as one of the original Lego sets, but it is less likely for a young boy to be playing with Lego Friends or taking one of the online quizzes about hosting a cupcake party. Put another way, it is "normal," and can even be "cute" for girls to be tomboys, like to get dirty, and play sports, but far less acceptable for little boys to wear tutus or want to host a tea party. This disparity sends the subtle message that it is okay and perhaps even natural that girls would want to be one of the guys, but it is not okay for a man to find interest in or desire to participate in activities designed for the lesser or second sex. This binary not only creates a power imbalance between genders, but also limits choices for both men and women in terms of hobbies, careers, and the way in which we engage in relationships and with the world.

The activities that children are socialized to play, then, also have a role in how men and women are treated differently as adults. Boys play sports such as football and other physical, rough-and-tumble activities, which position them to be leaders and more outgoing as adults, whereas girls are socialized to make friends, share secrets, and engage in more passive leisure. This type of gendering is associated with essentialist notions of identity and leads to gender binaries and stereotypes. As discussed by Laura Mulvey, these gender binaries result in active/passive and mind/body dichotomies, where women are valued for their appearance, creating a passive objectification that relies on over identification with the physical body. Males, on the other hand, are positioned as active subjects, more valued for their mind than their appearance, seen as powerful and whole, as opposed to powerless and looked upon the way women are. Women are seen as more emotional, whereas men "man up" and keep a stiff upper lip.

Although research consistently points to no statistical difference between gendered cognitive skills,[12] boys are quickly taught that they are good in math and science, and girls are taught that they are better suited for things like English and art. Popular culture helps perpetuate these myths in a number of ways, not only with toys and advertising, but even clothing. For example, in the fall of 2011 JC Penney came under fire for featuring clothes in their back-to-school line that were printed with the sayings "I'm too pretty to do homework so my brother has to do it for me" and another one stating, "my best subjects are 'boys shopping music and dancing.'" In response to a change .org campaign, JC Penney pulled the "I'm too pretty" shirt, acknowledging, it "does not deliver an appropriate message," and apologizing to customers.[13] How the shirts were ever deemed acceptable in the first place is questionable, but consumer outrage in demanding the shirts be pulled not only suggests the power of individuals speaking back to popular culture, but also is indicative of recent trends in recognizing the negative gender stereotypes that circulate in popular culture.

In 2015 Target made headlines by proactively being ahead of the curve on this issue, announcing:

Historically, guests have told us that sometimes—for example, when shopping for someone they don't know well—signs that sort by brand, age or gender help them get ideas and find things faster. But we know that shopping preferences and needs change and, as guests have pointed out, in some departments like Toys, Home or Entertainment, suggesting products by gender is unnecessary.

We heard you, and we agree. Right now, our teams are working across the store to identify areas where we can phase out gender-based signage to help strike a better balance. For example, in the kids' Bedding area, signs will no longer feature suggestions for boys or girls, just kids. In the Toys aisles, we'll also remove reference to gender, including the use of pink, blue, yellow or green paper on the back walls of our shelves.[14]

Target's announcement was newsworthy not only because of the decision they made, but in their acknowledgment of changing times and attitudes. While the decision, in itself, may have only been a savvy marketing move on Target's part, at the very least it proved to be another example of popular culture responding to shifting cultural attitudes and trends, particularly in thinking of gender in more fluid terms.

Increasingly, popular culture is responding to the notion held by many that gender is not a strict binary of male/female, but rather gender is fluid and exists on a continuum. As mentioned at the beginning of the chapter, Bruce Jenner's transition to Caitlyn Jenner has made her one of the most visible spokespersons for the transgender community. In bringing transgender terms to the national spotlight, gender, itself, as a cultural construct continues to be an increasing part of mainstream conversation. The term **transgender** refers to gender identity or gender expression that is different than what was sexually assigned at birth. This term is more commonly used than **transsexual**, which refers to individuals who have undergone medical intervention such as hormone therapy or surgery. Not all transgender individuals are transsexual, and some feel the term "transsexual" is outdated and/or offensive since it is a label that originated in psychological and medical discourse. It also places the emphasis on medical interventions, which not all transgender individuals choose and/or can afford to undergo. Other terms associated with gender identity include cisgender, which refers to non-transgender individuals, those whose gender expression matches their gender assignment from birth, and **gender queer**, which refers to both a social movement resisting gender binaries, and those who identify outside the male/female binary.

Let's talk about sex, baby

It is important to note that gender and sexual orientation are not the same thing. Comparing them to "apples and oranges," Jenner explained in her *20/20* interview, "Sexuality is who you personally are attracted to—who turns you on. But gender identity has to do with who you are as a person and your soul and who you identify with inside."[15] Sexuality, and the sexual scripts presented in popular culture, however, often rely on gender binaries in maintaining heteronormative ideals. **Heteronormativity** is used to describe the belief that heterosexuality—sexual relations between a man and a woman—is "natural" and that sexual practices outside of this paradigm are seen as deviant.We can see this marginalization in the lack of Valentine's Day or wedding cards for same-sex couples, to the fact that it was not until 2015 that same-sex marriage became legal in all fifty states. In terms of representation on film and television, Diane Raymond argues that there has historically been a "containment" of queerness, where heteronormativity is maintained through a lack of gay characters in meaningful lead roles, a difference in portrayals of heterosexual and homosexual relationships, and the trope of comedic plotlines of straight characters "pretending to be gay" or being mistaken for homosexual.[16] While shows like Bravo's *Queer Eye for the Straight Guy* (2003–2007) have been hailed as helping to pave the way for inclusion of LGBTQ individuals and characters on television, in many ways the show played into regressive and offensive stereotypes of gay males as one-dimensional, with the show's premise of gay men "making over" clueless heterosexuals, perpetuating the false belief that gay men are inherently stylish and that their value is in their ability to accessorize and support straight people.

National attitudes toward homosexuality have shifted a great deal in the past twenty or so years, with popular culture serving as a staging ground for the "culture wars" around sexuality. For every *Modern Family*, there is a *19 Kids and Counting*. Although the Duggar family does not officially identify with the Quiverfull movement (a conservative fundamentalist Christian practice that includes, among other tenets, having as many children as the Lord will provide) and members of the family have come under scrutiny for sexual misconduct, they still represent values associated with ultra-conservative beliefs regarding sexuality, courtship and marriage, and gender roles. And although *Modern Family* prominently features homosexual couple Cam and Mitchell, for the first three seasons Cam is a stay-at-home parent (mirroring traditional family values), and the two are rarely seen as physically intimate as the show's other couples. Similarly, while LGBTQ characters are onscreen in record numbers, original programming on premium cable channels and streaming television services such as Netflix and Amazon Prime far surpasses the rates of representation on broadcast networks.[17]

Money can't buy you class

It is important to note that the discussion of identity and its representation in and through popular culture is bound up in larger discourses and structures of power that intersect gender and sexuality with race and class. Caitlyn Jenner, for example, has the money and means to finance her transition any way she wants. She also models her idea of womanhood on very traditional notions of white femininity, as evidenced by her *Vogue* cover, with hair, makeup, and fashion choices echoing the "beauty myths" outlined by Naomi Wolf. While Jenner first entered popular culture consciousness via the 1976 Olympics, Millennials are more familiar with her through her marriage to Kris Jenner and their blended family, chronicled on the reality television series *Keeping Up with the Kardashians*. As discussed in earlier chapters, the conspicuous consumption and consumerism displayed by the Kardashians promotes a certain type of celebrity lifestyle. Wealth, however, does not necessarily translate to class, which is embedded with not only financial freedom and unlimited access to premium goods and services, but is also imbued with US foundational notions of breeding and gentility originating back to the United States' history as a former British colony.

One of the reasons F. Scott Fitzgerald's novel *The Great Gatsby* endures as an American classic is its ability to demonstrate the ways in which social mobility in the United States is tied up with more than a person's bank account. Jay Gatsby (played by Leonardo DiCaprio in the 2013 film version) throws the most outrageous parties and has the money to bankroll them, but his humble background all but guarantees he'll never have the future he so desperately desires with Daisy Buchannan. While the novel reflects changes to American society at the beginning of the twentieth century in part brought on by the First World War's crumbling of European aristocracy, waves of immigration, and the beginning stages of a breakdown in class differences based on inherited status and wealth, the story's continuing appeal and the success of its movie adaptations rest on our collective sustained hope of the American Dream, despite continued disparities in wealth and an ever-shrinking middle class in the twenty-first century.[18]

Broadly, popular culture represents the interest of certain groups, and historically the distinctions between "high culture" (Culture) and "low culture" (culture) have been deeply ingrained with socioeconomic status and class. While some of the earliest arguments about the relationship between social class and popular culture came out of British models of cultural studies with theorists such as Matthew Arnold, F. R. Leavis, and Dick Hebdige, the distinctions between "Culture" and "culture" have an impact on contemporary US popular culture's relationship to identity. As discussed in earlier chapters, "high" or "elite" Culture was traditionally associated with upscale creative output, often produced in limited quantities and/or reserved for only a select few with the funds and means to access these high-end cultural productions. As a result, a certain type of bourgeois or upper-class identity became associated with expensive leisure activities such as horseback riding or sailing, hobbies such as antiquing or art collecting, and appreciation of music forms such as opera or classical music. Of course, these are all stereotypes associated with wealth, and while many of them are outdated, they represent the way in which class has shaped not only individual identity, but also the historic identities of different groups and individuals here in the United States.

As industrialization and mass-production changed both labor forces and the production and access to goods, popular culture responded to these shifts in terms of a growing commercialization of society. With larger numbers of Americans gaining access to consumer goods in the second half of the twentieth century, popular culture became an increasing force in maintaining the stratification of American society while creating an illusion of equality. The media further perpetuates cultural myths about class, by either ignoring issues of poverty with disproportionate representations of wealth as the norm, or by relying on outdated and overblown stereotypes of lower-class individuals, all with the effect of distorting a national understanding of class in the United States.

In 2015, 51 percent of Americans identified as middle or upper-middle class, a percentage that has continually seen a decrease since the turn of the twentieth century.[19] Given the large swaths of income represented under the label "middle class," it is hardly a homogeneous group of individuals. Despite the vast differences in defining who actually constitutes the middle class, the term is often synonymous with the "every man" or "average American." Media representations, however, often skew the reality of class in society, with extreme representations of wealth and poverty. In terms of identity and stereotypes, lower class individuals are often portrayed as deviants (*Cops*, *Making a Murderer*), buffoons (*Here Comes Honey Boo Boo*), and/or uneducated (*Joe Dirt*, *Shameless*), and while their wealthy counterpoints are frequently portrayed displaying similar behavior (*The Real Housewives* franchise, *The Wolf of Wall Street*), there are different value judgments associated with these characters. The differences in the portrayal and reception of these class differences is important, because these stereotypes work to mask the way in which social structures in the United States systemically disadvantage certain populations (such as poor, rural whites and poor, urban blacks). As sociologist Diana Kendall notes, this can have a negative effect on identity and public policy, as individuals of lower classes tend to rightly shy away from these negative stereotypes and self-identify with a higher socioeconomic bracket.[20] True representations of poor and working class Americans are often hard to find in popular culture, and as a result, inaccurate portrayals and representations of poverty and the working poor often influence public policy and oversimplify general understandings of wealth inequality in the United States.

Race matters

In our discussion of identity so far, it is important to note that individuals embody a number of different identities, based on their gender, sexuality, class, and race (among other factors). When considering identity as a whole, though, it is important to look at the relationship of these identities on each other, taking the theoretical approach legal scholar and critical race theorist Kimberlé Crenshaw defined as **intersectionality**.[21] This term refers to a frame of analysis that takes into account the ways that elements of identity such as race, gender, and sexuality mutually construct one another. That is, when considering an individual's identity and its associated identifications of race, class, gender, sexuality, etc., these elements cannot be individually examined or ranked, but must always be considered in relation to each other. Intersectional analysis is important not only on an individual level, but also when considering society as a whole, as it helps to point out the power dynamics and relationships between various social locations and cultural processes.

After the 2008 presidential election of Barack Obama, there was talk that perhaps Obama's election signaled a turn toward a **post-racial** US society, one where racism or discrimination based on the color of one's skin no longer existed. This belief is untrue, and such suggestions fail to take into account the long and complicated history our country has had with race. From the forced removal and extermination of indigenous peoples, to slavery, to the Jim Crow laws of segregation, America's history and foundations are grounded in racial strife. While the rule of **hypo-descent** (assigning race based on an individual's socially subordinate heritage) no longer governs law, its cultural effects are still felt well into the twenty-first century, despite scientific evidence that there are no biological indicators of race. Instead, through the process of **racialization**, individuals, social practices, and cultural processes are given racial identity. The Dolezal case mentioned at the beginning of the chapter is an extreme example of self-racialization, with Dolezal herself remarking, "If people feel misled or deceived, then sorry that they feel that way, but I believe that's more due to their definition and construct of race in their own minds than it is to my integrity or honesty, because I wouldn't say I'm African American, but I *would* say I'm black, and there's a difference in those terms."[22]

Music, clothing, hairstyles, and food are all elements of popular culture that have been racialized and contribute to racial stereotypes in American culture. Dolezal's identification as black seems to rely on these superficial identity markers and points to the ways in which elements of race are performative in contemporary US society. This social construction both relies upon and results in stereotypes, which, as we have previously discussed, are based on relations of power. It is in this way that racial stereotypes have been used to maintain racial hierarchies throughout America's history. Building off of Crenshaw's theory of intersectionality, sociologist Patricia Hill Collins has argued that race, class, and gender form a "matrix of oppression" that is experienced at the levels of individual, institutional, and symbolic oppressions.[23] Those who argue against Dolezal's identification as a black woman point to the fact that her ability to choose to take on a black identity, without the legacy of discrimination or routine prejudice that African Americans face, is in actuality an example of her **white privilege** that ignores the existence of this matrix of oppression.

In the article "White Privilege and Male Privilege," Peggy McIntosh refers to white privilege as "an invisible package of unearned assets" that result from the social advantage white people have by being given the benefit of the doubt, just for being white.[24] Despite the way that some have interpreted this term, white privilege is not accusing all white people of being racist, nor is it apologizing for being white. White privilege, instead, is the way that whiteness in American society is taken for granted as the norm, and therefore masks the ways in which "whiteness" is also a racial social construct. To draw an example from popular culture, let's think about race and Halloween costumes. From "Chop Suey Specs" designed, according to its packaging, to "fool your friends with this oriental disguise" to the "Hot on the Trail Dress," a "Native american [sic] styled ultra suede fringed dress with colorful bead neckline detail" that includes "elaborately beaded authentic native american belt and head piece,"[25] these costumes point to the ways in which we exoticize the Other as scary, funny, or just plain different. While these examples are extreme in their cultural insensitivity (the "Hot on the Trail Dress" manages to be both sexist *and* racist in its marketing of the Trail of Tears and Native American women as sexy), the **cultural appropriation** displayed by costumes such as these demonstrate the ways in which white privilege allows individuals to see the cultures of others as a costume, something that can be put on or borrowed at a whim, without thinking about the actual lived experiences of individuals that do not see their cultures as jokes and live with the very real consequences of **microaggressions** and racial stereotypes that persist in their everyday lives.

In her essay, McIntosh lays out a number of microaggressions, subtle and not-so-subtle ways white privilege functions, such as the ways in which white people are never asked to speak for or represent their entire racial group in ways that other races are, to the point that a white person can be pretty sure that if he or she asks to speak to "the person in charge," they can assume that they will be facing a person of their race. Being mindful of one's white privilege, though, does suggest, at a minimum, an acknowledgment of the existence of white privilege and its system of advantages and disadvantages. And for those benefiting from white privilege, this privilege could be used to speak out against injustice while creating opportunities for equality.

Similar to McIntosh's call to action in "unpacking the invisible knapsack" of white privilege, the goal in Collins's theory of the matrix of oppression is to find new ways of understanding ourselves and others, as well as situations, in order to bring about positive social change. At the individual level, people are challenged to think of their own personal histories and the choices they've made based on their positions of both privilege and oppression. Alongside our individual experiences, institutional oppression takes place at the structural level of society through social establishments such as education, health care, or the criminal justice systems. Michelle Alexander's *The New Jim Crow: Mass Incarceration in the Age of Colorblindness* and Ta-Nehisi Coates's *Between the World and Me* gained considerable press given race relations between African Americans and the police in the wake of deaths such as Michael Brown, Freddie Gray, and Sandra Bland. After the acquittal of George Zimmerman in the death of Trayvon Martin, the Black Lives Matter movement was started by Alicia Garza, Opal Tometi, and Patrisse Cullors as "an ideological and political intervention in a world where Black lives are systematically and intentionally targeted for demise. It is an affirmation of Black folks' contributions to this society, our humanity, and our resilience in the face of deadly oppression."[26] The Black Lives Matter movement mobilized through social media and gained traction across multiple platforms of popular culture.

More than ever, popular culture and the media have become a staging ground for exploring the matrix of oppression that Collins suggests. She argues that symbolic oppression relies on identity stereotypes of race, gender, and class and are deployed as part of the media's image culture. And while many people dismiss popular culture and media representations, particularly when it comes to issues of gender or race, as Collins and others suggest, there are very real consequences to these kinds of symbolic oppressions. These include an overreliance on stereotypes resulting in one-dimensional caricatures, the casting of white actors to portray characters of color (such as the casting of Joseph Fiennes as Michael Jackson in an un-aired episode of the British comedy *Urban Myths*, Angela Jolie as Dutch Afro-Chinese Cuban Mariane Pearl in *A Mighty Heart*, or Emma Stone as Chinese-Hawaiian Allison Ng in *Aloha*), as well as a general lack of diversity on screen. In 2016, then-president Barack Obama even weighed in on the #OscarsSoWhite debate about the lack of diversity of actors nominated for Academy Awards, noting that the concern about casting in Hollywood is part of a larger question of equality in the United States, which is, "Are we making sure that everybody is getting a fair shot?"[27]

That is not to say, though, that popular culture does not also provide crucial commentary on issues of race in order to point out some of these injustices. When Beyoncé dropped the surprise video for her song "Formation" on the eve of Super Bowl 50, the song and her Super Bowl performance all but overshadowed the big game between the Carolina Panthers and the Denver Broncos. The strategic timing of the video release was not only a marketing coup, but underscored the importance of the issues Beyoncé explores in the song and video. After the "warning" of a parental advisory for explicit lyrics, the video opens with Beyoncé atop a New Orleans police cruiser partially submerged in floodwaters, reminiscent of Hurricane Katrina (the same event which led Kanye West to quip live on national television, "George Bush doesn't care about black people."). The image is accompanied by the voiceover of slain New Orleans' YouTube celebrity Messy Mya querying, "What happened at the New Orleans?" From there, the next four minutes and fifty seconds are a both a celebration of Beyoncé's black heritage and a commentary on the complicated history of race relations in the United States. With lyrics such as "I like my baby heir with baby hair and afros/I like my negro nose with Jackson Five nostrils," Beyoncé calls out the ways in which standards of beauty are based on Caucasian aesthetics and the ways in which black celebrities—including her husband and daughter (who is featured in the video)—are criticized for not conforming to white beauty standards. In addition to celebrating her own heritage ("My daddy Alabama, momma Louisiana"), Beyoncé transforms historical and contemporary black images into a celebration of black lives and culture. The video's depiction of a young black boy break dancing in a hoodie in front of a row of police in riot gear, along with the graffiti message "Stop Shooting Us," is reminiscent of Trayvon Martin and the Black Lives Matter movement, while offering a hopeful message of peace as the officers raise their arms in the air in response to the boy's stance.

The day after the video's release Beyoncé performed during the halftime show of Super Bowl 50, complete with a wardrobe and backup dancers that paid homage to both Michael Jackson and the Black Panther Party. Reaction to the performance was a mixture of both outrage and praise, with conservative commentators offering the most negative response. Appearing on *Fox and Friends* the Monday after the game, former New York mayor Rudy Guiliani criticized the performance stating, "This is football, not Hollywood, and I thought it was really outrageous that she used it as a platform to attack police officers who are the people who protect her and protect us, and keep us alive."[28] As we have noted earlier, popular culture is never "just a game," despite the ever-present proclamations that popular culture is fluff or entertainment, and not a potential platform for politics. Both liberal and conservative media outlets are well aware of popular culture's ideological stakes, though, and their framing of Beyoncé's performance was yet another staging ground for debates over race in contemporary culture.

Saturday Night Live responded with their own take on the Beyoncé backlash the following Saturday with their skit "The Day Beyoncé Turned Black," poking fun at reactions to the song. Framed as a trailer for a horror movie, the parody described a world in chaos (the day that "shook the whole white world" and America "lost their damn white minds") once they realized that "their" beloved Beyoncé is, in fact, black. As a satire, the humor resides in pointing out racial constructions, such as when a black woman is forced to explain to her friend, "I'm black" despite her friend protesting, "What? No you're not. You're my girl." "But I could still be black," the friend replies, before pointing out that there are black people everywhere, including a black man nearby dressed in a puffy jacket, baseball cap, and a large gold chain. "I know *he's* black" the white friend replies, gesturing with her head and speaking out of the side of her mouth, suggesting that those who conform to stereotypes of racialized masculinity are black, while those who "act white" are somehow racially different. The skit also points out white privilege when a white woman listens to "Formation" and confusedly confesses to her coworkers, "I don't understand this new song." When a white male coworker replies, "Maybe this song ... isn't for us," the woman shrieks in panic, "But usually everything is!" As the world continues to deteriorate with more celebrities being identified as black, two horrified men hide under a table, with one lamenting, "I don't understand, how can they [Beyoncé and Kerry Washington] be black? I thought they were women?" To which his friend replies, "I think they might be both!"[29] Both men scream in terror, presumably at the thought of either women and/or minorities existing outside of a single stereotyped role, pointing to the one-dimensional media portrayals of women and minorities. This skit's framing as a trailer for a horror movie points to the very real fears that exist not only around race relations in society, but of even deeper fears of "blackness" and the expression of open pride in racial heritage.

The new normal?

As our most visible markers of the self, bodies are integral to the social construction of identity with respect to gender, race, and even class. While it is unlikely that we will wake up one morning another sex or race, the vulnerability of bodies to aging and accident makes constructions of ability and disability a more tenuous identity category. Although we may not think of disability as a social construction, there are many ways in which we as a society have shaped our physical environments to privilege those who embody an idealized norm. For example, more people can navigate ramps than those who can navigate stairs, yet we have far more stairs than we do ramps with respect to accessibility in homes, offices, and public spaces. As opposed to thinking about disability as a defect within an individual, disability scholars such as Tobin Siebers argue for a social model of disability, where disability is considered not "as a personal misfortune or individual defect, but as the product of a disabling society and built environment."[30] This understanding of disability works against medical models that posit disability as a limitation that exists within an individual as defined by medical diagnosis.

In helping to found the field of disability studies, Lennard Davis's *Enforcing Normalcy: Disability, Deafness, and the Body* describes the ways in which "normalcy" as a category is a cultural creation originally tied to twentieth-century developments in the fields of eugenics and statistics, which resulted in the invention of questionably scientific models of an ideal body. While these models lacked actual biological definition or grounding in reality, they became the standards by which bodies were measured using Galton's bell curve of normalcy. In turn, disability became socially constructed in society through expectations that were developed in terms of what is "normal" based on what bodies can and cannot do and the ways in which both physical and social organizations of society are modeled around a small percentage of actual bodies—those that are young and physically ideal in terms of strength and health.

Despite a growing awareness of neuro and physical diversity, popular culture continues to perpetuate ableist beliefs and outdated stereotypes that advocate a medical understanding of disability. This not only includes the lack of realistic depiction of disability in the media, but the casting of able-bodied actors as disabled characters (what disability rights activists refer to as "crip face"); the continued use of disability as a metaphor for social ills; the narrative reliance on disability tropes in film, television, and literature as a problem to be dealt with or something a character must overcome; and the overall lack of disability represented despite individuals with disabilities comprising our world's largest minority group.[31] Able-bodied author Jojo Moyes's bestseller *Me Before You* and its film adaptation provide evidence of this. The plot of both versions of the text centers around character Louisa "Lou" Clark's growing attraction to Will Traynor, the wealthy quadriplegic she is hired to care for. Able-bodied actor Sam Claflin portrays Traynor in the film, and in both the film and novel his character is described as surly and defeated, unable to cope with the physical limitations that result from an untimely accident. Despite having the financial means necessary for the best medical care and a fully accessible home (a reality experienced by few individuals with actual disabilities) and the love of the beautiful and charming Lou, Will ultimately chooses physician-assisted suicide over living with a disability. While marketed as a romance, or even a modern-day fairytale, the novel and film perpetuate a number of gender stereotypes while presenting the ableist messages that Will is better off dead than disabled, and Lou is better off alone than burdened by a disabled partner. Romantic, indeed.

Conclusion

As poet and essayist Audre Lorde noted, "Somewhere, on the edge of consciousness, there is what I call a mythical norm, which each one of us within our hearts knows 'that is not me.' In america [*sic*], this norm is usually defined as white, thin, male, young, heterosexual, Christian, and financially secure. It is within this mythical norm that the trappings of power reside within this society."[32] In this chapter we deepened our understanding of the role of popular culture in shaping one's identity in response to this "mythical norm." Particular attention was paid to the role of stereotypes and their relationship to the identity markers of gender, sexuality, class, race, and (dis)ability. The power relations that these stereotypes reveal, and their circulation in and dependence upon popular culture, allowed us to more fully understand the ways in which identity is a social construction that both shapes and depends upon popular culture. When we think about the different stereotypes associated with identity and its visible markers, we begin to see the ways in which identity is not just about an individual, but reveals the ways in which identity has both private and public dimensions. It is our personal conception of who we are, as well as the outward expressions of a host of values, traits, and beliefs. In the next chapter we will consider how these outward expressions of identity form networks of connection creating groups and communities of identification.

Notes

1   Wesley Morris, "The Year We Obsessed Over Identity," *New York Times*, October 6, 2015, http://www.nytimes.com/2015/10/11/magazine/the-year-we-obsessed-over-identity.html?_r=0#.

2   Justin McCarthy, "Americans Losing Confidence in All Branches of US Government," *The Gallup Poll*, June 30, 2014, http://www.gallup.com/poll/171992/americans-losing-confidence-branches-gov.aspx.

3   Michel Foucault, *Discipline and Punish: The Birth of the Prison*, trans. Alan Sheridan (New York: Vintage, 1975), 25.

4   Anthony Giddons, *Modernity and Self-Identity: Self and Society in the Late Modern Age* (Stanford, CA: Stanford University Press), 99.

5   Alec Gallup and Frank Newport, *The Gallup Poll: Pubic Opinion 2007* (Lanham, MD: Rowman & Littlefield, 2008), 317.

6   Judith Butler, *Gender Trouble: Feminism and the Subversion of Identity* (New York: Routledge, 1999), 25.

7   Judith Bridges, "Pink of Blue: Gender Stereotypic Perceptions of Infants as Conveyed by Birth Congratulations Cards," *Psychology of Women Quarterly* 17, no. 2 (1993): 193.

8   A. C. Hurston, "Sex Typing," in *Handbook of Child Psychology: Vol. 4. Socialization, Personality and Social Development*, ed. E. Mavis Hetherington (New York: Wiley, 1983), 387.

9   Valerie Grant, "Sex of Infant Differences in Mother-Infant Interaction: A Reinterpretation of Past Findings," *Developmental Review* 14, no. 1 (1994): 1.

10   Naomi Wolf, *The Beauty Myth: How Images of Beauty Are Used Against Women* (New York: W. Morrow, 1991), 10.

11   Ibid., 14.

12   American Psychological Association, "Think Again: Men and Women Share Cognitive Skills," *APA*, August 2014, http://www.apa.org/action/resources/research-in-action/share.aspx.

13   Jessica Wakeman, "Kill Me Now, Please: JC Penney's 'I'm Too Pretty to Do Homework' T-Shirt for Girls—UPDATE," *The Frisky*, August 31, 2011, http://www.thefrisky.com/2011-08-31/kill-me-now-please-jc-penneys-im-too-pretty-to-do-homework-t-shirt-for/.

14   Target Corporate, "What's in Store: Moving Away from Gender-Based Signs," *Target.com*, August 7, 2015, https://corporate.target.com/article/2015/08/gender-based-signs-corporate.

15   *20/20*, "Bruce Jenner—The Interview" [TV program], *ABC*, April 24, 2015.

16   Dianne Raymond, "Popular Culture and Queer Representation: A Critical Perspective," in *Gender, Race, and Class in Media: A Text Reader*, ed. Gail Dines and Jean M. Humez (Thousand Oaks, CA: Sage, 2003), 100.

17 GLADD, "2015 Where We Are On TV," *GLADD.com*, December 2015, http://www.glaad.org/files/GLAAD-2015-WWAT.pdf.

18 Pew Research Center, "The American Middle Class Is Losing Ground," *Pew Research Center Social and Demographic Trends*, December 9, 2015, http://www.pewsocialtrends.org/2015/12/09/the-american-middle-class-is-losing-ground/.

19 Frank Newport, "Fewer Americans Identify as Middle Class in Recent Years," *The Gallup Poll*, April 28, 2015, http://www.gallup.com/poll/182918/fewer-americans-identify-middle-class-recent-years.aspx.

20 Diana Kendall, *Framing Class: Media Representations of Wealth and Poverty* (Lantham, MD: Rowman & Littlefield, 2011).

21 Kimberlé Crenshaw, "Demarginalizing the Intersection of Race and Sex: A Black Feminist Critique of Antidiscrimination Doctrine, Feminist Theory and Antiracist Politics," *University of Chicago Legal Forum* 1, Article 8 (1989), 140.

22 Allison Samuels, "Rachel Dolezal's True Lies," *Vanity Fair*, July 19, 2015, http://www.vanityfair.com/news/2015/07/rachel-dolezal-new-interview-pictures-exclusive.

23 Patricia Collins, *Black Feminist Thought: Knowledge, Consciousness, and the Politics of Empowerment* (Boston, MA: Unwin Hyman, 1990).

24 McIntosh, "White Privilege and Male Privilege: A Personal Account of Coming to See Correspondences Through Work in Women's Studies," *Working Paper No. 189* (Wellesley, MA: Center for Research on Women, Wellesley College, 1988).

25 Dreamgirl, "Hot on the Trail Dress," http://www.amazon.com/Dreamgirl-Trail-Dress-BrownMedium/dp/B007N1CY1C/ref=sr_1_46?s=apparel&ie=UTF8&qid=1457366709&sr=1-46&nodeID=7141123011&keywords=native+american+costume.

26 Alicia Garza, "Herstory," *Black Lives Matter*, http://blacklivesmatter.com/herstory/.

27 Associated Press, "President Obama Responds to #OscarsSoWhite Controversy," *The Hollywood Reporter*, January 27, 2016, http://www.hollywoodreporter.com/news/obama-responds-oscarssowhite-controversy-860008.

28 *Fox and Friends*, Fox, February 8, 2016.

29 *Saturday Night Live*, "The Day Beyoncé Turned Black," NBC, February 13, 2016.

30 Tobin Siebers, *Disability Theory* (Ann Arbor: University of Michigan Press, 2008), 3.

31 United Nations, "Convention on the Rights of Persons with Disabilities," *UN Division for Social Policy and Development: Disability*, 2006, http://www.un.org/ disabilities/convention/facts.shtml.

32 Audre Lorde, "Age, Race, Class, and Sex: Women Redefining Difference," in *Sister Outsider: Essays and Speeches by Audre Lorde* (Berkeley, CA: Crossing Press, 1984), 116.

8

Material Culture

You know that we are living in a material world

And I am a material girl.

—Madonna

The phrase "big-box store" sums up a lot about our spending in the United States. Massive shrines to consumption, they line four-lane highways across the country and are stocked full of objects and goods that make up our everyday lives. The buildings, as their name suggests, look like big boxes: huge, square-shaped, single storied, and windowless (other than their glass doors at the front). They are marked by impressive slabs of concrete; parking lots with rows upon rows of spots just waiting to be filled by thousands of shoppers daily. Brightly lit and towering above the entrance, the store's name and logo call out, assuring shoppers they are where they are supposed to be. Upon entering, the size can be overwhelming, particularly in stores like Walmart, which have the large open ceilings of a warehouse or airplane hangar. Other stores have a cozier feel, such as Target with its drop ceilings, but are still brightly lit with the assaulting fluorescents that reflect in the polished beige square tiles of the floor. Regardless of the size, ceilings, name, or colors, inside these stores is a great museum of contemporary American life. From the moment you wake up in the morning until the second you go to sleep, from the time you are born as a soft-skinned bundle and into your elderly "golden" years, for all of the chapters and seconds which fill these spaces of time, everything you could possibly need line the enormous shelves: food, drink, clothing, furniture, bedding, medication, toiletries, electronics, household items. Everything.

Our stuff of everyday life fills our homes, our public spaces, our city streets, our office buildings, and our free time. These things become the record of our existence; a living museum of contemporary culture. By studying or "reading" these objects like a book, we learn not only about the individuals in possession of these items, but about larger society as well. Our cultural myths and priorities emerge from our stuff, as do our individual and group identities. Examining these objects—what we use and how we use them—reflects who we are and what we believe while tracing larger cultural shifts. While Chapter 4 focuses on the culture industries and the production of culture, this chapter turns its focus to various contexts of consumption: what you buy today, use tomorrow, and throw away next week. In order to examine the objects of our everyday life, this chapter lays out theories of material culture and offers methods for the contextual study of everyday objects. Explorations of creation, communication, and consumption of objects as common as the basic necessities of food, shelter, and clothing reveal both larger cultural trends and smaller individual identities. Over time and through repeated use, objects gain meaning, turning them into icons and further revealing complexities and hidden meaning buried just under the surface of our daily lives.

Material culture

The study of objects of everyday life, of our stuff, is referred to as the study of **material culture:** the physical and tangible (material) objects the members of a particular culture use on a regular basis which, in turn, provide insight into the way of life and beliefs of said individuals. This term encompasses all of the things we eat, what we wear, the structures in which we live, what we drive, and everything we use. Changes in culture can be traced through material objects and how they are made, distributed, and consumed by specific groups of people. The materials of our daily lives that we often overlook provide a wealth of information, if we only listen to what they have to say.

The history of the study of material culture has roots in many disciplines as scholars in various fields have found that objects are useful tools to begin an examination of everyday life. For example, much of what is known about past cultures and ancient, or even prehistoric, people across the world comes from the objects they left behind. The field of archaeology examines the remnants of artifacts in order to understand how life was lived by different societies that came centuries and decades before us. Whether they are prehistoric (before written record) or historic (with a written record), objects can provide a glimpse into life not always part of the official record. Folklorist Warren Roberts explained this failure of history to include the full population of a culture by explaining that the written record only accounts for 5 percent of people. This 5 percent is the privileged minority and is not typical or representative (although claims may be made to the contrary) of average people.[1] Therefore, in order to understand the other 95 percent of the population, Roberts and other scholars argue that we must rely on other sources of information.

Beyond the written record, what is most abundant and available for this study are the longer-lasting artifacts that ordinary people leave behind. Because objects are tangible and endure, they remain to be studied long after people are gone. For example, North American prehistoric archaeological finds reveal flint formed into arrowheads and shards of pottery, providing clues into food sources and hunting methods used by ancient Native Americans. These objects point to the resourcefulness of ancient cultures, using the available natural materials and skilled craftsmanship to create tools necessary for survival. These objects also provide a different record than written accounts showcasing a white, European perspective.

The study of material objects is also significant when studying historic cultures that existed during the time of recorded history. It is important to remember that literacy was not always widespread. Historically, education was limited to wealthier citizens, with women, slaves, those in lower socioeconomic classes, and other minorities less likely to be literate. Though there are recorded accounts of various cultures throughout the world, such as letters and journals from Christopher Columbus, John Smith, Cotton Mather, and other European explorers and early settlers, these accounts were written through a lens of exoticism. Differences were highlighted and often the individuals being written about were seen as barbaric. There was no way for the European colonizers to understand the lives of those they were colonizing, and their accounts of the native populations were harsh and critical, portraying them in such a way in order to justify the mistreatment of them. These accounts demonstrate early inequalities and assumptions based on race, which allowed for the unequal treatment of people to the point of genocide and enslavement. Of course, a one-sided story does not supply the whole truth and the recorded "history" can be supplemented with the enduring material objects of those civilizations and cultures. They can tell a different story left out of the written accounts about the individuals whose voices were silenced, erased, or distorted through written documentation.

Even after European settlement of the United States, the objects left behind help to complete the tale started by recorded historical accounts. Objects such as houses, farm implements, clothing, and household items have endured and been preserved in official locations such as historic homesteads and museums or packed away in attic trunks and passed on for generations. These objects were used by average people and can therefore speak to the ways of life of those people, filling in the gaps left in written histories and documents. In conjunction with written testimonials of those who came before us, these objects complete the story of people's daily lives and how their environment shaped their methods of survival.

Museums, ranging in size from the larger natural history museums in major American cities to small local historical society museums peppered across tiny towns, feature these types of lasting exhibits. They range from the prehistoric archaeological finds to the colonial period and the artifacts of those who settled each respective town. Being in the presence of the objects representative of different times and people can be a more effective tool than simply reading. Seeing allows people to imagine what it would be like to live in those houses, wear those clothes, and use those tools. Through the process of imagination, visitors gain insight into the lives of the people from the past. Objects tell us the stories of their creation and use, and these stories are necessary to gain a fuller understanding of both our history and our current society. For example, common to many local history museums are centuries-old medical tools that would make you cringe to think of being used today. Reading up on the advice and procedures of medical professionals in the past forces visitors to imagine what it must have been like to be sick or injured a hundred years ago. Another common display at museums of this sort are old tools and farm implements. The heavy and crude metal and wood equipment look confusing and impeding. Imagining the hard work involved in farming before the mechanized processes of today, along with the pain and dangerous medical practices of yesteryears, tells a very different, yet accurate story of what life was like in the past, painting a picture that no words could alone describe.

Understanding the value of objects and material culture has had a significant influence on the study of people. It not only fills in the gaps of history, but it also provides direction for examining what is happening now in societies all over the world. For cultural studies scholars with an interest in material culture, it is important to gain insight into those still living, using performance theory and other methods to study not only the objects of groups of people, but also what they do with them. Scholars of material culture emphasize the different contexts related to the study of material objects, making way for a more focused study of individuals, creativity, and the ways in which identity and group membership are expressed.

Context: Creation, consumption, and communication

In *Material Culture*, folklorist Henry Glassie presents a clear method to the study of material culture. Having studied material culture through the lens of performance for decades, he simplifies his approach based on context, beginning with the explanation that, "All objects are simultaneously sets of parts and parts of sets."[2] Referring to objects as "sets of parts" frames them as texts, things we can observe and describe through an examination of their formal qualities and component parts. A car, for example, has four tires, a metal body, an engine, brakes, seats, a steering wheel, and so on. Each item listed is a part of a car, something that can be bought and sold separately at an auto parts store. When put together, these objects make a set, which in this case is a car. The first step in the study of material culture is, therefore, description and documentation at the level of the object, what it looks like, the parts that make it up, and all of the various qualities of it.

The "parts of sets," however, is important because it indicates that objects exist in different contexts and that these contexts are what give objects their meaning. Therefore, each object is significant because of its relationship to other objects, people, or places. Going back to our example, a single car is just one part of the larger set of cars on the road, along with the road itself, traffic signs, and everything else that makes up the driving landscape. But what if the car is a rare Corvette, and instead of being driven on the road, sits in the Corvette Museum in Bowling Green, Kentucky? Or, what if the car is beaten up, spray painted, hacked apart, and entered into a demolition derby at a county fair? These cars have different meanings because they each exist in different contexts; they constitute different parts in very different sets.

To assist in the study of material culture, Glassie divides the contexts into three categories: the contexts of creation, consumption, and communication.[3] When studying creation, the researcher studies the process: every stage of development from the learning of skills, to planning, to the execution. Unlike the mass production of the culture industries outlined in Chapter 4, the study of material culture with respect to **creation** explores the ways in which the artist or creator interacts with his or her environment—natural, social, cultural. Consider pottery; its materials come directly from the ground, and the methods of its production depend on the type of ground available. Some places in the United States, such as the South, are rich in malleable clay with the right amount of moisture to sculpt pottery. Other areas, such as the arid West, are much drier, and their ability to make pottery depends on scarce water being made available. Beyond the natural environment and resources available for the production of pottery, there is also the social environment. This includes how people live and socialize. The examination of the types of pottery produced in different regions can determine what kind of food was traditionally consumed, how water was carried and transported, and the nature of mealtime and social structures. This bleeds into an understanding of the cultural environment because aesthetic values can be determined through the pottery designs, beyond just the functional elements, and provide insight into the values and the beliefs of the individuals using the pottery.[4]

Researching material objects using folklore methods and focusing on the context of creation allows for the creator's voice to come through and for a new level of understanding of the meaning behind the objects to be made clear. Many objects possess added cultural meaning, such as religious beliefs and values, which are placed in the creations themselves. For potters across the United States, from the east, south, and southwest, the pottery allows for a connection to their beliefs. From etching Bible verses into the bottom of jugs, to shaping the dry arid southwestern earth as a prayer for water, these creators use nature to express their beliefs.[5]

A close study of the context of creation demonstrates the ways objects are complex and carry many layers of meaning beyond their surface. Any number of meanings can be attached to an object. Additional meanings become connected to an object through additional contexts. The context of consumption allows researchers to explore how objects can fulfill several different functions for the individuals who consume them. As touched upon in Chapter 4, while creators imbue their objects with an intended purpose, it is up to the owner and user of the object to determine its ultimate use. If we continue with our pottery example, think of the different ways individuals use fine china, vases, or handmade mugs. The intended use of these objects is to hold materials, whether they be food, flowers, or hot beverages. Many people, though, save their china for special occasions, don't have a constant supply of fresh flowers, or are worried about breaking handmade objects. This is especially true if they know the artist, if the object is a family heirloom, or if it is a gift from a friend. In these cases, the objects have sentimental value. As a result, these items are rarely used regularly or for their intended purpose; instead, they are kept safe in china cabinets or on display on high shelves. In this instance, they may add color to a home while at the same time reminding the owner of family, friends, or travel. They become valued not for their intended use, but rather for their aesthetic and emotional value.

In between the contexts of creation and of consumption is the context of communication, which mediates the other two. This stage is where an object changes hands and, through this exchange, gains the meanings discussed above. A creator infuses an object with meaning during creation. This meaning could be very personal, as is the case with the talented potters described above; they are communicating something about their identity and their values through the creation of their art. What is communicated can resonate with those who will eventually consume (whether by purchasing or receiving) the objects and be upheld, or that meaning can be forgotten and buried beneath new meanings. Over time, meaning can fade. For some the originally communicated meaning will always be there, even while additional meanings come to the fore. Imagine an antique handmade rocking chair. I own one myself. I do not, however, know the person who made the chair, nor do I know why they chose to make it the way that they did. I lack the context to know what that chair meant to them. The chair, however, still has and can continue to communicate this meaning. At the same time, new meanings are communicated. To me, the chair connects me to my mother and grandmother, as my grandmother gave it to my mother when she had me, thinking that my mother would need a rocking chair. To my grandmother it communicated motherhood. To my mother, it communicated a bond she had with her mother-in-law and her new child, and now for me, it communicates that connection to the strong women in my family. The chair is now the sum of all of those meanings and, depending on to whom you talk about the chair, different meanings are highlighted. Thus, understanding various meanings along the way and the different ways an object can be positioned within the various stages of its lifecycle develops what an object communicates.

Contexts of mass production

These different contexts trace the life of an object from its creation through its many transformations and transitions. With this in mind, we can begin to see how the stuff that we use each day is not as simple as we think. There is a great deal wrapped up in each object. The examples above, which use the exploration of material culture as outlined by Henry Glassie, emphasize the role of the individual creator in the meaning of the object. While we are undoubtedly blessed with an abundance of traditional artists who consider themselves members of folk art, craft, or hobby communities, like the online marketplace Etsy, who would be well-suited to examine through the context of creation, it isn't necessarily what immediately comes to mind when thinking about popular culture. However, that doesn't mean that these same contexts cannot be applied to the objects we use every day. Given the dominance of mass production in today's society, we as consumers are generally more removed from the original context of creation. Consider again the big box stores from the beginning of the chapter. For most of us in the United States, when we need milk, soap, or bed sheets, we don't run to milk the nearest cow, boil down lard and lye, or take our homegrown cotton to the loom in the back room. Instead, we go to Walmart or Target to purchase such necessities of our everyday life without considering the context of creation behind the item's production. When mass culture is designed to make a profit, meaning and communication originates with the goal of the object's sale. As discussed in Chapter 4, through branding, advertising, store displays, and other methods of selling items, corporations pass on additional meanings to consumers in order to make them buy particular objects. The culture industries instill a need in consumers encouraging people to purchase things that they may not have a use for, but fulfills some desire. As we discussed, advertising often creates desire in order to sell a product.

Once the object is under the ownership of someone else, however, new things can be communicated by it based on the way it is consumed. Where the object is purchased, the process of the purchase, the actual moment when the object changes hands from creator (potentially through many middlemen) to the consumer are all aspects to consider in the context of consumption. Store displays, flea market haggling, high-end retail service, online browsing, art galleries, nation-wide advertising campaigns, and craft fairs all have different ways of doing business and transferring objects. How this transfer occurs frames the object for the consumer and can add to its meaning.

The rise of the culture industries and their resultant organization of contemporary life around consumption have resulted in a consumer culture, with "Black Friday" and "Cyber Monday" serving as the high holy days of this cultural practice. We buy everything that we need and even things that we don't need and, before we know it, we have too much stuff. If you've ever moved or decided to do some spring-cleaning, you most likely became aware, however briefly, of just how much stuff fills our daily lives. Often it is not until we are confronted with the weight of the boxes or the overwhelming feeling of not knowing where to begin with the cleaning and organization that the burden of our stuff becomes overwhelming. In a society that is based on consumption, where we fill our time shopping in stores and online, and have sayings like, "he who dies with the most toys wins," it can be hard at times to know whether we own our stuff, or if our stuff owns us. While most of us have a handle on our consumption, popular culture demonstrates the danger of overconsumption through the popularity of shows like A&E's long-running *Hoarders* and TLC's shorter-lived *Hoarding: Buried Alive.* Rather than diagnosing our culture as a whole, though, these shows pathologize those featured, labeling them abnormal and extreme cases, or as suffering from mental illnesses more serious than what the rest of us experience with our constant need to acquire. However, they still serve as a cautionary tale reminding average Americans of the control that objects and things have in our life.

Obviously, not all consumption is bad, and even though we are a culture of consumers, we are also creators as well. While working with the raw materials of earth is one way to create, as is the case with individual folk artistry, people also create out of the objects they purchase. The distinction is one between objects made out of nature and objects made out of culture.[6] In a culture like the one in which we live today, not many of us are in contact or working with natural materials. Instead, we interact with and use things that have already been made and/or are far removed from nature having gone through various mechanized processes. Yet as consumers, we can engage these objects and manufactured materials in such a way as to continue the context of creation. This is described as creation out of culture. This creation can be anything from using materials purchased at a store to make a quilt to arranging mass-produced home décor items purchased at Target, Home Goods, or Ikea to decorate a dorm room. In this case, it is not just in the manufacture of the pillows, wall art, or lamps that creation takes place, but through their arrangement new meanings are made, adding to the layers of the study of material culture.

It is through this context that we want to consider popular culture's relationship to material objects, and to do this, we will consider the three basics of survival—food, shelter, and clothing.

Food: You are what you eat

As anyone who has ever been hangry will tell you, food is an absolute necessity for life. We must have access to clean water and adequate nourishment in order to survive. In the history of this nation, and the world, much of one's day was spent securing substantial and adequate food. From hunter-gatherer societies to the agrarian societies that later emerged, a day's toil was for food and survival. Though people today can forage, hunt, garden, and farm their own foods, very few are fully self-sustaining and supplement what they get through different methods of consumption. Local farmers' markets, community supported agriculture (CSA) programs, co-ops, grocery stores, super markets, box stores, food trucks, local restaurants, and fast food chains are all places to purchase and consume food in various forms and degrees of preparation. Some of these outlets allow for individuals to produce a meal out of nature, from scratch. An examination of the various contexts of the study of material culture (creation, communication, and consumption) as applied to food, then, would be to follow the individual as they procure their food from the natural environment, prepare the food, and consume the food.

Foodways is the academic term used to describe the study of food, which includes all of the actions and practices connected to food within a particular culture or group and how food is used in everyday life. The method to the study of foodways follows five phases: procurement, preservation, preparation, presentation, and consumption.[7] To begin, the food object is the text to be read and each of these phases indicates a different context in which the food should be viewed and examined. These phases parallel the study of material culture, covering the various contexts of objects through creation, consumption, and communication.

Let's begin with procurement: how one receives his/her food. In cultures and societies of the past, food was procured by living off of the land. While some societies still operate in this way, today, food procurement is much different for most of us in the United States. We go to the grocery store or to a restaurant and procure our food through the monetary transaction of paying for a pizza, burrito, or groceries. On closer inspection, though, examining the values and beliefs expressed in the way in which we procure our food suggests a great deal about our culture. The prevalence of convenience stores, quick checkout lanes, and fast-food points to a fast-paced lifestyle with individuals on the go looking for inexpensive and instant gratification. On the other hand, organic food products and stores like Whole Foods cater to a growing "foodie" culture, and are suggestive of values associated with health, quality, and sustainable food practices. That's not to say that wealthy people don't eat fast food and that poor people don't care about eating healthy, but the growing disparities around food justice in our culture points to broader inequalities with respect to various identity markers and demonstrates that more goes into what we eat than what is on our plate. Despite being one of the wealthiest nations in the world, over forty-two million Americans live in households experiencing food insecurity, a condition characterized by hunger, skipping meals, compromising on food nutrition, and/or a reliance on emergency food sources.[8] Further, many areas, despite being heavily populated, are considered food deserts, areas where affordable, fresh, good-quality food is unavailable and/or difficult to access within a one to two-mile radius.

With respect to preservation here in the US, food doesn't present the challenge it once did, as we live in a country where most of the darkest corners can easily be tapped into electricity and wired to support refrigeration and freezer units. Refrigerated and frozen foods allow us more time to consume otherwise quickly perishable foodstuffs, particularly meat, dairy, and vegetables. At the same time, our food is also loaded with scientifically advanced preservatives to maintain freshness, while canned and dried foods can maintain a shelf life of several years. Our preservation techniques point to our reliance on technology and science, and allows for food to be readily available, even when not in peak season. Once again, like many of our procurement methods of food, advances in food preservation suggest a need Americans have for instant gratification of all whims, a desire to eat fruits and vegetables when we want, whether or not they are in season. Our accessibility also allows for a wider variety of food as well. We are no longer limited to what naturally grows where we live, allowing for more diversity in our diets.

Preparation is a very important and telling phase of the foodways model. The methods of preparation, as well as the dishes chosen to be prepared, tell us a great deal about the individuals and cultures involved. Meals and their methods of preparation transmit regional, ethnic, cultural, and individual identities and expressions.[9] In the United States, there are many regional foods (often tied to what is naturally available in that area). In the northeast, fresh seafood and clam bakes are common, while in New Mexico, the question, "Red or green?" accompanies most meals, in reference to the color of chilies preferred on the dish. The South has spice and the North has cheese. When traveling in the United States, people often dine out to sample the local cuisine. At home, what one prepares is also affected by region and familiarity, and is often connected to ethnicity and culture. Italian-Americans are known for their food, as are Mexican-Americans. From lasagna to tamales for holiday meals, what is prepared often is determined by family tradition passed down through generations. Those practicing strict Judaism follow a kosher diet with many restrictions: pork, shellfish, and mixing meat and milk, just to name a few. Beyond these markers of identity that individuals are born into, some of the factors that go into the decisions for food preparation are by choice. For example, vegans, vegetarians, and others who opt for restrictive diets due to health concerns, weight loss, or moral and ethical reasons express their values and beliefs through their choices of which foods to prepare. What is on the plate, in the refrigerator, or being served up at a restaurant speaks volumes about the person who is eating the food.

As anyone who has ever watched television series such as *Hell's Kitchen*, *Top Chef*, or *Chopped* will tell you, the presentation of food concerns how it is plated, served, and presented to those eating it. Food served on a paper plate means something very different from a meal served on fine china. Food could be wrapped in bright yellow paper and put into a brown paper bag or plated beautifully with a decorative garnish and glaze. The presentation determines the degree of formality or of celebration, often dependent on those who will be sharing in the food.

All of these different phases ultimately end with the context of consumption. While the word consumption has been used in this chapter to point towards the purchasing of objects, in this case it means the actual physical consumption of food. How this is done, with whom it is done, and the rules necessary for consumption is the culmination of all of the other phases of the study of foodways. Examining meals and food in our daily lives, with a focus on these phases, can reveal a significant amount of information about our culture and what we value most. Starting in the 1980s, an often-cited indicator of the problems with contemporary US society was that families no longer had meals together. Hurried meals at fast-food restaurants or frozen ones heated up in microwaves—designed to be consumed in cars, in front of the television, or while glued to computer screen as opposed to around the family dinner table—spelled trouble for the crusaders of family values. To them, the fundamental structure and identity of what it meant to be "American" was attacked. Single-parent homes or homes which had two working parents meant that no one was home to toil over the family meal for hours. Because of work and extra-curricular activity schedules, less time was spent preparing meals or worrying about the nutrition. Rather than eating together, a social and bonding experience for families, people were doing so separately. Food was no longer about maintaining ties and connections, but rather about basic survival. While this is only one side of the argument, it speaks to the ways that focus on foodways suggests something broader about our culture.

A more recent conversation circulating about food has to do with the politics surrounding the national push for healthy eating. With former First Lady Michelle Obama's health initiatives such as "Let's Move" and working to get healthier food options into public schools, there was an acknowledgment of the disparities in food availability. The push towards organic food comes at a cost as the methods used to grow and make organic foods are more expensive. Therefore, the consumer is left with the financial burden. This makes healthy eating a luxury that only the more affluent members of a society can afford leaving those individuals lower on the socioeconomic ladder eating the unhealthier foods full of preservatives and empty calories, contributing to a nation-wide health crisis. Despite this, many Americans balk at the idea of the government trying to regulate what should and should not be served in public schools, while others oppose taxes on sugary drinks such as soda.

Food also points out the diversity among individuals in the United States as well. As mentioned, regional and ethnic identity are extremely important when it comes to food. Not only what is eaten, but how it is prepared and consumed speak to the many different backgrounds that make up the country. Values connected to identity, on the larger cultural and smaller individual levels, are abundant in any examination of food. It tells a great deal about heritage and about social interactions.[10] A close study of food such as that presented by the different phases of foodways reveals a lot about people and their daily lives. As a vital material for the sustenance of life, food is a common, everyday, and an essential component to our popular culture landscape.

As an example, let's briefly compare two meals: a pizza party among friends and a first date. We'll start with the pizza party. One friend decides that she is going to host a pizza dinner in her home, inviting some of her closest friends. Though one individual is hosting, her friends are going to assist in obtaining the necessary materials. The host tells her friends that she will pick up the necessary toppings for the pizza. She goes to the grocery store and buys premade sauce, cheese, fresh mushrooms, jalapenos, garlic, jars of olives, and packages of pepperoni. One friend, who used to work for a pizza restaurant, offers to make and bring fresh dough. Another friend lives on a farm and offers to bring whatever vegetables he picks that day. Another friend offers to pick up snacks and beverages, another offers to bring materials to make a salad, and yet another brings a vegan cake for dessert. Through this procurement phase, a great deal can be learned about the friends. First of all, they all have their own strengths: some of them live off of the land, others have skills in the kitchen, and still others only consume what is available to them at the grocery store. However, they all use their strengths to support the dinner the best that they can while sharing in the financial burden and responsibility, which suggests a mutual respect and close comfort level.

In a situation like this, preservation isn't necessarily one of the more important phases, as all of the friends prepare for what they will bring the day of the party. As they all have access to refrigeration systems, there isn't a concern for how to preserve the food ingredients or even the leftovers. The pizza dinner really is all about the preparation phase. As one friend is making the salad, another is tossing the dough, and others are preparing the vegetables and other toppings. The friends play music and catch up on their lives as they prepare the food. While waiting for the pizza to cook, they share in snacks and drinks. It's an egalitarian meal in the sense that they all share in the burden and work of preparation. The food itself is secondary to their relationships, but gives them something to do and something to eat when they gather.

The presentation of the pizza is not of the utmost importance. As the friends are very comfortable with one another, they do not feel the need to show off and are happy when the pizza emerges from the oven fully cooked, but not burned. This casual feel feeds into the consumption phase of the evening. One friend cuts the pizza while others gather a stack of plates and utensils. After cutting the pizza and taking the pieces each wants, the friends don't even all sit at the table. Some sit while others remain standing at the counter. The casual way the food is eaten suggests a level of comfort and familiarity among the friends. Analyzing this meal using foodways, it becomes clear that while the food is present and vital to the gathering, it is not the main focus. The shared roles in the procurement, preparation, and ultimate consumption unite the friends.

This is a meal that stands out from most, whether a traditional family meal or a quick drive-through fast food meal. To compare it to another meal, let's think about a first date. During a first date, the outing is about getting to know another person in a more intimate way. People tend to go out for a meal on dates, rather than stay in, because of the comfort level. Going somewhere in public guarantees a neutral ground that traveling to someone's home when you don't know them would not. Further, going out to eat eliminates the stress of the procurement, preservation, preparation, and presentation of the meal. Instead, it is up to the restaurant staff to otherwise arrange the meal. Depending on the region, socioeconomic class, and age of the individuals going on the date, the restaurant choice varies. Some locales, particularly cities, are known for having a wide variety of restaurants and fine-dining experiences, while more rural or suburban areas rely more on chain restaurants. Though nice, the dining experience is less refined than in the upper-scale restaurants with well-known chefs in charge of the kitchen. After picking the restaurant and selecting a meal choice from the menu, the burden of the meal is on the staff, leaving the two individuals on the date to get to know one another. Since learning about another individual on a first date can be an uncomfortable situation, the topic can turn to the meal and the restaurant experience. By sharing a meal, the individuals are sharing an experience and will forever have that time together. Again, the food is not necessarily at the center of the meal, but it serves a valuable function as a reason for the two individuals to come together to get to know another.

Meals can take many forms with many meanings, and these two instances were selected to demonstrate the way food is used in our everyday lives to bring individuals together. Whether it is friends coming together to share food and each other's company, or strangers getting to know one another, potentially starting a more meaningful relationship, food becomes key to these interactions, telling us a great deal about daily life and values such as love, socialization, and friendship. Not only that, but close examinations of the food that people prepare and consume, as well as how they procure, preserve, and present it, can serve as an indicator of many different identities.

Shelter: Tiny houses, fixer uppers, and design stars

Similar to how most of us no longer procure our own food from toiling in the Earth, most of us don't spend our days cutting and hewing logs from the forests of our surrounding areas, shaping and baking clay or mud into bricks, or hauling stone from dry creek beds to build our homes and other buildings. The shelters in which we spend a great deal of our time, both sleeping and awake, have been contracted and built by others using a variety of different materials and equipment not natural to the world in which we inhabit. As discussed previously with respect to the "American Dream," the buildings too are things that we consume and usually pay for throughout most of the years of our lives. Whether paying for a college dorm room with student loans, renting an apartment in a complex of cloned spaces, buying a small suburban home, or funding the building of a dream home from the literal ground up, shelter is a huge and primary expense in the lives of Americans.

With respect to material culture, our homes tell a significant amount of information about their inhabitants, as well as their location. Shelter is different from food, clothing, and the other objects we're examining in that it doesn't necessarily move. There are the rare occurrences of buildings being moved from one location to another and some homes are meant to be moved (such as mobile homes, trailers, and tiny houses), but, for the most part, our shelters are fixed in place. As our private dwellings, they are not public in the same way other expressions of our identity are, as we typically only share our homes with friends and family. Of course, what is outside of a house is more public than what is inside, and this difference can express a variety of different codes and meanings. On the surface, what a house looks like from the outside can suggest something about socioeconomic class, region, and some values with how the yard or façade may be maintained, but inside can be a completely different code where more personal details can be revealed. And while most people aren't necessarily building their home from scratch with raw materials they've collected, that doesn't mean individuals are removed from the creation of their own spaces through the creation from culture in their homes.

The objects we put into a home are most often mass-produced and purchased. Once purchased, they are taken home and displayed in the space in a way that gives them added value and meaning. This action is an example of what is called **assemblage**, the arrangement of objects in a particular context or location, with meaning created through their grouping. In many fields of study, the term assemblage is often used in connection to, or conflated with, the term **bricolage**: the creation of something new from different and unrelated parts. Claude Lévi Strauss explained that the "'bricoleur' is still someone who works with his hands and uses devious means compared to those of a craftsman."[11] This "bricoleur" is "also adept at performing a large number of diverse tasks; but, unlike the engineer, he does not subordinate each of them to the availability of raw materials and tools conceived and procured for the purpose of the project. His universe of instruments is closed and the rules of his game are always to make do with 'whatever is at hand.'"[12] Bricolage is often referred to as DIY, or "do-it-yourself," as individuals rely on their own abilities and what is available to them rather than on an expert or trained craftsman. It is a response to one's environment and creating within it.

Folklorist Jack Santino explained assemblage as "combining of a variety of symbolic elements within a single frame, and the creation of a single aesthetic entity by grouping together disparate things."[13] Assemblage is therefore a contextual understanding of how nonrelated objects can work together in one "frame" rather than put together to form one object, bricolage. Together they make an aesthetic statement, as decorations on a mantle do, but they all have not been adhered together as one object to remain connected for the rest of their lifespan. To illustrate his point, Santino looks at the outside of homes, focusing on holiday decorations. For example, the store-bought decorations mixed with home-carved pumpkins on the outside of a house around Halloween work together to make one "aesthetic entity." However, when Halloween is over, the rotten pumpkins can be thrown away and the more durable decorations can be stored for next year. When they emerge for the following year's holiday, they can be placed outside of the house and on the lawn in a different setup than they were before. They are not one object, but a system of objects that work together to create a spooky Halloween yard. Here we can see how assemblage is the creative and meaningful arrangement of unrelated objects which reflect the beliefs of the creator. With the rise of the culture industries, assemblage has become "a major expressive mode of industrial civilization."[14]

Homes are very personal spaces and what is communicated through them points to how individuals consume, live, and identify. When people live alone, they are free to make that entire space their own, decorating and personalizing it to fit their needs and their desires. If the living space is shared, however, there is more of a compromise on how it is decorated and what it communicates. It can suggest not only information about the individuals, but also their relationships. In these shared spaces, there is often a mix of communal and personal spaces. Communal spaces, such as kitchens, living rooms, family rooms, dens, or dining rooms, are designed for gathering. A kitchen requires appliances, counter space, and cabinetry. Seating is available, whether it is an island with stools, or a full table. The kitchen is defined by the presence of objects such as cooking utensils, pots and pans, dishes, and silverware. Spaces such as living rooms or dens are designed to accommodate more people relaxing, so there tends to be plenty of comfortable seating. These rooms also feature electronics like a television, stereo, video game consoles, and any number of corded metal boxes to occupy time. Each room in a home is decorated differently and contains items which further communicate how the space should be used and gives clues about the individuals using it. Beyond the more obvious objects that are common for different types of rooms, design details depend on the individual; from the paint and art on the walls, to the choice of furniture and the objects on display, and even to the order and cleanliness, a great deal of information can be inferred. For example, a sitting room featuring ornate antique chairs and beautiful hand-woven rugs over white carpet communicates wealth and class, while a similar room with a large, broken-in sofa and toys in a bin along the wall suggests a more comfortable and relaxed space.

In contrast to these communal spaces, bedrooms are private spaces, whether they are occupied by a single person or shared by a couple or by siblings. By definition, bedrooms are defined by sleeping and should contain some sort of bed and the type of bed or beds would indicate the number of people who share the room. Within such a space are also more personal items such as clothing and sentimental objects and keepsakes. Although these items do communicate identity and contain meaning, the fact that they are tucked away from the communal space speaks of their personal nature. Other personal spaces in homes, like the rising popularity of "man caves" and "she sheds," are also designated spots for one particular individual and are somewhat off-limits to others without invitation.

Further, as anthropologist Daniel Miller notes, "material objects are a setting. They make us aware of what is appropriate and inappropriate [...] But they work most effectively when we don't actually look at them, we just accept them."[15] Therefore the objects we surround ourselves with, in our homes and offices, as well as the objects we encounter that are not ours, subconsciously work to shape our expectations about the spaces they occupy and the individuals who own them. They can help dictate what we wear, how we speak, and the ways in which we interact with others in public and private spaces.

Though individuals decorate and create their space through assemblage, most of the objects are purchased separately and carry a number of different meanings. The popularity of HGTV and shows like *House Hunters*, *Design on a Dime*, and *Fixer Uppers*, demonstrates our cultural interest not only in the homes in which we and others live, but also our desire to communicate our identities through our living spaces. Each of the objects we inherit, buy, collect, and display express individual meanings, and as sets and systems communicate larger messages about our social locations, values, and beliefs. The understood permanence of homes and other building structures also means that they are more likely to endure beyond our lifetime, granting them the power to speak for us when we are no longer able.

Clothing: In fashion, one day you're in, the next day you're out

After the basic needs of food and shelter have been met, the protection of the body with clothing is the final requirement for survival. Clothing functions to protect the vulnerable, hairless human skin against the elements: the frostbite of the bitter cold or the severe burns of the hot sun. Beyond protection from the environment, clothing has also become a cultural requirement in our society. While there are some exceptions, in general, nudity is not accepted in most public spaces, and it is expected that when going out into the world, people do so fully clothed. The value placed on covering the human body, the rules of what can be shown and to whom, and what passes as acceptable garb express the values and beliefs of a culture and of an individual. Reading the codes connected to clothing reveals significant details about human interactions, social expectations, and a variety of identities. As clothing's original function was protection of the body, style, taste, and norms weren't of primary concern. Early clothing was made of what was available in nature, such as leather and pelts from hunted animals. Over time, adornment, the act of decorating the body, became a function of clothing in order to signify status in culture or to align with particular beliefs.

Like the shelters in which we reside and the food we eat, the clothing that we wear today is not solely organic. While the materials used to make clothing may come from nature (such as cotton and wool), there is quite a process before those materials are transformed into wearable objects. Though many items are still produced by hand, they are done so on a massive scale with the assistance of machines and inexpensive labor. Before being worn, garments go through many other phases such as branding, shipping, selection by vendors, etc., before they are available for purchase in the market place. This can happen on a small scale with high-end designers and craftsmen or on a much larger scale with factories, or even sweatshops, and huge warehouses of stocked items. As with the other objects we have discussed, in addition to the original context of creation, the other contexts of communication and consumption, as well as creation through assemblage, apply to the daily decisions made when it comes to what we wear.

Clothing, whether one likes shopping for it or not, is a necessity. When considering the contexts of communication and consumption, the place to begin is the process of purchasing articles of clothing. Many stores carry clothing: those in malls, smaller boutiques, outlets, second-hand stores, online retailers, and even the larger chain stores. Some individuals embrace the ethos "shopping is my cardio," their blood pumping with excitement as they search out the latest styles and sales. Others see shopping as a form of relaxation and entertainment, flipping through catalogs, scrolling through online sites, or actual window shopping at malls and retail stores. For others, shopping is something done only out of necessity. Attending a wedding, funeral, job interview, or first date might be occasions for those who do not enjoy shopping to find themselves in a last-minute rush to buy an acceptable outfit. This can be stressful, as it forces individuals to adhere to social rules that might divert them from their regular fashion palette. Holiday gift shopping and back-to-school shopping are regular rituals associated with the purchase of new clothing. The look that someone is going for or the purpose for which they need clothing will dictate the types of stores and departments where they shop. Factors such as region and socioeconomic class also determine shopping habits. Living in a rural area limits choices, while cities are full of eclectic shops. Those with ample funds for extravagant clothing might find themselves drawn to designer show rooms or upscale boutiques, while those on a tighter budget may opt for the fashion selections at second-hand stores. One's style preference also plays a huge role in where one chooses to shop. If one wants to stay on trend, they may shop at stores like H&M, Forever 21, or Zara, which are constantly changing merchandise to cater to "fast fashion" that is cheap, trendy, and designed to be worn for just a season. However, for individuals who want to stand out and wear more unique items, they might revel in the rare finds at vintage clothing stores or lesser-known boutiques tucked around US cities.

Regardless of where it is purchased, clothing is worn daily, with individuals creating an endless number of style options by mixing items together, donning them, and going out into the world. By putting different outfits together, the context of creation comes through, as well as that of communication, as individuals send messages about themselves and their values through their chosen wardrobe. Many forms of coded communication exist within dress, such as age, marital status, economic status, religion, occupation, personal style, and much more. The details provided by what we wear speaks to the usefulness of the approach of the study of material culture as it relates to identity and popular culture. The outfits that individuals create regularly are an example of bricolage, as dress is made up of different objects that don't necessarily naturally belong together, but which are brought together as a collection and work together in a system. The system the objects form makes statements and create meaning which allows for self-expression.

Consider your own routine and approach when it comes to dress. Each day, certain concerns must be taken into consideration before the clothing choice for the day is decided. Imagine it is a regular Wednesday morning and you have to get to a 9:00 a.m. class. Most likely, you'll not spend too much time on your appearance, opting for something comfortable, quick, and convenient. Most likely this approach and your choices are different from a Thursday evening when preparing for a night out with friends. With different expectations and goals, you may spend more time on your appearance, whether it is working on hair, adding makeup, adding accessories, or carefully considering the clothes being worn. Reality television shows featuring young twenty-somethings highlight this ritual. When lounging around the house, one's appearance isn't flawless and clothing choices tend to be much more causal. When going out, however, much more is to be considered. The men in *Jersey Shore* gelled their hair, chose their sneakers, and waited until the last minute to yell "T-shirt time" in an effort to keep T-shirts clean and fresh looking for the evening. The girls were often seen primping in the mirror, examining themselves from every imaginable angle in very tight and revealing dresses, high heels, and hair coiffed just as high. Taking a moment to consider your own wardrobe is an opportunity to reflect on how your choices of what to wear vary significantly depending on whether you are preparing for a worship service, job interview, class presentation, or workout.

The first context of communication expressed by clothing is its functionality and the day's goal. Beyond that, individuality is expressed as people develop styles of their own. One of the first studies to explore this with respect to popular culture was Dick Hebdige's *Subculture: The Meaning of Style*, which examined youth subcultures such as punk and the varying inspirations and offshoots of culture that stood apart from the mainstream significantly in their style of dress. By choosing elements of clothing which deviated from the mainstream culture, the individuals were expressing their working-class values in opposition to the consumerism on the rise and the disorder felt by the increasingly marginalized. Ripped up clothes, safety pins, spiked hair, and other unique style choices defined not only the movement, but the individuals involved in that movement. While those styles originally stood apart from the mainstream, there was also an element of conforming to a punk uniform embedded in the movement. Further, the concept of a punk infiltrated culture, becoming a form of commodified rebellion that eventually could be purchased at mainstream retailers. This development of punk in the mainstream is critiqued by those who strongly identify with the subculture and dismiss the poseurs who attempt to easily conform or the trendy adoption of the style on fashion runways and museum displays.

As touched on in Chapter 4, the rise of the Internet has created a space for blogs for a number of consumer habits, including fashion. While they may seem silly or frivolous, fashion blogs help to explain the role of clothing in our contemporary society. For example, fashion blogger Becky Haltermon Robinson explains her process of getting dressed through the contexts of material culture. She describes it as such:

> My philosophy on dressing revolves around balance: Balance of conservative and sexy, professional and playful, classic and wacky. If my starting piece is an evening gown, I might want to make it more fun with bizarre 1960s plastic earrings. If I know I want cowboy boots, I might balance their bulky silhouette with a fitted dress…. My process for getting dressed for work is a streamlined version of this: I have a selection of dresses and pants that are work-appropriate, and I use them as a starting point for outfit construction, usually adding from a selection of sweaters/ blazers, fancy tops and heels or flats.[16]

Becky's approach to dress is very much a creative process. She uses trial and error, test and tune, and many glimpses in front of the mirror before finalizing the day's look. Her arrangement of various pieces of clothing in order to balance one another to her liking is an act of assemblage. The ways in which she puts items and accessories together is both an act of consumption and communication. She elaborates on this, explaining:

> Wherever I'm headed, I leave the house feeling like the best version of myself is visible to everyone around me. My goal is to be perceived as interesting more than attractive, though I try to make sure my garb compliments my physicality. While I live for compliments, my fun is really in the process

of constructing an ensemble that communicates complicated messages. Those messages might include, "I am professional but creative," "I am here to party but I will talk to you about 19th century American fiction," or "I am indifferent to the passing of ridiculous trends but I did just happen to find this completely on-trend item at a thrift store."[17]

Becky is particularly aware of what her clothing is communicating about her on a daily basis. She embodies Miller's notion of style, "that is, the individual construction of an aesthetic based not just on what you wear, but on how you wear it."[18] The dedication with which she approaches her dress is more than just a necessity; it is an art form. Her creativity isn't limited to the bricolage of putting pieces together, she also makes and alters many of the garments she wears. She is also extremely aware of the power clothing has in different situations and the importance of accommodating one's dress to fit those situations, whether it be work or play. Through her creations out of what she has consumed, she can communicate significantly to the world about herself, her interests, and her values.

Conclusion: Popular culture icons

What the examination of food, shelter, and clothing demonstrates is that we create and communicate significantly and regularly through the material objects we use each and every day. The basic needs of survival are wrapped in meaning and are quite complicated when broken down and examined closely. Through regular use and association, objects have been studied in popular culture as **icons**.[19] The use of the term icon is significant because it carries the connotation of a symbol, of something that is more than it appears and has meaning beyond the obvious. The term originally was reserved for images of Christian religious figures such as Jesus. As Jesus was not Himself standing before worshipers, depictions of Him were used in His place. Therefore the object on which the image appeared became venerated as a sacred stand-in for the Savior in Christianity. Religious iconography was especially useful when most people were illiterate. When not able to read holy texts, icons stood in for those sacred stories. Consider the cross in Christianity; it summarizes the entire crux of the religion. The cross stands for the ultimate sacrifice made by God by giving up his son to forgive believers of their sins. Without actually reading the text of the New Testament, the cross stands in for the Biblical tale of selflessness and forgiveness.

Beyond religion, icons are objects that come to represent other cultural markers. They are the material objects of popular culture which serve as representations of a culture's ideologies, values, and beliefs. Flags, for example, are icons for nations. Even within the United States, each individual state has its own flag. Those flags stand for that particular territory. The American flag has great significance. The thirteen red and white stripes stand for the original thirteen colonies and the fifty stars stand for each of the fifty current states. It is therefore an icon of the unified, or "united," territories of the United States. Because of its significance as an icon of the nation, it is treated carefully. It shouldn't touch the ground, should be revered, not desecrated, and folded with respect and ceremony. Because its only use is to stand for the United States, it is what is considered a pure icon: it has no other function beyond the symbolic.[20] On a less grand scale, the term icon has been adopted and used in varying ways and applied to normal everyday objects. As soon as objects carry a meaning that goes beyond their intended function and purpose, they become icons. From Mickey Mouse to the golden arches of McDonalds, we see iconography across the popular culture landscape of the United States.

We are surrounded by the objects of popular culture, the stuff of our everyday lives. They are the things we make, eat, live in, wear, buy, and work on. The prevalence of things in our life can make it so they are overlooked. That prevalence, however, is the exact reason why we should examine them closely. The objects that make up our everyday existence provide clues and information about the nature of our lives. Things as broad as the entire belief system of a culture to the more specific individual interests we all have are, whether we mean to or not, expressed through objects. By using material culture as a starting point and understanding the various contexts in which objects can exist, a great deal is revealed about the popular culture of our everyday lives.

Notes

1   Warren E. Roberts, *Log Buildings of Southern Indiana* (Bloomington, IN: Trickster Press, 1996), vii.

2   Henry Glassie, *Material Culture* (Bloomington: Indiana University Press, 1999), 47.

3   Ibid., 48–59.

4   Henry Glassie, *The Potter's Art* (Bloomington: Indiana University Press, 1999).

5   Ibid., 36–47.

6   Pravina Shukla, *The Grace of Four Moons: Dress, Adornment, and the Art of the Body in Modern India* (Bloomington: Indiana University Press, 2008), 387.

7   Lucy M. Long, *Culinary Tourism*, ed. Lucy M. Long (Lexington: The University Press of Kentucky, 2004), 8.

8   Alisha Coleman-Jensen, et al., "Household Food Security in the United States in 2015," *Economic Research Report No. 215*, USDA, 2016, https://www.ers.usda.gov/publications/pub-details/?pubid=79760.

9   Linda Keller Brown and Kay Mussell, ed., *Ethnic and Regional Foodways in the United States: The Performance of Group Identity* (Knoxville: The University of Tennessee Press, 2001).

10 Ibid.

11 Claude Lévi-Strauss, *The Savage Mind* (Chicago: The University of Chicago Press, 1966), 16–17.

12 Ibid., 17.

13 Jack Santino, "The Folk *Assemblage* of Autumn: Tradition and Creativity in Halloween Folk Art," in *Folk Art and Art Worlds*, ed. John Michael Vlach and Simon J. Bronner (Logan: Utah State University Press, 1992), 159.

14 Glassie, *Material Culture*, 84.

15 Daniel Miller, *Stuff* (Malden, MA: Polity, 2009), 50.

16 Becky Haltermon Robinson, e-mail interview with Callie Clare, August 9, 2016.

17 Ibid.

18 Miller, *Stuff*, 15.

19 Jack Nachbar and Kevin Lause, ed., *Popular Culture: An Introductory Text* (Bowling Green, KY: Bowling Green State University Press, 1992), 169–85.

20 Ibid., 172.

9

Community

I've never been held hostage, but I have been in a group text.

—Anyone who has ever been in a group text.

The FX series *Sons of Anarchy* is a violent, bloody, and ruthless show which assisted in the transformation of quality, serialized, hour-long television dramas during its seven-season run (2008–2014). Depicting an extremely dramatized version of a fictional motorcycle club (MC) in Northern California, the show focuses on the original chapter of SAMCRO: Sons of Anarchy Motorcycle Club, Redwood Original, as they live together, die together, party together, peddle illegal guns together, murder together, go to jail together, but, most importantly, ride together. Over the course of its run, the show regularly killed off the beloved, yet perpetually flawed, main characters and pushed the boundaries of what could be said or shown on television, contributing to its popularity and its continued appeal. However, behind the flashiness of the sex and violence, *Sons of Anarchy* is a well-executed portrayal of a very particular type of community: the community of an outlaw motorcycle gang.

While we may not all be gang members, most people do tend to gather in groups; it is part of our most elemental biology. The old adage of "safety in numbers" speaks to our need to come together. Survival depends on cooperation and unification of strengths and resources. Humans are social animals, and socializing makes the coming together of individuals easier and more enjoyable. Today in the United States, more than mere survival, people gather for a variety of different reasons. Sometimes it is circumstantial; people spend time with the individuals they happen to be around due to factors such as where they live, work, or go to school. Other times, it goes beyond the circumstantial and is sought after; people form friendships and groups based along their lines of interests, hobbies, or beliefs. Coming together in this more intentional way demonstrates that people seek out others who share their interest because it reflects a deeper and more significant shared mindset and outlook on the world. For the bikers in *Sons of Anarchy*, a common interest in motorcycles acts as that bridge. This is also the case with real-life automobile enthusiasts and motorcycle groups, but gathering around common interests also extends to people who have similar tastes in music, video games, comic books, and many other types of pastimes.

As we've explored in the last two chapters, people come to identify themselves in a variety of ways. Expressing one's individual identity comes from an intersection of many group identities. While it is important to understand how individual identity develops, it is also important to understand the meaningful relationships that contribute to that identity and the various ways that identity can be expressed through membership in a larger group. We all belong to many communities and although those communities may look very different, they do in fact serve important functions for the individuals involved and further our study of popular culture by helping us to understand people and why they commune.

This chapter is about groups of people, what that means, and how they have been studied. Beginning with the broad terms such as the often-used culture and society, this chapter focuses on community. Studying community based on the understanding of what folklorists refer to as folk groups, **community** emerges as a democratic way to understand the everyday experiences of groups of people as they gather together and express themselves through their shared characteristics and interests. Applying this analysis to modern-day trends of networks and online communities reveals that even though technology and communication forms change, the basic need within individuals to gather remains a strong unifying and expressive force.

Societies, culture, and community

Before exploring community, we can begin by addressing the larger terms that group people into categories: culture and society. **Culture** is often described as a set of shared meanings, practices, and beliefs that constitute a way of life for a specific group of people coexisting in a particular place and time. People of a particular culture typically share a **mindset** and look at the world in similar ways. Being raised in the same culture shapes and molds people to believe certain things. However, to define where one culture ends and another begins can be difficult. Part of that is because culture is somewhat abstract with no clearly delineated lines. Culture unites people who believe in the myths that shape and constitute it. Of course, these myths adapt and change as people and daily life evolve.

Society, on the other hand, is a much more structured and organized system for grouping people. It has more intention behind how it is set up, whereas culture tends to emerge on its own with no overarching plan. We can all live in a society, but that doesn't mean we share the same mindset or worldview. Instead, society sets the expectation that we all agree to abide by certain regulations, order, and organization. It also doesn't imply personal relationships among members beyond everyone following the agreed-upon rules set forth. A well-organized society resembles a well-oiled machine where everything runs smoothly. Although everyone isn't necessarily equal in a society, nor do they have the same stake in it, the premise behind functioning societies is that, in the long run, everyone benefits through the maintenance and observance of society's set standards. As an abstract idea, society can be difficult to put borders around. Although it may be easier to delineate than culture, it is a dense concept and different fields of study approach it in different ways.

As a culture, people are defined by their beliefs and mindset. This can be narrowed down to **subcultures** and **countercultures**, depending on how those beliefs align (subcultures) or contrast (countercultures) with the overall beliefs of the larger culture. People also live in a society, which keeps organization and manages people in a civilized way. Although culture and society work to describe large groups of people, not all people in specific cultures and society have relationships with one another. This is where community is instrumental to our study. **Community** refers to smaller groups of individuals with shared identities and worldviews and emphasizes the importance of interpersonal relationships.

Community, like many of the terms we are identifying and defining in this book, is a common word, used by everyday people in their everyday lives.

However, the weight the term carries is significant. If we break it down like we did with the term "popular" in the first chapter, it becomes clear that community and popular have quite a few similarities. As stated way back in the introduction to this book, the intentional use behind the label of *popular* culture is that it is of the people, coming from the people. It doesn't mean it is necessarily liked by all, but rather common for most. It comes from average individuals and provides insight into how they live their lives. This leads to the examination of popular culture through the lens of democracy by recognizing the importance of the contributions of all people. Community works the same way. Its root word is "common," meaning shared or public. This idea of common relates significantly to the concept of a commune, or communal living, where people work and live together, sharing their resources and contributions for the greater good. The related term "communism" was chosen for these connotations. As defined by Karl Marx and Friedrich Engels in *The Communist Manifesto*, "Communism is the doctrine of the conditions of the liberation of the proletariat."[1] As a theory of political practice, it was meant to stand for the shared means of production, and therefore wealth, by all people to better serve the marginalized working class (proletariat). This system would do away with the stratifications created in the capitalist hierarchy of socioeconomic classes, creating a communal society based on sharing and equality. Of course, this doesn't exactly work in practice, but the intention behind the naming suggests community and sharing.

Beyond these connotations of equality, at the heart of community, and the ways the term is regularly used, are personal connections and the maintenance of interpersonal relationships. While the terms culture and society suggest a much larger scale, community focuses on the smaller individual relationships and regular interactions among people. These interactions exist for various reasons. One situation that leads to regular contact is proximity to others. The towns and cities we live in have delineated borders and use those borders to define the individuals within them. This proximity determines things such as schools, local government, parks, public spaces, and, therefore, the people who interact with one another on a daily basis. The people, places, and activities that exist within those boundaries are important elements that make up a community. Community action, outreach, development, resources, and service apply to the individuals who share the space of the defined borders. Living together can create many complications, so community building is an essential element of towns and neighborhoods across the country. Ultimately, however, it is up to each individual to define their own level of involvement in the community. Some choose to be very active in their communities through volunteering, partaking in local events, participating in the local political process, or through efforts to better the community. Others might choose to remain more closed off from their community and limit their interactions with others.

Beyond proximity, communities can also be defined by effort to connect with others based on similarities and shared identities. Instead of making connections through regular interactions determined by where one lives, people often seek out others who share their interests. By frequenting a certain place or purposefully putting oneself near individuals who share similar hobbies and pastimes, relationships and communities can develop through these more intentional behaviors. Sites such as workplaces, parks, watering holes, or even clubs can develop communities with those we share deeper interests with beyond the happenstance of where we live.

Beyond how communities are built, there is more to consider: what does community mean, how has it been conceptualized, and how has it been studied? To start this discussion, let's first turn to the relationship the term community has with what cultural anthropologist Victor Turner referred to as "communitas." Turner used communitas over community "to distinguish this modality of social relationship from an 'area of common living.'"[2] The "common living" would be the proximity element of community discussed earlier. For Turner, however, communitas is different because physical closeness isn't enough to bring people together meaningfully. One also needs to consider the order and structure associated with society, as there are certain power dynamics and rules associated with community when thinking of it as the town or city where one resides. Communitas, on the other hand, is less structured; it develops in a more egalitarian way making everyone more equal. It is therefore more democratic than society.[3]

Turner's division mirrors Ferdinand Tönnies's dichotomy of gemeinschaft and gesellschaft.[4] **Gemeinschaft** roughly translates to community and depends on personal interactions. These interactions are social and can develop into relationships. **Gesellschaft**, on the other hand, is connected to society and, therefore, more impersonal. In gesellschaft, interactions between people are more structured and don't necessarily develop into relationships. The structure isn't as spontaneous or natural in its creation as community is. As mentioned, society is based on power, with certain individuals having and yielding more of it than others. The implication of equality doesn't exist within society or gesellschaft. Real and personalized relationships aren't as important or necessarily fostered or created beyond the necessity of continuing society.[5]

Looking at the differences between gemeinschaft and gesellschaft, communitas, as well as the "common" root to the word community, it becomes evident that community is about people. It is about ordinary people and the ways they come together and make meaningful relationships beyond the circumstance of being in proximity to others. This relates to the study of folklore, which heavily influenced the development of popular culture studies. Like the academic study of popular culture, folklore, too, values all people, not just those who have traditionally held the power within a culture or society. Our understanding of the use of the term community comes from an understanding of the term "folk" as it has been studied by folklorists across the globe and adapted for use in the study of the United States. As pointed out distinctly by Ray Browne and other scholars, what was traditionally recognized in the academy tended to ignore the regular, everyday people. The study of folklore and popular culture work to shift the focus of study onto the everyday lives of average inhabitants of society and culture. Understanding the development of folklore, then, is key to understanding this text's approach to popular culture and our study of community and groups.

What the folk!?

The term "folk-lore" was coined by William J. Thoms in 1846, borrowed from the German "volkskunde," termed in 1782.[6] Folklorist Alan Dundes suggested that in order for the term "folk" to exist, it must do so in opposition to another group of people. In this way, it can be defined as something other than "elite" culture or even separate from popular culture. This opposition exposes how "folk" was used to stand in for the "primitive" societies of Europe. The folk weren't seen as elite. They were considered less evolved and, according to Dundes, "were the uncivilized element in a civilized society."[7] The folk were the peasants who may have existed nearby a civilized society, one that was more modern and resembles society as we think of it today. Literacy and the ability to share the written word, and therefore spread beliefs, customs, and laws, was a key component of civilization. However, the folk weren't always literate, which set them apart. Their ways of life and ignorance of the written word were believed to signify that they were more primitive people living among the civilized world. Since the peasant, or the folk, lived close to civilization, there was the potential for literacy, but they still remained on the fringes.[8] They existed outside of this literate circle explicitly because of their location; they were rural while the elite were urban. Implied within Dundes's explanation of this is that the folk were also of a lower class than the elite and, therefore, through both lack of funds and lack of availability, could not afford to learn to read or write.[9] These elements of location, access to education, and divisions of cultural capital carry over today in our stereotypes related to socioeconomic class in the United States.

These stereotypes and understanding of the folk stem from evolutionary theory which ranks different societies by their level of civilization. The most advanced societies were referred to as civilized, the least advanced were considered savage, and the middle ground was considered barbaric.[10] Within the realm of evolutionary theory falls the comparative method through which researchers could study particular societies based on where they stood, evolutionarily speaking. Societies could be understood by where they had been and where they were going. For those researchers who existed in civilized society who wanted to understand their own society and their origins, they could examine the barbaric societies closest to them; they felt that they could understand their pasts through the barbaric society's present. According to these guidelines set by European researchers, only European peasants could be considered folk since they were the only ones within close proximity to a civilized society. Anthropologists were left to study the remaining societies too far away from civilization to be considered peasants while historians studied their own civilizations.[11]

For individuals such as the Grimm brothers, who were studying and publishing folklore in the early nineteenth century, the collection of material from the folk was seen as a valued pursuit. First of all, this type of study was thought to tell about a civilization's history mostly through the use of "survivals," a term coined by Edward Burnett Tylor to refer to traditions that existed from an earlier developmental stage.[12] Second, it also served a nationalistic purpose. By self-reflexively looking at one's folklore and survivals, the researcher can discover qualities and characteristics that exist for a particular nation and demonstrates its cultural independence. This is especially the case for smaller nations.[13] These hierarchal notions and methods should stand out as contrary to what this text is working to express. The scholarship of popular culture (and folklore) is focused on equality and the democratic study of all individuals and how they live their daily lives. No group should be highlighted over another because of their level of education or place in the socioeconomic ladder. However, how the study began would suggest that the folk, or real people, were only being used as a means to study mainstream culture and not valued for being their own individual communities. Ultimately over time, this began to change.

Influenced by various scholars outside of the United States, American thinkers put down their research about Europe and began studying their own continent. As Dorothy Noyes suggests, the Americans put a spin on the old approach in the form of resistance to the grand theory of evolutionary biology.[14] One such scholar was William Wells Newell. Although he subscribed to some of the tenets of evolutionary theory, he took a less heavy-handed approach. He was not looking to study the folk in order to understand civilization. Rather, he was more concerned that cultures of some groups, such as Native Americans, would soon vanish making it imperative to collect their traditions before that happened. In that salvage attempt, there was a recognition that the culture, though not European, was worthy of study itself. This thought process was eventually applied to many different groups in the United States, including the study of Old English traditions which were thought to be in danger of going extinct. As Scotch-Irish settlers moved into the remote Appalachian region of the United States, they were cut off from other ways of life, thus preserving those traditions they brought with them.[15] Appalachia has been a thoroughly examined region of the United States because of these reasons. It is rich in folklore and because of its isolation for centuries developed many small communities which contrast the rest of the United States. The publication of JD Vance's *Hillbilly Elegy: A Memoir of a Family and Culture in Crisis*; Nancy Isenberg's *White Trash: The 400-Year Untold History of Class in America*; recent studies pointing to the declining life expectancy of rural, white Americans; and the 2016 election's focus on the "forgotten" working class of the region has led to a recent resurgence of interest in this group.

In post–Civil War United States, Newell considered the collecting of folklore from southern African Americans to be extremely imperative, emphasizing the importance of animal tales, music, and beliefs. They, like the poor rural whites, existed on the fringes of civilized society, in opposition to it, and made up another American folk. As time went on, the historic conceptions of African Americans changed to mean ex-slaves which had both African retentions and Anglo influences, then rural peasants with their own folklore (as exemplified in Zora Neale Hurston's *Mules and Men*) and finally into urban dwellers which ushered in a whole new idea of the folk.

The last type of folk that Newell emphasized was the folk outside of the United States and in the rest of North America, the hemisphere, and the world. Initially this began when folklorists first were tracing the origins of certain folklore texts, taking a diffusionist approach, found in America. Eventually, however, folklorists who went to live in other societies found these cultures complex and interesting and began to view them as the folk, and not just a means to an end.[16]

In the tradition of American folklore, of expanding the definition of folk to mean groups of people that had traditionally been ignored, more and more people came to be encompassed in the study of the folk. It has expanded from the narrow view of the peasant into a more inclusive concept that acknowledges both value and importance in all groups of people. Special attention was paid to women and the folk arts traditionally dominated by them. Women, like minorities, the poor, and the illiterate were also left out of much of history so the recognition of experiences of women are valuable. The expansion also went beyond these obvious markers of identity and expanded to more nuanced groups. For example, occupational folk groups; much of this country's occupational folklore was developed early on with groups such as cowboys, lumberjacks, miners, and railroad men who, because of their occupations, were cut off from the rest of society and therefore developed very rich traditions based on what they were experiencing on a daily basis. Some of these existed in rural settings but others also developed in urban and industrialized areas. Up until the recognition that folk existed in urban settings, American folklorists, such as Leonard Roberts and Richard Dorson focused their studies in rural settings which were most commonly delineated by region, whether that be as broad as North and South, Appalachia and Ozarks, or more narrow, such as by state.

As folklorists and other disciplines began to extend their scope of study to more and more different groups of people, it expressed that all groups are therefore worthy of study. Focusing on the democracy of the study of popular culture, this is an important turn and acknowledgment. According to Noyes, this was including "the people whom grand theory had set asunder."[17] This move to all of these various groups also led Dundes to claim "folk" can mean "any group of people whatsoever who share at least one common factor" no matter what that linking factor may be.[18]

Evolving the definition of folk to mean any group of people who share something in common is important to the study of popular culture as we are defining it in this book. Every one of us is a member of folk groups. We all have defining aspects of our identity which link us to other individuals. Some of those are natural and dictated by where we are born, the parents to whom we are born, and other irreversible factors. Markers such as gender, race, and ethnicity also put us in various folk groups. However, other groups form around our likes and those whom we choose to be around, creating the chosen communities. By recognizing that we all belong to folk groups, that we are all the folk, we can then recognize commonality and value in all living individuals. Studying popular culture through this lens is an egalitarian attempt to give a voice to all.

Group speak

This conceptual leap not only broadens the concept of the folk, but it also transforms the term. Rather than relying on just "folk," it evolves into the word "group." Folk contains judgments about race, class, and even level of civilization due to its early associations with marginalized people. Group is a term which was originally used by sociologists in the 1950s and eventually came to mean the same thing as folk, but group was seen as a less loaded term.[19] Group is therefore a safer and more acceptable option that also leaves out the concept of tradition that is still heavily connected to the idea of folklore and folk studies, thus opening the doors for the individuals in groups to be considered creators, rather than just bearers, of folklore.[20] Group does, however, maintain elements of folk. These include the necessity of a shared reference group, a shared tradition or characteristic, and capable of face-to-face communication.[21] This led to Dan Ben-Amos's famous definition of folklore: "artistic communication in small groups," which points to a fundamental change in the field of folklore. It took it from a discipline whose basic method was collecting folklore items from a designated folk to a field that is concerned, instead, with a process of communication and interaction within a group.[22]

As theorists continued to use the term group to study what was once traditionally called folk, the conception of group evolved. With the rise in popularity and acknowledgment of cultural differences, groups such as ethnic groups, religious groups, occupational groups, and even generational groups were examined. Of course, groups can exist between people of different identities. Not everyone in each group needs to be the same. However, what echoes is the portion of the definition of group which claims that people must "share at least one common factor." This acknowledgment of something being common brings us back to this chapter's main concern: community. As defined earlier, community is a smaller group of individuals with a shared identity and worldview that emphasizes the importance of interpersonal relationships. In order for individuals to create bonds, a natural starting point is with what they have in common. This is a group identity, which is central to the creation and maintenance of bonds between individuals.

Like much of what we do on any given day, the groups and communities we belong to are significant to how we identity ourselves and make sense of the complicated world in which we live. Understanding one's individual identity is explained in the previous chapters, but central to individual identity are the groups and communities that one belongs to and where exactly each person fits into each particular community. Identity is a delicate balance between fitting in and standing out. The element of fitting in is reflected as a collective identity, an identity that one shares with others of a similar culture or group shaping their sense of self. People often identify by where they come from, their gender, race, ethnicity, interest, or certain characteristics. How that aligns with other people would be the collective identity. Of course, people who belong to the same group or community are not all the exact same, standing apart from one another. This is the individual identity. Not everyone in each group needs to be the same.[23] In fact, diversity is extremely important to any group as it makes life more interesting and dynamic. Different people offer different strengths and weaknesses and through coming together can make more happen.

This balance between individual identity and group identity is important. For example, coming to college, you may have moved away from your hometown. At school, you become part of a new community, but the ties you have to your hometown community and groups of family and friends are still extremely significant in how you identify. If you have moved very far, then some of the differences are even more obvious. The names used for different things, the way one pronounces certain words, or one's hobbies all may be in contrast to one's new community. We are all simultaneously part of different communities, and the characteristics that make us fit into one are what make us stand out in another. While this will differ depending on the context, all of these identities and groups contribute to who we are as individuals.

Whatever, let's ride!

Returning to our example of bikers can help us understand the ways in which the study of popular culture teases out the difference between individual and group identity, community and group, and society and culture. Biker culture permeates the larger culture of the United States. Bikers are some of our favorite bad-boy, outlaw antiheroes. They are modern cowboys on iron horses. The stereotypical image of biker culture, portrayed most recently on *Sons of Anarchy*, has a long history based on actual communities. The bikers portrayed in the series resemble what are referred to as "one percenters." This term for outlaw bikers is a nod to a statement the president of the American

Motorcycle Association made in response to the fear that swept the nation after an infamous motorcycle gathering-turned-drunken riot in Hollister, California in July of 1947. The president, as the story goes, said that 99 percent of actual bikers are law-abiding citizens, leaving 1 percent marked as dangerous outlaws. The Hollister incident inspired the famous Marlon Brando film *The Wild One*, which helped perpetuate the image of the outlaw biker.

In the United States, motorcycles became a cultural mainstay after the Second World War when returning veterans, who rode them while serving overseas, drove up sales domestically.[24] The image of the biker grew in popular culture, and MCs, such as the infamous Hells Angels, began to form. While popular, biker culture also reflected conflicting American values. As "outlaws," bikers stood opposed to what was mainstream at the time, with mainstream used to describe the "norm" and practices that most closely resemble and follow the beliefs, values, and myths of a particular culture. Outlaw bikers were rebels with aggressive style, in black leather and untamed facial hair. They were in definite contrast to the sanitized version of 1950s America, which focused on the conformity of suburban living that was being sold to the general public. At the same time, while rejecting these aspects of American culture, bikers also subscribed to and supported the superiority of postwar United States. Their hypermasculine and, at times, white supremacist tendencies reflected traditional conceptions of a version of American identity. They were dedicated to American-made motorcycles and expressed a loud opposition to foreign made ones, particularly those which were Japanese-made. As many of the founding members of early MCs were veterans of the Second World War and/ or the Korean War, there was a sense of loyalty to their country. Sonny Barger, famed member of the Oakland chapter of the Hells Angels, gives credit to the military for many of the group's traditions, where groups of men formed close connections, named their squadrons, and even sewed those names on their bomber jackets. These leather jackets with patches resemble the common image now associated with bikers.[25] Even the name "Hell's Angels" has a history in both the American military and popular culture, with bomber squadrons naming themselves in the Second World War after the 1930 Howard Hughes film *Hell's Angels*, which portrayed a First World War squadron and their fancy military flying.[26]

In tracing their history, we can see how bikers have a culture, and that owning a motorcycle is only a part of that culture. The rest is an attitude. Earlier in the chapter, we briefly mentioned that there are **subcultures** and **countercultures**. Subcultures are a group or subset of the larger culture that shares its own interests, practices, and beliefs, that, while unique, are not aggressively in opposition to the dominant culture. Countercultures, as their name suggests, are subcultures whose values, practices, and/or beliefs actively go against those of the dominant culture. While the stereotypical attitude of bikers might be tough, for the most part, we can consider this group a subculture. Contemporary Outlaw Motorcycle Gangs (OMGs), while a small percentage of bikers, can be considered counterculture in their actions. According to the FBI's 2013 National Gang Report, some OMGs are, "organizations whose members use their motorcycle clubs as conduits for criminal enterprises. OMGs are highly structured criminal organizations whose members engage in criminal activities such as violent crime, weapons trafficking, and drug trafficking. There are more than 300 active OMGs within the United States, ranging in size from single chapters with five or six members to hundreds of chapters with thousands of members worldwide."[27] Some of the MCs recognized by the FBI as OMGs include the Hells Angles, Outlaws, Bandidos, Sons of Hell, Iron Horsemen, and Warlocks. They make up 2.5 percent of all gang activity in the United States and, based on research, they "present a significant threat."[28]

While all countercultures are subcultures, not all subcultures are countercultures, nor do they pose a significant threat. One of the most influential studies of subcultures is Dick Hebdige's *Subculture: The Meaning of Style*. In his research, Hebdige looked at the rise of British postwar punk culture as it derived from several other movements happening before it. Of particular interest to Hebdige was the actual style involved; this doesn't only apply to musical style, but to the whole lifestyle including clothing, body modification, and other sensibilities. Punk, he traces, is a conglomeration of many other styles such as reggae, teddy boys, beats, and mods. Those who identified with a punk culture tended to identify more with marginalized working class groups. Their styles were adapted to stand out against something, to define themselves through what they were not. Therefore, these groups would rebel against what was considered to be mainstream style, adapting looks, lifestyles, and values outside of that. According to Stuart Hall, under whom Hebdige studied and developed his ideas, culture is "that level at which social groups develop distinct patterns of life, and give *expressive form* to their social and material life-experience."[29] This relates to the shared meaning and the mindset explained earlier in the chapter as characteristic of a culture. However, on a large scale, there can be interruptions to this. Not everyone, for example, in American culture will agree. As a whole society much more centered on organization and order, there are naturally some groups who gain a structural advantage over others. When groups of the same society, and even the same culture, begin to see things in different ways, they can be categorized as a subculture. According to Hebdige, "subcultures are therefore expressive forms but what they express is, in the last instance, a fundamental tension between those in power and those condemned to subordinate positions and second-class lives [...] I have interpreted subculture as a form of resistance in which experienced contradictions and objections to this ruling ideology are obliquely represented in style."[30] Though a subculture exists within the larger culture, it is different from that culture and stands apart from it.

Bikers are, therefore, a subculture. Though they themselves have a certain style and way of looking at the world, they stand in some opposition to the larger American culture. While there is patriotism with the military tradition, there is also at times a distrust of the government. In the case of modern-day OMGs, there is a tendency to engage in behavior outside of the law, as dramatized on *Sons of Anarchy*. There is also a shared cultural identity among bikers. First, they are unified by their general interest in motorcycles, which they illustrate through their style of dress, music, and choice of bikes. Along with the interest in motorcycles, there is also a general mindset or way of looking at the world that comes through. It can be read as anti-authority, pro-freedom, and with a different set of morals. While this may be seen in opposition to the culture at large, they also represent some of the founding principles of our country, such as rebellion, sovereignty, and individual liberty. Therefore, bikers are a subculture of the larger United States. Subcultures, although rebelling against some of the standard norms of society and culture, do differ from countercultures. Countercultures are like subcultures but are in more direct opposition to mainstream culture. Counterculture is a term which more appropriately applies to movements like hippies who challenged traditional structures of society and were outspoken when it came to revolutionizing civil rights and opposing war. Hippies are sometimes connected to the image of a commune, which is a culture that stands apart from the larger culture when it comes to the economy and belief system. Coming from this larger movement were smaller movements that were sometimes even fractured into standalone cults. So, while bikers do have their own style, opinions, and way of life, those are not in direct opposition to the mainstream culture. Although they may appear and sound radical, they are not calling for a complete overhaul and question of the system or culture. Instead, they are working at surviving within that system all the while maintaining traditional gender roles and conservative protection of the constitution and tenets of American identity and individual freedom.[31]

Sons of Anarchy's complicated storylines reflect these tensions and seem to come directly from real-life OMGs. The illegal gun running of SAMCRO, as well as the regular investigations into their dealings by ATF (Bureau of Alcohol, Tobacco, Firearms, and Explosives) on RICO (Racketeer Influenced and Corrupt Organizations Act) charges, mimic the well-publicized allegations of the criminal activity of MCs. Although *Sons of Anarchy* is clearly a fictionalized portrayal of OMGs in the United States today, its handling of the topic is quite relevant. As mentioned above, the FBI's gang report lists OMGs as a major source of illegal activity in the United States. In May 2015 in Waco, TX, what began as a turf war occurred at the Hooters-like restaurant called Twin Peaks. During that all-out, bullet-filled brawl, nine were left dead, eighteen more wounded, and over 170 arrested between two rival clubs: the Bandidos and Cossacks. However, to echo the comment about the "one-percenters" made above, 99 percent of bikers are law-abiding making it so that most motorcycles you see on the road on any given day aren't outlaw bikers with gang affiliations, but everyday folks who enjoy some other aspect of the motorcycle world.

Although fictionalized, *Sons of Anarchy* does a good job demonstrating the various levels of community. In the first sense of the word, there is the town of Charming, California, which is the larger community to which the MC belongs. Many of the townspeople are wrapped up in the MC even if they are not members themselves. SAMCRO has their hands in many of the local businesses and maintain the goal of protecting their hometown from other gangs who threaten the safety of the citizens. They also stand up to the more corrupt members of the business or political world whose dealings could potentially destroy their small-town way of life. The police are involved with SAMCRO and often work with them towards these same ends. It would appear as if the people of Charming want to be left alone, just as the members of the MC do. The club itself, as a community or even a family, is at the heart of the show, though. The complicated relationships and politics within the club, as well as their shared space and time, is an intense dramatization of a very natural tendency for human bonding and connection. The men in the club (women are excluded from membership) come together because of their common interests in motorcycles and the alternative lifestyle of the outlaw motorcycle gang. They have a similar mindset about what their freedoms are and how laws and regulations should and should not impact their way of life. Through continued exposure to these ways of life, the members of the community become more and more indoctrinated into the club and build a stronger community.

Material culture, discussed in Chapter 8, is another way in which individuals can express their identity and group membership. This is seen with the iconography and clothing worn by the characters in *Sons of Anarchy*. The members of the SOA club all wear their "colors." On black leather vests, a variety of different patches are showcased. Most notable are the patches on the back. In the center is the emblem for the club, its colors. Above that is the "top rocker," named for its resemblance of a rocker from the bottom of a rocking chair in shape, but upside down. The top rocker provides the name of the club. Below the top rocker and club colors patches is the bottom rocker which indicates the chapter or location of the club. These types of patches are relatively standard for most of the more prominent biker clubs. The characters on *Sons of Anarchy* also assigns patches to its members based on other factors, such as their individual standing in the club, offices held, years of membership, memorials to lost members, or other personalized features.

These expressions of material culture demonstrate various levels of identification. Group identity is strongly expressed through the patches, with specific group identity communicated through the designation of a particular chapter of the organization. The members quite frequently refer to their involvement with the club as a brotherhood. They are more than members; they see themselves as family. A unique individual identity is expressed through the various patches which explain each member's position in the club or personal preference when it comes to clothing adornment. Not only does this point out their individual ranks, but hints at the larger group structure and relationship between members. They all drive different motorcycles as well, with the style of the bike seemingly reflecting personal characteristics of the riders. Some of the bikes are more traditional in their look with a chopper style bike, which suggest that the rider built or had a significant role in the creation of the motorcycle. Other riders appear to want a sleeker and more modern look, reflecting a break from tradition.

Beyond what is associated through membership, community expands outside the confines of the clubhouse. Outside the brotherhood, they have an extended family of wives, children, and friendly citizens in Charming. These are the people who support them and who they, in turn, support. When dangerous drug dealers come to town or corrupt big-money investors threaten to take over and develop Charming, CA, they go to battle for their community. When SAMCRO is triumphant, the extended community supports and celebrates with them. When they are not, the community mourns, or even dies, with them. Though these outside characters can't express themselves as connected to the club through their colors and patches, the club's protection extends to them as they all share the same identity as members of the town of Charming. This demonstrates one of the ways in which some identities can be shared while others are not.

When studying community, it must be acknowledged that communities may appear differently on the inside than they do to those on the outside. Understanding a community from the inside is called an esoteric perspective; members have reasons for being a part of a particular community and a general understanding of what identities and beliefs they share which contributes to their belonging. Views from the outside of the community, from those observing without being members themselves, is called an exoteric perspective. It can be easy to judge a particular community without having a significant amount of knowledge, but rather based on general observation. The danger in this is that it can lead to stereotyping and misunderstandings. Communities may mean a lot more to the individuals involved than can ever be imagined or understood by those looking from the outside-in. Hearing about the activities of biker gangs in the news might lead to a particular exoteric understanding of communities, their activities, and their members. Those with an esoteric perspective, however, may have far different and more accurate understandings of the community in question. These two perspectives are explored in *Sons of Anarchy*, drawing in exoteric perspectives from audiences who get hooked on the plotlines' juicy details and reeled into the drama. At the same time, the series complicates its characters and works to paint a portrayal of a group of people who depend on one another, form valuable relationships, and, when not killing one another, really love and appreciate each other. The view from the characters themselves provides the complicated esoteric understanding that the outsiders wouldn't gain simply driving past a MC on the road.

The social network: More than fake news and fake friendships

Beyond the relationships that exist between individuals in a community, relationships can form between members of one community and members of another. For some scholars, the term "network" has been introduced to describe these interactions. Groups are not homogenous, and individuals exist at different status levels within those groups.[32] It is the individual, and therefore not the whole collective "group" or "folk," that maintains a status. Individuals may interact with others of a different status within their own group or they may even interact and make connections with individuals outside of their own group. Therefore, the individual is in the middle of a web of interactions of their own creation, tied to individuals and not necessarily to whole groups. These individuals may or may not share common identities or characteristics but have interacted on an individual level nonetheless. Not everyone in one network will share traditions or identify with everyone else in the network. While networks have always existed, this idea is especially pertinent in our contemporary American society since, with technological advancements, individuals can more freely move about and interact with the larger society and make connections outside of their particular group. These connections must be maintained, however, in order for them to last, since they cannot fall back on shared characteristics and identities to sustain them.

Consider the role of technology in contemporary United States. Members of older generations often bemoan the loss of social interaction and strong in-person community connections that they feel generations who come after them lack. Often blamed is the rise in cell phone text messaging and social media. Young people's preoccupation with these technologies and forms of communication have them staring at their screens rather than interacting with the individuals around them. While this can be observed nearly everywhere one travels today, it is more complicated than that. First of all, it isn't just Millennials who are preoccupied with the Internet and cell phones; individuals of every age group are engaged with social media and technology. Second, understanding social interaction as limited to only in-person relationships is problematic. Social media and cell-phone use allows for extensive communication and relationship-building and maintenance with people across the world. This technology allows for the breaking down of barriers that were once insurmountable. Maintaining relationships across various geographical boundaries just a few decades ago was much more difficult. Today, with various technologically-mediated communication options, relationships can develop, grow, and exist without any physical in-person interaction. While these can be one-on-one relationships, a significant amount of them are much larger, fulfilling the requirements of both community and network.

Networks are often described as a web. When thinking about each individual as a random dot, lines can be drawn from dot to dot based on the relationships and connections people have with other people. Sketching this out on a piece of paper quickly creates a structure that resembles a web. Perhaps the ultimate web of human interaction is the world-wide web, the Internet, the "www" before each of our web addresses. Computing devices communicate to other devices in this complex web of interaction. The people on either end of those devices are also communicating through this connection. Through these online interactions, people can develop networks with other individuals based on shared interests, characteristics, and identities. Regular interaction forms bonds and relationships between people who have never met. There is also the opportunity for more than two individuals to connect and interact regularly, usually over a shared interest. The phrase **online community** has come to stand in for those regular group interactions and relationships that exist through mediated forms rather than in-person connections.

Online communities are very common, but also can be difficult to delineate. What might be regular interaction between friends in online format doesn't necessarily indicate an online community, yet the phrase online community is used regularly to describe many online formats where people can gather and communicate. For example, whether the entire extent of Facebook constitutes a community or a network can be difficult to distinguish. As it is a place where people can connect with others on an individual basis, it resembles a network. However, Facebook "Groups" can form. Some of these groups are particularly active and the members are in regular contact, establishing and cultivating meaningful relationships. The groups are smaller and therefore allow for that type of deeper connection to be made. In that case, Facebook itself could be classified as a network of people, but the smaller groups that individual users can create would come closer to our understanding of an online community.

Online communities are often formed based on a common interest. For example, for most **fandoms**, there are online communities where individuals who are drawn to particular popular culture texts can go to connect with others who share their interest. Although fandom, the broad term for the subculture of communities that form between audiences and media texts, existed before the Internet, new media and convergence technologies have increased the visibility of and possibilities for these communities. From comics and video games to television and music, people connect with others who share their interests and build relationships through blogs, wall posts, and discussion boards, as well as face-to-face at conventions, fan events, and other club and group gatherings. Tumblr, for example, caters to fan communities, making it easy for individual users to make connections and form relationships. Online communities exist for motorcycle enthusiasts, MCs, and even fans of *Sons of Anarchy*.

As discussed in chapter five, audience functions in the maintenance of the celebrity ecology. More than just the stereotypical "fanatic" devoted to their favorite show, celebrity, or sports team, fans are a mode of social interaction that aids in the formation of community across socioeconomic class, regional, and racial identities. Further, as opposed to more passive understandings of media consumption, fans and fandom demonstrate the ways in which individuals are active participants with respect to the media they consume. This not only includes the formation of fan communities where individuals gather, share information, and make connections based on their shared interest, but also takes into account the active creation of texts that span across artistic media.

Henry Jenkins's *Textual Poachers: Television Fans & Participatory Culture* was one of the first texts to consider fans and fan communities outside of the stereotypical image of a fanatic. Instead, Jenkins used an ethnographic approach to reject "media-fostered stereotypes of fans as cultural dupes, social misfits, and mindless consumers," and instead argues for an understanding of fans "as readers who appropriate popular texts and reread them in a fashion that serves different interests" and transform the experience "into a complex participatory culture."[33] While we are all fans of aspects of popular culture, there are varying levels of engagement in fan communities. Media theorist John Fiske outlined three levels of fan production: semiotic, enunciative, and textual, which occur "at the interface between the industrially-produced cultural commodity (narrative, music, star, etc.) and the everyday life of the fan."[34] Semiotic production is mostly interior, and applies more broadly to the ways in which people, in general, make meaning and understand cultural texts. When these meanings are shared, or made public, they move into the realm of enunciative productivity. This can include talking about the latest episode of *Grey's Anatomy* with your friends, posting on social media about the awesomeness of your favorite musician, or even styling yourself like *Scandal*'s Olivia Pope. The point of this type of production is to enunciate, that is visibly or vocally communicate, your appreciation for a particular celebrity, sport team, or media text. Fiske's final level of fan productivity is textual and involves the actual creation of modified or new textual forms. These include fan art; fan vids; fan fiction (including slash fiction, which contains erotic elements); shipping, which supports fictional romantic relationships; mashups or remixes of digital media; and filk, fan folk music. Fan costuming is another form of textual production, whether it be dressing up for latest *Star Wars* film, standing in line at midnight for a *Harry Potter* book release, or attending a fan convention, fans often express their community identity through costuming. For many, the creative outlets of fandom allow for the expression of an aspect of one's identity that cannot necessarily be expressed during daily life. These textual productions are not only an outlet for creativity, but also a form of coded communication that connects individuals to others who share a common interest.

While fandom was once associated with marginalized groups and subordinate forms of media production, today the stigma around fandom has lifted significantly and has been made mainstream through events such as San Diego Comic-Con and popular television series such as *The Big Bang Theory*. Documentaries such as *Trekkies* and *Bronies: The Extremely Unexpected Adult Fans of My Little Pony*, also helped bring visibility to fan communities. *Bronies* follows individuals who identify as fans of *My Little Pony: Friendship is Magic* as they navigate the brony community. A common way for fans of this particular text to find one another and connect is through fan sites dedicated to the show. The documentary demonstrates that though individuals don't get to meet very often, their friendships are formed online due to the acceptance of other fans providing them with a safe space to share themselves and form lasting relationships. For some, the online communities to which they belong, fandom or otherwise, are just as important, if not more important, to their lives than the in-person communities of their everyday life as they can connect around shared interests and passions with individuals outside of their immediate proximities.

Conclusion

In the summer of 2016, Niantic, Inc. released the hugely successful *Pokémon Go*, the latest release in the long-running Pokémon franchise, beginning first with video games and then heading into an animated television series, movies, trading card game, and numerous merchandising. However, the phenomenon of *Pokémon Go* went past the screen, asking individuals to engage with their environment, in order to "catch 'em all." Using GPS capabilities on smartphones, the augmented reality game maps a virtual world over the actual physical surroundings of each of the players as it scans for nearby Pokémon and locate nearby Pokéstops (to fill one's virtual backpack with pokéballs, potions to bring Pokémon to full health, and eggs to hatch) and gyms (where one could train and fight their Pokémon for prestige and to earn gold).

Many layers of networking and community exist in this particular game. First is the huge worldwide network of individual users. In its first month, 231 million people talked about the game on Facebook, engaging in 1.1 billion interactions that mention *Pokémon Go*.[35] *Go* players used a shared language to communicate with one another about the game whether it be about the location of certain Pokémon, Pokéstops, or gyms. This shared knowledge immediately connects players of the game. Online forums and groups quickly developed as individual users began sharing their experiences and expertise with others and forming relationships with other users, thus creating online communities of individuals not necessarily in close proximity to one another.

Another form of community that developed was through the Pokémon teams users were asked to join once they reached Level 5 of the game. With three teams to choose from (Red: Team Valor, Blue: Team Mystic, and Yellow: Team Instinct), users choose the characteristic that best fits their personality. Once a team has been chosen, users work together or against one another to dominate the Poké gyms. Each gym is controlled by members of one of the three teams, and working together, members of the same team can take over a gym from a rival team or train their Pokémon in a gym controlled by their team in order to gain XP (experience points). The alliances created through team membership also works to create a network of individuals who do not know one another, but who are working together in the game. When an individual wins a battle in the gym and comes to dominate it, only then is their user name public for all other users to see. Otherwise the game is anonymous and users cannot see where other users are located on the game interface.

While all that has been discussed above has been part of the virtual creation of networks and communities, there is a real-life component to the game as well which contributes to the game's overall success. The game forces individuals to interact with their environment and with other players near to them, whether they are previously acquainted or not. One cannot succeed in *Pokémon Go* by remaining indoors at home: in order to catch Pokémon, users must move around; in order to gain supplies necessary to continue in the game, players have to travel to Pokéstops; and in order to fight or train, trainers must take their Pokémon to gyms. These locations cannot be navigated to on the phone alone, but the player must be in the physical area, according to GPS, to these locations in order to engage. Both Pokéstops and gyms tend to be significant locations in the greater community; public parks, churches, businesses, public art (such as statues and murals), and historical marker signage are often used as the locations for these sites. As individuals playing the games travel around their neighborhoods, they are perhaps taken to places they have never been, noticing the beautification or historic preservation taking place in the areas where they live, potentially leading to greater community appreciation. On another level, traveling around on the search for wild Pokémon, stops, and gyms brings people together. At popular gathering spots where the pocket monsters tend to collect or battle, real communication and bonds are made between the individuals drawn to those areas because of the game. Discussions and alliances can create bonds as players recognize others on their same team or who they may be battling against. Learning when others play the same game can create unlikely friendships and strengthen the sense of community among people who would otherwise remain strangers. *Pokémon Go*, therefore, hits many different qualifiers and ways of examining community. While it was a huge cultural phenomenon when it was released, it allowed for individuals to connect and form relationships on many different levels: the initial networking by being a part of the game and understanding the way to navigate the virtual world. However, as users became further engrossed in the game, it resulted in avid online communities, team alliances, and engagement in one's real-life community.

As stated at the beginning of the chapter, whether we like it or not, people need one another. They find each other by chance of where they live and frequent, or intentionally by connecting with those individuals with whom they share common interests and ways of seeing the world around them. The study of community forces us to recognize the many different types of people around us and the value in the diversity of identities and human expression. In the tradition of giving equal voice to all people as championed by the fields of folklore and popular culture studies, examining community gives researchers and interested individuals an entry point into the fascinating study of people and everyday life. Whether it be bonds created as physical neighbors, motorcycle enthusiasts, fans of *Sons of Anarchy*, players of *Pokémon Go*, or members of Team Mystic, community takes many different forms and is vital in defining individuals based on their group identities. The way these communities and group identities are celebrated and marked will be the focus of our next, and final, chapter.

Notes

1   Karl Marx and Frederick Engels, *Manifesto of the Communist Party*, 1848, trans. Samuel Moore, *Marxists Internet Archive*, 2010, https://www.marxists.org/archive/marx/works/download/pdf/Manifesto.pdf, 41.

2   Victor Turner, *The Ritual Process: Structure and Anti-Structure* (Chicago: Aldine Publishing Company, 1969), 96.

3   Ibid., 94–165.

4   Ferdinand Tönnies, *Community and Civil Society*, trans. Jose Harris and Margaret Hollis (1887; repr., Cambridge: Cambridge University Press, 2001).

5   Ibid.

6   Alan Dundes, *International Folkloristics: Classic Contributions by the Founders of Folklore*, ed. Alan Dundes (New York: Rowman & Littlefield, Publishers, Inc., 1999), 9.

7   Alan Dundes, "Who Are the Folk?," in *Interpreting Folklore*, ed. Alan Dundes (Bloomington: Indiana University Press, 1980), 2.

8   Elliott Oring, "On the Concepts of Folklore," in *Folk Groups in Folklore Genres: An Introduction*, ed. Elliott Oring (Logan: Utah State University Press, 1986), 5.

9   Dundes, "Who Are the Folk?," 2.

10   Simon J. Bronner, "The Intellectual Climate of the Nineteenth-Century American Folklore Studies," in *One Hundred Years of American Folklore Studies: A Conceptual History*, ed. William Clements (Washington: American Folklore Society, 1988), 6.

11 Dudes, "Who Are the Folk?," 2–4.

12 Hugo A. Freund, "Cultural Evolution, Survivals, and Immersion: The Implications for Nineteenth-Century Folklore Studies," in *One Hundred Years of American Folklore Studies: A Conceptual History*, ed. William Clements (Washington: American Folklore Society, 1988), 12–13.

13 Richard Dorson, "Current Folklore Theories," *Current Anthropology* 4, no. 1 (1963): 96.

14 Dorothy Noyes, "Humble Theory," *Grand Theory* special issue of *Journal of Folklore Research* 45, no. 1 (2008): 41.

15 Sylvia Grider, "Salvaging the Folklore of 'Old English' Folk," in *One Hundred Years of American Folklore Studies: A Conceptual History*, ed. William Clements (Washington: American Folklore Society, 1988), 26.

16 Eric L. Montenyohl, "The Folk Abroad: American Folklorists Outside the United States," in *One Hundred Years of American Folklore Studies: A Conceptual History*, ed. William Clements (Washington: American Folklore Society, 1988), 37.

17 Noyes, "Humble Theory," 41.

18 Dundes, "Who Are the Folk?," 6.

19 Dan Ben-Amos, "Toward a Definition of Folklore in Context," in *Toward New Perspectives in Folklore*, ed. Americo Paredes and Richard Bauman (1972; repr., Bloomington, IN: Trickster Press, 2000), 14.

20 Dorothy Noyes, "Group," in *Eight Words for the Study of Expressive Culture*, ed. Burt Feintuch (Chicago: University of Illinois Press, 2003), 11.

21 Ben-Amos, "Toward a Definition of Folklore in Context," 14.

22 Ibid.

23 Richard Bauman, "Differential Identity and the Social Base of Folklore," in *Toward New Perspectives in Folklore*, ed. Americo Paredes and Richard Bauman (1972; repr., Bloomington, IN: Trickster Press, 2000), 49.

24 Ralph "Sonny" Barger with Keith and Kent Zimmerman, *Hell's Angel: The Life and Times of Sonny Barger and the Hell's Angles Motorcycle Club* (New York: Perennial, 2001), 29.

25 Ibid., 27.

26 Ibid., 28.

27 *2013 National Gang Report* (Washington: National Gang Intelligence Center, 2013), 8.

28 Ibid., 18.

29 John Clark and Stuart Hall, "Subcultures, Cultures and Class," *Resistance Through Rituals*, in *Resistance Through Rituals: Youth Subcultures in Post-War Britain*, 2nd edn., ed. Stuart Hall and Tony Jefferson (1976; repr., New York: Routledge, 2006), 4.

30 Dick Hebdige, *Subculture: The Meaning of Style* (1979; repr., New York: Routledge, 2002), 132.

31 Theodore Roszak, *The Making of a Counter Culture: Reflections of the Technocratic Society and Its Youthful Opposition* (New York: Anchor Books, 1969).

32 Noyes, "Group," 13.

33 Henry Jenkins, *Textual Poachers* (New York: Routledge, 1992), 23.

34 John Fiske, "The Cultural Economy of Fandom," in *The Adoring Audience: Fan Culture and Popular Media*, ed. L. A. Lewis (London: Routledge, 1992), 36.

35 Johnson, "231 Million People Talked About Pokémon Go on Facebook in July," *Adweek*, August 9, 2016, http://www.adweek.com/news/technology/231-million-people-talked-about-pokemon-go-facebook-and-instagram-july-172891.

10

Rituals and Ceremonies

Celebrate good times, come on!

—Kool & the Gang

Each day of the week has its own personality. Monday is notoriously horrible. People across the United States awake on Monday morning having to return to the daily grind of the workweek, whether that means going back to their 9:00-to-5:00 job or going to school. The ease back into the workweek causes grief, frustration, and general feelings of malcontent. Having a "case of the Mondays" isn't anything to look forward to, but something that must be overcome. Tuesday has a bit more hope to it; outlooks might not be as dismal because at least Tuesday isn't Monday. Waking up, the morning commute, and the daily grind aren't quite as daunting on Tuesday. Wednesday, hump day, provides some excitement. It is halfway through the workweek and the promise of the weekend just over the horizon makes it easier to work through the frustrations of the day-to-day. Thursday, or Friday Eve, builds on this excitement. The assurance of the next day being Friday carries people through. The celebration of the end of the workweek coming near culminates in the best night for television, local and school events and performances, or, if you're a college student, a party night. Finally, Friday rolls around; the air at work or school is different as people anticipate the break from the long days of tedium. Knowing there will be a respite from the early morning wakeup call or intense job labor makes Friday a day where people are more likely to stay out later, seeking opportunity for entertainment not usually sought Monday through Thursday; it allows for much-needed decompression. Saturday is a free day, a fun day, to do what one wants. People can sleep in, explore their neighborhoods or beyond throughout the day, and celebrate again like they did the night before. Sunday, to some extent, is also seen as a free day. As the United States is ideologically influenced by Christianity, in the past, Sunday was marked as a day of rest and worship. Nowadays many people don't restrict themselves as was once expected on Sunday, but people still rest, attend church service, enjoy Sunday football, or participate in events and activities under the name of "Sunday Funday." Eventually, for many, the reality of Monday morning sets in and "Funday" transforms into the "Sunday Blues."

Of course, not everyone has a Monday-through-Friday work schedule, or even a 9:00-to-5:00 workday. There are many variations on the forty-hour workweek depending on one's field, position, or number of jobs. Even for those individuals, however, there are similar notions of a day's personality. "This is my Monday," or, "this is my Friday," on any day of the week still communicates something about how the person is feeling, something that is understandable even to others on a different work schedule. Monday is the first day back after having some time off, and Friday is the last day left of work before having a day or more to relax and do what one pleases. What is being expressed is the relationship to a day off and all of the freedoms that having a day off allows. Built into the standard system is two days off per week, but for many, that could be more or less, depending on individual circumstances.

Even if you have a day off from work, it doesn't guarantee you have the day off from school, or vice versa. There are many factors, but the understanding is that we conceive of our time—days, weeks, months, and years—by the structure in which our daily life, our work, the hustle and bustle, is suspended. Our free time, our time out of time, away from authority, is what we live for and is just as important to defining us as individuals, a culture, and a society than the regular every day. Days off aren't just the built-in weekends, but are also observed holidays. These days, which occur annually and regularly throughout the year, are often marked by particular activities and beliefs. A study of these occasions, how they help to define us, and how we come together in diverse communities and celebrate, makes up the study of rituals in contemporary US culture and is the focus of our final chapter.

Celebration

This book has focused on the everyday life of average people. The exploration of our cultural myths, the genres we rely on to entertain us and the stories they sell us, the celebrities we worship and love to hate, the identities we construct, the material objects we use, and the groups to which we belong weave together as the fabric of the everyday. Some of the most obvious times that these elements come together, though, are on the days that don't appear to be the norm at all. It is through our celebrations—holidays, festivals, and various rituals—that beliefs and aspects of our identities are highlighted and exaggerated through the coming together of various communities and the use of particular objects in a collective performance of celebration.

Our time, whether it be a day, week, month, year, or lifetime, is punctuated regularly with events and celebrations that stand apart from the monotony of the everyday. **Celebration** is the term given to something that stands outside of the ordinary in a positive way. Celebrations are enjoyable, light, entertaining, joyous experiences focused on bringing people together in order to acknowledge some particular event or cause. Celebrations can take on as many different forms as there are actual celebrations. Some are large, others small. Some celebrations honor particular individuals, while others can honor an entire group of people. Even events that might have a more reverent or somber tone, such as funerals, can still be included in celebration, as they incorporate elements that highlight a particular individual, belief system, or group, despite lacking a cheery and lighter mood. No matter what the occasion, celebrations stand apart from the activities of daily life, while at the same time reinforce the values needed to carry us through the regular day-to-day. Scholars in various academic disciplines have used numerous approaches to the study of celebration. Sorting through these studies under the guise of rituals, festivals, carnivals, and holidays sheds light on what can be a very complicated and contested topic. First of all, not all who have studied and defined these concepts would agree with the term "celebration." For this chapter, "celebration" has been chosen as an umbrella term under which many other concepts fall. All of these terms have dense and complicated histories from their use in the fields of anthropology, folklore, communications, and cultural studies, and the purpose of their use here is to streamline them and relate them to modern life in the United States. While this can be a confusing and highly contested study, it can also be simplified; underlying all of these ideas and occasions is an expression and reinforcing of particular beliefs, values, or identities. The breakaway from daily life in these socially and culturally sanctioned celebrations may temporarily remove individuals from daily life, but are necessary to keep order and perpetuate the cultural myths that shape our everyday lives.

Before beginning the discussion of the United States today, it is important to recognize that although there is no official religion of the United States, the United States is still influenced and overwhelmingly organized by Christian values. To say that the United States is culturally Christian suggests that though there are many religions accepted and recognized within the nation, the official and observed holidays are tied to Christianity. While an individual may not believe every aspect of what is taught in Christianity, they may still observe and celebrate these holidays. Many holidays, even if not explicitly celebrated in a religious way, are therefore culturally Christian. The purpose of this chapter is not to explore too much of the sacred or holy, but rather secular practices not tied to any particular religion. Though many of the celebrations in the United States are secular or increasingly secularized, this topic is difficult to explore without some discussion of religion, as the roots of many of these celebrations are steeped in religious beliefs and were converted from pagan practices in the Middle Ages.

The first of the terms important to the understanding of the complexities of celebration is **festival**. In its simplest form, festival comes from "feast." Throughout history, feast days have existed to break up the monotony of the everyday. They are celebrations centered around communities coming together to enjoy excesses of food. Festivals were often related to agrarian cultures and the cycles of farming. To celebrate the hard work of the warmer times of year and the harvest, feasts were held. Before the spread of organized religions, feasts and their occurrences were tied to seasonal shifts, which influenced many pagan celebrations throughout Europe. Still today, many of our holidays centered around the notion of feasting, such as Thanksgiving, are about bringing people together around a dinner table and celebrating the strength that comes from this unity.

As Christianity spread throughout Europe in the Middle Ages, what were once pagan or Roman festivals were repurposed to spread Christian values and beliefs and dubbed holidays. As festival comes from feast, **holiday** comes from holy. The transition from pagan festival to Christian holiday made it easier to convert masses of people to Christianity by assigning the traditional celebrations and symbols new religious meaning. Today in the United States, there are many official holidays where work and daily life are suspended. Though some of them are based in religious traditions, there are many other holidays that are more secular and related to the nation and politics, called civic holidays. These holidays are related to the act of citizenship in a particular area or nation and, since there is a separation of church and state, not necessarily tied to any particular religious tradition. The beliefs exhibited in these holidays are not spiritual in nature, but rather reflect broader national values. However, what all holidays have in common, besides being a day off from work or school and a reason to celebrate, is that they uphold specific ideologies. These range from religious belief systems instilling one with a sense of meaning, purpose, morals, and faith to ideologies tied to nation, politics, and civic duties.

One thing that remains constant is that festivals and holidays are often marked by ritual, though the forms those rituals take change over time and vary significantly between different groups. **Rituals** are rigidly structured actions and performances that, throughout their enactment, carry meaning. Rituals often bring about some sort of change through the process of enactment.[1] A common change elicited through ritual is one's standing within a specific group. In these instances, the ritual's purpose is to transform an individual's status from one stage to another, whether that be an elevation or demotion. **Ceremony**, on the other hand, is broader and more encompassing. While at the center of ceremony is a ritual, ceremony also involves the celebration of the ritual's transformation. The ritual is the specific act being highlighted, while the ceremony is the larger gathering of people surrounding that act and includes all aspects and elements of the performance of the specific ritual.

Performance, another commonly used term, is also one that has been complicated by various academic disciplines. In its various uses, performance is the stylized, repetitive acts that communicate the expression of self or the enactment of beliefs to audiences. With this definition, we can see that performances are not limited to the realm of entertainment. Central to understanding performance is the recognition of both a performer and an audience and, that within a performance, the performer must consider the audience, the audience's desires, and their own wants and expectations with respect to the performance. Further, it should be noted that the audience can voice their approval or disapproval of a performance, thereby impacting its result. Viewing ritual through the lens of performance demonstrates the role of celebrations in highlighting rituals, putting them on display for specific groups of people gathered. All of these elements—the gathering, ritual, performance, and audience—combine to form the ceremony. Upon completion of the ceremony, celebration commences with a party to commemorate the transformation that has just been witnessed.

Rituals, such as a traditional wedding in the United States, are formulaic and require certain actions and participants. While conceptions of marriage and family have expanded in the new millennium, there are certain wedding conventions that are recognizable to most. Customarily, a wedding party walks down an aisle to an officiant, religious or not, followed by the bride arm-in-arm with her father to preselected music such as Mendelssohn's "Wedding March." After the father gives the bride away, the officiant takes charge expressing the importance of marriage, leading the couple in their recitation of vows. After the pronouncement of "husband and wife" comes the announcement of the first kiss, followed by the march of the happy couple and wedding party down the aisle. Those in attendance are invited to the official celebration— the wedding reception—where more ritualized performances such as dinner, speeches, a first dance, throwing of a bouquet and garter, cutting of a cake, and dancing continue.

Using the traditional American wedding as an example, we can see how, "in ritual life, for example, performances encode and transmit the core values of society, implanting ideologies."[2] The "giving away" of the bride is a patriarchal holdover from chattel marriages, where women were literally property being exchanged from father to husband. The vows and officiant, who is often a religious clergy, reflects the sacrament of marriage within the couple's religion. The throwing of the bouquet to single women reinforces the marriage tradition, with the flowers representing fertility; she who catches the bouquet is supposed to get married next. Similarly, the garter represents the sexual aspect of marriage. Together, these elements reinforce values that work in the maintenance of society through the creation of families, our built-in support systems. The cultural myths of heteronormativity and romantic love encourage this system.

There is a season—turn, turn, turn

Rituals and their understandings are, therefore, complex. They come in various forms and, depending on their purpose and social and cultural contexts, are accompanied by different types of celebrations. They can be a part of festivals or holidays, or be the occasion for their own ceremonies and celebrations. The types of rituals celebrated in various cultures points to different ways of considering and punctuating time. Though time is something that US culture tends to regard as measurable, exact, finite, and factual, time can also be understood as a social construct. Anthropologist Edward T. Hall has studied the concept of time in various cultures. His division of monochronic and polychronic time explains how time is not as exact as we might think. Monochronic cultures tend to focus on one thing at a time and are concerned with scheduling and breaking things down into small increments of time dedicated to different tasks and activities. Polychronic-oriented cultures are different in that they acknowledge that many things can be going on at once. There is less concern for scheduling and structured time and more of a focus on relationships.[3] Despite the fact the United States tends to lean heavily toward the monochronic side with scheduled work/school weeks, meetings, opening and closing times, meals, television schedules, celebrations, and nearly every other measurable aspect of daily life, there are still different ways to conceptualize time when studying rituals, festivals, celebrations, and holidays: cyclically and linearly. Cyclical time focuses on the reoccurrence of events and rituals, with celebrations, happening yearly which focus on a group of people and their relationships. Once the cycle ends, it begins again, suggesting renewal. Linear time, however, looks at time as having a beginning, middle, and end. It doesn't rotate again and again, but follows a timeline. Rather than having the hope of renewal, it is finite. Celebrations that occur with reference to linear time are not as collective or tied to unification of a large group as cyclical celebrations are. Instead, they tend to honor an individual or small group.

To understand time cyclically, think about an individual day. As the Earth spins from darkness into light, from day into night, and back again, it is clear that time is cyclical. Everyday life is punctuated by those hours of waking and sleeping, of working and resting. As each day ends, a new day begins in an ongoing cycle. As discussed at the beginning of the chapter, weeks are also cyclical. Each week begins a new cycle, and each day is measured in relation to how close to the beginning or the end of the week it happens to fall. At the end of each week a new week, and new cycle, begins again. Similarly, our years are also cyclical; through the changing of the seasons, our calendar starts in the midst of the cold dark winter, brightens in the rebirth of the spring, flourishes in the heat of the summer, changes and dies in the fall, and retreats once again into the dark cold of winter. There are many celebrations along the way to punctuate the progression of the year, and they happen annually at the same time or on the same day.

Though they may not be at the forefront of our celebrations, the seasons are tied to and inspire many of our holidays. Consider wall calendars, the kind with images of cute animals, sports teams, cartoons, celebrities, and nearly everything else one can imagine. Regardless of the subject, one prominent and common characteristic is the themes that are highlighted and define each month. January might have a New Year or snow theme. February, undoubtedly, features Valentine's Day. Perhaps March highlights St. Patrick's Day, while April has a spring or Easter theme. May features flowers, and this bright lightness transcends into the beauty of June. July, in the United States, should highlight Independence Day. August continues the summer fun or brings it to an abrupt end with the start of school. September highlights the harvest and the coming of fall. October continues the fall theme, but defines itself by the month's culmination in Halloween. November, as fall gets colder, continues to celebrate the harvest with Thanksgiving. Lastly, December ends the year with its recognizable religious holidays such as Christmas or Hanukkah. Of course, not every calendar follows these themes, but a significant amount of them do, with their symbolism pointing to the personality of each month.

The months and their personalities are defined by the changing of the seasons. Understanding the year as a cycle—a circle with four quadrants that align with the four different seasons, beginning and ending on the solstices and equinoxes—makes clear the ways celebrations help to punctuate and mark the changing of the seasons. Across different religions and cultures is the constant recognition of the way nature influences our belief systems. Early cultural myth systems, such as those of the Romans and pagans in ancient Europe, were, more than anything, tied to nature and seasonal changes. Each year there are two equinoxes and two solstices. An equinox is when day and night are of equal length, when the light and the darkness are each half of the twenty-four-hour day. The equinoxes usher in the spring and the fall. The spring, or vernal, equinox happens on or around March 20, the first day of spring, and the autumnal equinox happens on or around September 22, the first day of fall. On these days, there is less of a tilt of the Earth, resulting in the northern and southern hemispheres receiving the same amount of light. The solstices, in opposition to the balance of the equinoxes, mark the shortest and longest days of the year. The shortest day of the year, the day where there is more darkness than any other day, is on or around December 21. This is only the shortest day, however, for nations in the northern hemisphere, as the North Pole is at its furthest tilting point away from the sun. In the United States, the days after the winter solstice leading up to the vernal equinox get longer than they had been in the darkest days of winter, and continue to get longer until the summer solstice, on or around June 21. In the northern hemisphere, the North Pole is tilted closest to the sun, making for the longest day of sunlight during the year. After that point, the days shorten until light and dark once again balance during the autumnal equinox and continue to shorten until after the winter solstice when the days begin to get longer, beginning the cycle again.

Along with this standard calendar, we have our own various seasonal and yearly cycles occurring. For example, an American, Christian college athlete exists on many different cycles. In addition to the standard yearly cycle beginning on January 1, there are religious and civic holidays to take into account given the student's identifications as an American and Christian. As a college student, there is also the academic calendar, a cycle that begins in late August or early September. Lastly, as an athlete, the student must also observe a different cycle of time depending on when their sport is in season. A sport like soccer, which peaks in fall, has a very different season and schedule than that of basketball in the winter or baseball in the spring. Practices, conditioning, training, and the competitive season vary for the athlete depending on their chosen sports. Though days are taken one at a time, they all fall within these various cycles. Distinct value and belief systems are highlighted in each of these different cycles, though they all have connections to each other as well. An exploration of these various cycles throughout the year reveal the complexities of everyday life as individuals balance their belief systems through assorted celebrations while also maintaining their daily life and responsibilities.

A year in the life

Building on our discussion of the seasons, let's examine a year in the life of our hypothetical college student, beginning with the start of the typical school year marking the unofficial end of summer. Shortly after classes begin we are awarded with a civic holiday. In the United States, Labor Day is observed on the first Monday in September. Its official purpose is the celebration of labor movements and their success in achieving workers' rights. Established unions, weekends, the standard forty-hour workweek, minimum wage, safe working conditions, and various other protections of workers are connected to this holiday. Unofficially, Labor Day also serves as an end of summer celebration. Having the day off is connected with many festivals and community celebrations, parties, travel, recreation, and fun. It is the last hurrah of the summer months when students don't have to go to school and responsibility is suspended. After these celebrations, summer comes to a close and individuals slowly acclimate to the shortening of days as fall approaches.

Along with the shortened days, temperatures begin to drop, and fall marks the end of the agrarian growing season and the time for the harvest. The flourish of life visible in summer plants begins to fade as they die or go dormant with the winter approaching. Though this could be a somewhat depressing time of year as the summer fun and the Vitamin D producing sunshine lessen, historically the end of the growing season also means the reaping of the rewards of the strenuous farming cycle. Soon after Labor Day and into October, fall festivals abound throughout the nation, with regional festivals focusing on local crops. Corn, beans, tobacco, wool, and the harvest in general are the perceived reason for the festivals throughout this time of year. The imagery associated with these festivals relates to this and is often rural and farm-related, with the fruits of the harvest spilling out of the cornucopia, hay bales, and corn husk adornments and symbols. The warm color palette of browns, oranges, and reds compliment the changing colors of the trees as the days continue to get colder and darker.

Rounding into October, as the weather changes and the school year begins to get intense and frustrating with midterms, many schools across the United States take a "Fall Break." Ranging from just one day to an entire week, this break provides a midpoint marker of the semester. It is something to look forward to, to work up to, and provides a much-needed respite. Many times, this break coincides with Columbus Day. As the imagery of Christopher Columbus's forceful and violent settlement of areas of the Americas become more widely known and not as glossed over in American mythology, less and less schools and organizations are observing this as a holiday to celebrate. In fact, increasingly cities are changing the name of the holiday from Columbus Day to Indigenous Peoples' Day to instead celebrate the cultures native to the Americas which were settled and destroyed by European explorers and colonists like Columbus.

Throughout October, anticipation for Halloween grows. Rather than focusing on the fading away of life in plants, an interest in the dead walking among us becomes the focus of this somewhat morbid holiday. Many cultures celebrate death around this time of year as a way to alleviate the anxiety of the changing season. Although pagan in its origins, the church adopted this holiday, like many others, and changed its meaning to something more Christian-focused. The name Halloween, or All Hallows' Eve, relates to hallows, another word for saints. Therefore, this celebration at the end of October is in preparation for All Saints' Day, November 1. In order to help the conversion from paganism to Christianity, "the church maintained that the gods and goddesses and other spiritual beings of traditional religions were diabolical deceptions."[4] Therefore the imagery of the devil with horns and hooves is meant to suggest that the pagan gods that were once worshiped were actually evil.

All Saints' Day ushers in November, but everyone knows that the month's real star is Thanksgiving. Ostensibly, this is a celebration of the rich harvest and the start of a season of giving thanks. The purpose behind the holiday, beyond giving thanks, though, is to stuff ourselves to the point of bursting. The season celebrates America's glutinous consumption, beginning with rich foods that would usually be a no-no for the health conscious among us. It starts the packing on of "holiday weight," as people eat their way through the upcoming holiday season. In the United States, Thanksgiving also abets the great cultural myth of Europeans peacefully coming together with Native Americans to celebrate cooperation. Although all history points to the romanticization of this point, the persistence of this myth speaks to our cultural desire to believe the founding of our nation was a peaceful occupation of a foreign land where natives and newcomers worked together in a blend of diversity and freedom.

After Thanksgiving, we immediately shift gears to the cheery winter holidays. The Thanksgiving break is the perfect time to begin holiday shopping and decorating. Black Friday, the day after Thanksgiving when retail businesses go from the dreaded red numbers of debt to the positive "in the black" numbers of profit, is known for doorbuster sales, early morning wake-up calls, outrageous lines, and, increasingly, violence erupting over limited quantities of sale items. After giving thanks and spending time with family, Americans turn around and express another great pastime and belief system: consumerism. The value systems expressed in Black Friday, Cyber Monday, and Small Business Saturday highlight our modern capitalist economy and national emphasis on individual freedom and success measured through monetary and material goods.

Though Black Friday is the kickoff of the shopping season in preparation for Christmas, post-Thanksgiving ushers in the holiday season in more ways than just material consumption. The cold and dark of winter, though quickly approaching, is hidden behind light and warmth: decorative lights adorn homes, trees are brought inside and prominently displayed in windows, and menorah candles are lit. Whether it is for Christmas, Hanukkah, or Kwanzaa, what is the darkest and coldest time of year, on or around the winter solstice, becomes bright, warm, and festive. As has been readily pointed out throughout history, there is no mention of the actual date of Jesus's birth, the intended purpose of celebrating Christmas, in the Bible. Instead, December 25 was chosen because of its proximity to the beginning of winter when pagans had been celebrating the solstice, often with an abundance of food, alcohol, and public revelry.[5] The family focus of Christmas today is a relatively modern take on the holiday and reflects changing perceptions of children in late nineteenth and early twentieth centuries. Christmas trees, the buying of presents, and the invention of the benevolent Santa Claus were all markers of this changing mindset. With the shift in focus to highlight children, the celebration of Christmas became, in some ways, more civilized. There were less obvious public displays of drunken revelry and more focus on the family in a child-centric celebration.[6] Of course, there are still examples of the debauchery that once defined the season, such as the infamous work Christmas/holiday parties, where coworkers who are usually known for a maintaining a level of professionalism let loose. It has become a motif in modern US culture as people share the stories of their work holiday parties with others, highlighting the more unprofessional aspects including office flings and public drunkenness. Seasonal episodes of serialized television shows, holiday movie scenes, and even feature-length films such as *Office Christmas Party*, highlight this annual event.

As holidays, Christmas Eve and Christmas are days that break away from the norm. They are official holidays where government offices, schools, and most businesses are closed. The school break that coincides with these holidays marks the end of a semester, a halfway point through the standard school year. Finalizing one's courses and then shifting focus toward holiday celebrations and the meanings of those rituals is a necessary pause from work. It punctuates the progress of the school year and is something to look forward to, beyond the end of the semester and calendar year. As the temperatures change and things begin to die, our celebrations seem to prepare us for that long and cold winter.

Folklorist Jack Santino summarizes this transition between holidays in his book *All Around the Year*, writing:

> Christmas and New Year's share midwinter symbolism and the use of a baby as a symbol of rebirth and renewal. Halloween has images of death in anticipation of sustaining life through the coming winter; Christmas and New Year's have images of life that remain through the winter. Thanksgiving

is about the life of the family unit; its focus is on past generations. Christmas is about new life, and its attention is devoted to children and future generations.[7]

The new life celebrated at Christmas is the birth of Jesus, with the symbol and celebration of this birth the crux of Christianity. Immediately after Christmas, one week to be exact, the calendar comes to an end and the year transitions into a brand new one. The image of time as an old man, Father Time, suggests the continuation and passage of time. At the New Year, however, rather than Father Time, the image of Baby New Year is common, another symbol for rebirth, fresh starts, and opportunities in the year ahead. Like our New Year's resolutions, the baby is a promise of a young year full of potential to mold, shape, and grow our own way.

As the New Year progresses in the northern hemisphere, it becomes increasingly colder. Groundhog's Day reflects our desire for spring, and Valentine's Day warms the heart. Santino notes that mid-February is a time of fertility, when nature begins to reawaken and seek out mates.[8] Like other holidays named for saints, pagan imagery of sex and fertility were downplayed, and the holiday was refocused on more chaste notions of love. The forced romanticism of Valentine's Day and the cultural myth of one true love have become increasingly challenged as divorce and remarriage is now normalized in society, as well as with the acknowledgment of platonic love. Leslie Knope, the heroine of the television series *Parks and Recreation*, invented Galentine's Day, where, "Every February 13," she and her lady friends leave husbands boyfriends at home, and "just come and kick it breakfast-style. Ladies celebrating ladies. It's like Lilith Fair, minus the angst, plus frittatas."[9] Though fictional, Galentine's Day has caught on with groups of women across the country who, instead of spending their energies preparing for or concerning themselves with the possible stigma of being single on Valentine's Day, celebrate their friendships with, and appreciation of, other women. This fun and lighthearted transformation demonstrates how the celebration and meanings of holidays are adaptable and evolve to better serve the people of the time, their beliefs, and their needs.

Regardless of whether the groundhog sees his shadow, the days get longer, and spring arrives with the vernal equinox. As the hemisphere begins to thaw, plant life emerges, animals awake from hibernation, and new life abounds. As a reward for surviving another cold winter, schools provide students with a Spring Break. It is a much-needed time for students and teachers to rest up before the final stretch of work and exams leading to the end of the school year. Spring Break has also become a cultural phenomenon, marking many young adults' first vacation without the rules and structure imposed upon them by family, with destination hot spots in warm locales in the United States, Mexico, and Caribbean.

Perhaps the most iconic and clearly spring-oriented holiday in the United States is Easter. Easter is one of the few holidays still observed that is based on the lunar calendar as opposed to the calendar year. Therefore it falls on various Sundays throughout March and April, changing annually, celebrated on the first Sunday after the first full moon after the spring equinox. One of the holiest days on the Christian calendar, Easter marks the day Jesus rose from the dead after his crucifixion on Good Friday. The popular celebration of Easter—dyed eggs, rabbits, and candy—would appear to have no connections whatsoever to the celebration of this resurrection of Jesus. These elements are, however, symbolic of rebirth. From the reawakening of nature in spring, to the fertility of rabbits, to the symbolism of birth with the egg, to the resurrection and rebirth of Jesus, Easter is all about new beginnings and new life. The colors are light and cheerful, like flowers, and in direct opposition to the darker colors that mark death and permeate the fall.

As this new life begins to take root, the school year comes to an end. May heats up quickly and by the end of the month, summer unofficially kicks off with Memorial Day. Like Labor Day at the end of summer, Memorial Day is the front bookend to the summer months and holidays. A day dedicated to the memory of those who lost their lives in service to the United States, Memorial Day's observance as a federal holiday on a Monday allows for a three-day weekend. Outdoor picnics, block parties, camping and recreational boating, and the opening of public pools are celebrated on this long weekend, serving as general markers of the beginning of the summer season.

Most of the summer holidays are about enjoying the season: being outdoors, backyard barbeques, and summer fairs and festivals. In the United States, the most definitive summer holiday is Independence Day, the Fourth of July, where Americans ignite the night sky with sparks and loud noises in honor of the US freedom from British rule. The holiday is characterized by outdoor activities including parades, picnics, neighborhood gatherings, and large taxpayer-purchased fireworks displays held in municipalities across the nation. As a celebration to the end of summer, the fairs are typically held in the weeks leading up to and after Labor Day and focus on prize-wining produce and livestock. With categories celebrating everything from homemade pies, quilts, and art, the county fair is a celebration of the crafts of rural life as the growing season winds down and folks turn their attention to the harvest after Labor Day. Individuals prepare to go back to school, and the cycle begins again.

This detailed description of holidays as the year spins around demonstrates the cyclical nature of our lives. The focus on the United States and the complicated interweaving of various different yearly cycles where we might find ourselves show that our lives are constantly looking forward. From one thing to another, we are making forward movement into the next season as a part of a repeatable cycle. While there is comfort in this predictability and ability to prepare, not everything can remain constant. As people develop individually and grow into different phases of life, their cycles may change. One cycle might become more prominent than another. The celebrations and meaning of holidays change as individuals grow older and perhaps start families of their own. Christmas, for example, is a much different experience for a child than for a parent, and it is still much more different for an adult with perhaps no children and little to no family. Adhering to the school year cycle will go by the wayside once an individual graduates, but might return again if that person finds themselves in the role of parent or teacher. This changing of ritual cycles points to the second nature of time, the linear.

Time marches on

From childhood into our teenage years, and later into adulthood, middle age, and our golden years, we mark changes along the way. Thinking of the milestone celebrations and rituals that carry an individual throughout these phases of life show a very different way to conceive time. Our last section focused on the repetition of life as evidenced in the cyclical year; now we will explore life as a timeline, tracing an individual's growth through the years.

The term for these types of rituals is referred to as **rite of passage**, which have been studied in great detail by anthropologists in various cultures around the world. However, at the heart of it, in the words of Arnold van Gennep, the French anthropologist who spearheaded this particular study, "The life of an individual in any society is a series of passages from one age to another and from one occupation to another."[10] This leads to the understanding that "life comes to be made up of a succession of stages,"[11] suggesting, again, not the cyclical nature of time and human life, but rather the linear progression of it. The stages and transitions in this progression are marked by ceremonies that delineate them from ordinary life and celebrate our transformation from one stage to the next. Therefore, a rite of passage is a ritual associated with the transition from one status to another. Sometimes the transition is specific to one individual, while other times these rites of passage apply to groups and communities of people.

Gennep defined the qualities and stages of these transitions into rites of separation, transition rites, and rites of incorporation. All three are important elements of rites of passage; however, depending on the occasion, different stages take the focus.[12] As rites of passage are concerned with transitions from one stage to the next, they are often referred to in terms of **liminality**, deriving from the Latin term *limen* for threshold.[13] A liminal period is an ambiguous stage in a rite of passage where an individual occupies a transitional space between their old and new identities. It is as if they occupy both and neither at the same time. Turner elaborated on Gennep's theories of rites of passage, further explaining that the first phase, the pre-liminal phase of separation, occurs when the individual or group detaches from their previous stage of life. This could take various different forms, but it is essentially a move away from the past life in preparation for entering a new stage. This then moves into the liminal period, which, as described above, is ambiguous. Turner refers to the third phase as "reaggregation or reincorporation" where "the passage is consummated" and the individual must then act according to their new rank and station.[14] Take, for example, pregnancy. It is a liminal phase, where the pregnant woman is at one time a parent and not. The moment a woman becomes aware of the potential child, she crosses the first stage of the threshold (the rite of separation) out of her old identity. However, she does not cross the next threshold into the new identity (rite of incorporation) until the child is born and she embraces her new identity as mother.

Turner's stages capture the essence of the journey that is the rite of passage; there is a strong delineation between the beginning, the middle, and end and their accompanying phases. The pre-liminal rites mark the time before the transition occurs, rites of transition refer to the crossings of the thresholds, and the completion concludes with the post-liminal rites.

There are milestones for every individual, beginning with our birth. As we are babies, toddlers, and children, different events deserve more celebration. Baby's first steps, food, word, tooth, and any number of personal markers may be cause for celebration. These are not, however, rites of passage, as they do not entail ritualized performances. There are, however, ceremonies for children at a very young age to initiate them into a culture, community, family, or faith. In Judaism, a boy's circumcision is ritualized as a bris. As the ceremony brings the child into the Jewish faith, it is a time for celebration. Various forms of Christianity have christening and baptism ceremonies to signify entrance into the Christian church. While these can happen at any age, quite often the ceremony is performed on babies and children, where the individual is washed of sin with holy water, from just a few drops to a full-body dunk, and brought into Christianity and religious life. Regardless of religion, more and more, parents in the United States are ritualizing birthdays, particularly the first birthday. This celebration is seen as both a milestone for the child and parents, marked with excessive footage of the child as he or she buries their face in cake made just for them. The adorable mess that is the child brings joy to everyone present as the child hits the highs of the sugar rush and soon passes out after the crash. This ritual suggests that the child is now past the infant stage, that the parents have survived (and kept the baby surviving) through the first year, and that development will increase rapidly now that both parents and child have a full year under their belts.

School is another major rite of passage for individuals in the United States. Even before school starts, many attend preschool, and even daycare centers are increasingly referred to as school by parents, children, and teachers. The shortened days of preschool and kindergarten serve as a liminal phase for children as they ease into the ritual of a daylong school routine. As they are only partial days of intense learning, the child has less of a demand put on them. It is a necessary point, however, to get them to school age. Once they transition from kindergarten to first grade, usually marked by a kindergarten graduation ceremony, the child has transitioned to a different life stage. No longer completely dependent on parents or family, the child will spend more time away from home, make their own friends, learn knowledge, and develop independently. With each passing school year, there is a smaller marking of a transition from one grade to another, especially when transitioning from one level of school to another. Going from elementary school to middle school and then to high school are worthy of acknowledgment.

Throughout this period in a child's life, most markers are related to academic growth and development. However, rituals such as Christian confirmations or Jewish bat mitzvahs usher children into different faith-based life stages. The rituals performed on babies are similar to insurance; if something were to happen to the child in that period between birth and deciding one's faith for oneself, the child is safe. However, as the child grows up and becomes more independent, the child should willingly choose their faith. These options transition the child into adulthood as they accept the faith for themselves rather than have it accepted on their behalf by a parent or spiritual counselor, such as a godparent.

In addition to the first birthday, some cultures have other milestone birthdays. For Latino cultures, quiñceaneras are celebrated when a girl turns fifteen, marking her entry into adulthood and the community. Similar birthdays are celebrated in the United States with "Sweet Sixteen" celebrations. Sixteen is a milestone birthday in the United States because, in many states, this is the age when individuals can begin driving or obtain a learner's permit. Depending on the state, the time that this permit is required varies. However, during this period, the individual is in a liminal phase. The student driver can drive on the road, with some restrictions such as needing a licensed passenger, but is not yet a licensed driver. However, once the required period is up and the individual passes the driving test, they then have their license. This is an entirely new phase toward adulthood because with driving comes a great deal of freedom but also new responsibility. Of course, many families will still institute rules and curfews but the driver is no longer at the mercy of parents or guardians for transport and decide for themselves who to spend time with, when, and where. However, driving is also expensive. Obtaining a car, insuring it, keeping it filled with gasoline, and regular maintenance and repairs require responsibility and money. This can be achieved through the acquisition of work, often one's first formal paying job. There is a cost to freedom, and that serves as a lesson in adulthood.

As far as school is concerned, the most monumental milestone is high school graduation, which occurs when most students are eighteen years old, the age when one enters adulthood. Again, with this milestone, we can see the three phases of the rite of passage. First, the separation can be considered the point when all schoolwork is completed, but final grades have not yet been submitted and the graduation ceremony has not yet occurred. The liminal phase would be the time leading up to the moment of transition when an individual's name is called, they are handed a diploma, and celebrate their new status. The integration phase would be the realization of the new status of adulthood and searching for a job, college, or whatever the next phase might be. More and more, however, the college period between high school and full-fledged adulthood appears to be more of an accurate representation of the liminal phase. The separation is the graduation from high school and moving away from the parents' or guardians' home. However, college is removed from the real world. Living in dorms, attending classes, and exploring oneself is still an in between phase where individuals come to terms with who they are, their beliefs, and what they would like out of life. The time in college, then, has increasingly become a liminal phase. Often it is not until the graduation from college that the individual truly crosses the threshold into adulthood and integration into society and culture at large.

As time and adulthood progresses, individuals find themselves transitioning into other life stages. Getting that first real job is a major milestone and transition. Marriage, with the liminal period of the engagement, is another major milestone. Of course, another possible rite of passage is divorce, when an individual transitions legally and emotionally from being in a couple back to the status of single. Parenthood is another significant rite of passage, as transitioning into the life of a parent changes nearly everything about one's life as a new level of maturity and priorities emerge. Still other milestones occur as one ages, from birthdays and anniversaries, to job advancement and retirement. The transition into retirement is the inverse of college graduation, where one, rather than preparing to work for years, shifts to enjoying their newfound freedom and life outside the mandates of work. Finally, regardless of your religious beliefs, the last rite of passage that any of us will experience is death, the ultimate final frontier.

Though the rites of passage are discussed in this chapter are specifically relevant to the United States, all cultures have similar markings of transition into the different life stages. Marriage, naming, initiation, and death rituals explain the universal need in humans to mark these important milestones and transitions as one progresses naturally on one's life path. It makes life appear linear, although one could also argue for a cyclical interpretation. From birth through the helplessness and dependence of childhood and then into the independence of adulthood and then once again to needing help in old age and eventual death, life is a cycle. However, not all of this happens in one year, like the seasonal cycles mentioned earlier in the chapter. There is more of a progression with a beginning, middle, and end to this marking of time.

Relax (don't do it)

While the rites of passage discussed in the previous section cover life's major milestones, these theories have been expanded on to help us understand activities more commonly associated with popular culture. Turner's concept of the **liminoid** describes liminal-like experiences that are temporary suspensions of the mundane, but do not signify major life transitions from one stage to the next.[15] The purpose in distinguishing between the liminal and the liminoid relates to modern society's division of work and leisure, where, "In the liminal phases and states of tribal and agrarian cultures—in ritual, myth, and legal processes—work and play are hardly distinguishing in many cases."[16] The investment of time and energy into rituals and ceremonies resembled work and, therefore, was different from what we today consider leisure time or time off, which is much more separated from what we designate as "work." The concept of having free time where one does not have to actively work toward sustaining life but can do exactly what one wants to do with one's time is relatively new. Turner defines leisure time in two different ways: "freedom from" and "freedom to." By thinking about leisure time as freedom from, you can think about it as time away from work, responsibility, the daily grind, and the 9:00-to-5:00. Thinking about freedom to, one can think about the freedom to truly do what one might want. It is the freedom to enjoy entertainment and play of all kinds, guilt free and away from the responsibility of usual time.[17] Therefore, the liminoid is the break from the normal, everyday requirements placed on us by modern society. It differs from the liminal because it isn't about marking a transition from one stage to another or occupying two different spaces or identities. Instead, the liminoid is about a temporary suspension of the mundane. Thinking back to the beginning of this chapter, we can see how the liminoid is an important way in which we structure our time and attention. We define our days by how close we are to the liminoid, whether that be a day off, vacation, holiday, concert, or other special event. The built-in liminoid and leisure time in modern society makes much of popular culture possible. The time we spend playing on our phones, reading books, watching television and movies, attending concerts, traveling for pleasure, shopping, consuming, and nearly everything else in this book is a celebration of the liminoid.

The liminoid is important because it is time that serves as a pressure valve and break away from the monotony. Our time away from work is seen as a reward, and mentally allows people to reset and work through the frustrations and fatigue that come from repetitive tasks, as is the case in modern industrialized society. At the same time, these days reinforce the power structures that benefit those in the upper echelons of corporations and society. By allowing people to let off steam and frustration the liminoid functions in maintaining systems, where once a brief, temporary release is experienced, people return to their routine of daily work refreshed with renewed energy.

While weekends and other days off from work serve this purpose, there are also more formal socially and culturally sanctioned days and celebrations that serve this function. These days, celebrations, and rituals are referred to as carnivals and are known for standing apart from—and even flipping—

regular days and social expectations. Historically, carnivals, festivals, and fairs of medieval Europe had, at the heart of them, a lot of play and laughter. These events were designed for the folk, with a clear purpose: "Carnival is not a spectacle seen by the people; they live in it, and everyone participates because its very idea embraces all the people."[18] With the focus on fun and play, Russian philosopher Mikhail Bahktin explains that "All these forms of protocol and ritual based on laughter and consecrated by tradition [...] were sharply distinct from the serious official, ecclesiastical, feudal, and political cult forms and ceremonials."[19] Carnival comes from "carne" or "carnal," meaning flesh, which can be indicative of a large feast and the consumption of meat, but it also speaks to the more base, natural, animal, and lascivious instincts of human kind. Both overconsumption and the taboo expression of the flesh's desire are generally forbidden, yet on carnival are permitted and encouraged. These days were also characterized by misrule, which means that things usually forbidden or seen as illegal can were done and achieved without fear of punishment.[20] This carnival quality makes for a different type of ritual.

Referred to as rites of reversal, these celebrations reverse social norms through the permitting of activities that are usually looked down upon or forbidden. Elaborating on this, Turner distinguishes between what he refers to as "rituals of status elevation" and "rituals of status reversal." Both of these have qualities of liminality and the liminoid, but are very different from one another. Those of elevation would be like rites of passage, where an individual transitions from one stage of life to another. Those of status reversal, however, are more cyclical and, therefore, tied to the calendar year. They also tend to be collective as opposed to individual, where those in lower status positions get to enact power and authority over their superiors. The result is a celebration that reverses the traditional social hierarchy.[21]

As Bahktin notices and expands upon, carnivals and these rituals of reversal are for the folk audiences, or the masses, rather than for the elite. The rituals of carnival, however, may mimic the official rituals of various religions and belief systems, but, in Bahktin's words, "All these forms are systematically placed outside the Church and religiosity. They belong to an entirely different sphere."[22] Beyond this spirit of fun and reversal, however, is a reinforcing of those very hierarchies that are being mocked. By providing this outlet for frustrations and perceived subordination, groups can let out their frustrations in the chosen celebratory fashion and then quickly resume the status quo and subordination the very next day. According to Turner, "the liminality of status reversal may be compared to comedy, for both involve mockery and inversion, but not destruction, of structural rules and overzealous adherents to them."[23] Rituals of reversal are merely a break from the norm, not an actual changing of them.

Here in the United States, one of the most celebrated rituals of reversal is Mardi Gras. Occurring on Fat Tuesday every year, which is the day before Ash Wednesday and the start of Lent, Mardi Gras is a famous New Orleans celebration. Though carnivals and different versions of Mardi Gras happen across the United States, the New Orleans celebration is the most famous. Marked by parades, costumes, public drunkenness, sexuality, and general merriment, Mardi Gras symbolizes a celebration of sin and gluttony before the period of Lent and abstinence begins. More broadly, cities like New Orleans and Las Vegas base their tourism on this suspension of rules and order, marketing themselves as places to play and celebrate carnival and the liminoid year round.

In terms of holidays, Halloween, in many ways, is also a ritual of reversal. In general, children are taught not to beg or ask for too much, particularly when it comes to candy and sweets, which are increasingly stigmatized as unhealthy. On Halloween, however, children walk door to door asking for those usually forbidden treats. While engaged in this taboo behavior, they are also dressed up as something they are not. As a celebration of the day when the dead walk among us, the ultimate reversal, other costumes also signify reversal. Gender can be more fluid and children can dress in ways that cross the hard lines of the gender binary. Children can also live out their fantasies as princesses, superheroes, or other famous characters. The freedom to be something that one isn't can be an exciting experience and one that breaks up the boredom of being the same person every day.

The 2013 film *The Purge*, along with its sequels *The Purge: Anarchy* and *The Purge: Election Year*, plays with this ritual of reversal to the extreme. Taking place in the United States after the fall of our current system of government, the purge is an annual celebration of the "new founding fathers" and a "nation reborn." Celebrated near the vernal equinox, it is a day when all crimes are legal, even murder, for twelve hours. The obvious reversal in the films takes the form of a lift of usual laws, both enforced by police and moral systems of belief. It is, therefore, a time of misrule and suspension of the usual ordered society. *The Purge* is heavy-handed in its discussion of the purpose that the ritual serves those in power. While masked as a day to let off steam, the ritual itself is a cleansing of the undesirables who are seen as a burden on society. The specific targeting of the poor and racial minorities reinforces the power of the rich white men, the new founding fathers. However, the maintenance of power and hegemony is, as discussed above, the purpose of these types of rituals. By allowing the things which are normally forbidden for one day, it allows everyone to more easily fall into line without question or desire to stray from what is expected of them during their everyday lives. This pause for play, for misrule, and for reversal is an important type of celebration for keeping us satisfied with maintaining the status quo.

That's all folks

Beyond all of these types of rituals and celebrations that are meant to help us punctuate our days, to break away from the mundane, to reinforce religious or cultural beliefs, and to let off steam by playing, there has also been a serious uptake in the creation of fake holidays. Invented traditions are nothing new. As new genres emerge from changes in old genres, new traditions and celebrations also emerge from others. Black Friday couldn't exist without Thanksgiving and the upcoming Christmas season, just as "March Madness" couldn't exist before college basketball. As times change, new celebrations and holidays naturally emerge. In our current culture, which is increasingly marked by the influence of social media and instant updates, every day seems to be a new holiday. From "Dress Up Your Pet Day" (January 14) to "International Talk Like a Pirate Day" (September 19), every day is a new reason to celebrate. While most of these "celebrations" are silly and tongue-in-cheek, their spread via social media suggests a desire to bring people together in an increasingly globalized world and the absence of physical community. Other similar celebrations, such as "Siblings Day" (April 10) or "Pro Sports Wives Day" (February 11), tend to focus on specific groups or identities and serve as demonstrations of appreciation and acknowledgments of accomplishments by these individuals and groups. Most of these days, however, are not tied to the yearly calendar in any meaningful way, do not contribute to the smooth transition of seasons, do not mark anything important, nor do they appear to celebrate any purposeful reversal of the status quo or anything of any religious, political, cultural, or historical significance. In fact, the only way they are disseminated, popularized, or even acknowledged is through the lackadaisical sharing of pictures, posts, and memes on social media. With the nature of social media, as well, these posts are not always shared on the same day making it so one arbitrary holiday is celebrated on various dates throughout the year depending on when an individual happens across a particular post. Considering the impulse to share these holidays on social media, and "celebrate" them however one chooses, would suggest a general malaise with everyday life and the mundane in modern society. People are not content with accepting any day for what it is and feel a need to make it special and to stand out. The *carpe diem* and #YOLO attitude emphasized and encouraged through the culture of the United States is taken to a whole new level with this phenomenon. Every day is expected to be imbued with more meaning, and the ritualization of this desire and reason to celebrate are ways to achieve that. Some of these invented holidays, famously October's "Sweetest Day," are meant to encourage the sale of certain products. Greeting card companies are often blamed for the perpetuation of some of these more meaningless, do-nothing holidays, as it stimulates their revenue and the masses are anxious for another reason to make a day feel different and special.

The everyday life of people in the United States is a great way to understand the human condition. Understanding popular culture as the study of the intersection of people, power, and politics, is best done by examining the practices, amusements, and activities of our everyday. Throughout this book, we have tackled our cultural myths and the way these myths are expressed through popular culture, from the genres of entertainment we enjoy to the celebrities we worship, from the material objects we need and want, to the ways in which these objects shape the formations and expressions of individual identities and communities. Concluding with this chapter, we end our study thinking about the everyday from the days that stand apart from it. Through the examination of personal celebrations and national holidays, we see the ways in which popular culture defines the various moments throughout our lives. Both linear and cyclical, these celebrations, like popular culture, endure. It may not always be pretty, and it certainly isn't perfect, but when it comes down to it, popular culture makes the world go round.

Notes

1   Jack Santino, *All Around the Year: Holidays and Celebrations in American Life* (Chicago: University of Illinois Press, 1994), 11.

2   Deborah A. Kapchan, "Performance," in *Eight Words for the Study of Expressive Culture*, ed. Burt Feintuch (Chicago: University of Illinois Press, 2003), 130.

3   Edward T. Hall, *Beyond Culture* (New York: Anchor Press/Doubleday, 1976), 14–17.

4   Jack Santino, *Halloween and Other Festivals of Death and Life* (Knoxville: The University of Tennessee Press, 1994), xvi.

5   Stephen Nissenbaum, *The Battle for Christmas: A Cultural History of America's Most Cherished Holiday* (New York: Vintage Books, 1997), 4.

6   Ibid., 176–218.

7   Santino, *All Around the Year*, 177.

8   Ibid., 68.

9   *Parks and Recreation*. "Galentine's Day." *NBC*, February 11, 2010.

10 Arnold van Gennep, *The Rites of Passage* (Chicago: The University of Chicago Press, 1960), 2–3.

11 Ibid., 3.

12 Ibid., 10–11.

13 Victor Turner, *The Ritual Process: Structure and Anti-Structure* (Chicago: Aldine Publishing Company, 1969), 94.

14 Ibid., 94–95.

15 Victor Turner, *From Ritual to Theatre: The Human Seriousness of Play* (New York: PAJ Publications, 1982), 32.

16 Ibid., 34.

17 Ibid., 36–37.

18   Mikhail Bahktin, *Rabelais and His World*, trans. Helene Iswolsky (Bloomington: Indiana University Press, 1984), 7.

19   Ibid., 3.

20   Nissenbaum, *The Battle for Christmas*, 6.

21   Turner, *The Ritual Process*, 167.

22   Bahktin, *Rabelais and His World*, 7.

23   Turner, *The Ritual Process*, 201.

Glossary

Antihero: Protagonists who fail to possess traditional heroic and admirable qualities, often embodying the opposite characteristics one expects from narrative heroes.

Assemblage: The arrangement of objects in a particular context or location, with meaning created through their grouping, reflecting the beliefs of the creator.

Base: Marxist term for the means and production of a society's economic system.

Biopower: Term coined by French philosopher Michel Foucault to describe the power of the state over people via controls over an individual's physical body.

Brand: Image cultivated in order to project a company, product, or individual's essence and associated values, skills, or qualities.

Bricolage: The process of creating through found objects or by rearranging elements of a text or object to create something new.

Celebration: Enjoyable, entertaining, joyous experiences focused on bringing people together in order to acknowledge some particular event or cause.

Celebrity: An individual who achieves fame not for any specific action or accomplishment, but through repeated exposure by and through the media.

Ceremony: The celebration and gathering of people surrounding the performance of a specific ritual.

Commodity fetishism: Term coined by Karl Marx to describe the "mystical character of commodities" where, in capitalist economies, value is not determined by the work related to an object's production, nor for its utility, but dictated by the market based on its perceived social value.

Community: A small group of individuals with a shared identity and worldview that emphasizes the importance of interpersonal relationships.

Conspicuous consumption: Term coined by Thorstein Veblen to describe the visible social and class markers associated with the purchase and use of specific goods and services, often in excess of what is necessary, as a means to indicate and represent an elevated social status.

Consumption: The ways that audiences purchase, borrow from, use, consume, and make meaning from the popular culture that surrounds them. The institutional structures and processes involved in the use and practice of popular culture.

Counterculture: A subculture whose values, practices, and/or beliefs go against those of the dominant culture.

Creation: Context of material culture that considers the ways in which an artist or creator interacts with his or her natural, social, and cultural environments in the development of an object.

Cultural appropriation: The adoption of elements of one cultural group by another.

Culture: The shared meanings, practices, and beliefs that constitute a way of life for a specific group of people coexisting in a particular place and time.

Culture industries: The individuals, companies, and institutions that shape and control the production of popular culture products and their associated cultural meanings.

Discourse: The ways in which the relationship between knowledge and power circulate in culture through speech and thought in order to exert control.

Exchange value: Refers to the value placed on goods in comparison to other products in the financial market.

Fandom: A subculture that refers to the communities that form around the relationships between audiences and media texts.

Feminism: The movement for social, political, and economic equality between men and women.

Festival: Celebrations centered around communities coming together to enjoy excess of food.

Folklore: Defined by Dan Ben-Amos as "artistic communication in small groups," the term applies to a field of study of the art, practices, communications, and beliefs shared and passed down through generations of small groups of people.

Foodways: The academic study of food, which includes all of the actions and practices connected to food within a particular culture or group and how food is used in everyday life.

Frankfurt School: Name given to the school of critical philosophy and social thought associated with Institute for Social Research (Institut für Sozialforschung) founded by Marxist intellectuals in Frankfurt, Germany, in 1923. Forced to flee Nazi Germany, theorists associated with the Frankfurt School were critical of both capitalism and Soviet socialism, and attempted to theorize on the social changes that saw the rise of fascism and the role of culture in upholding oppressive ideologies.

Gemeinschaft: Conceptual term used by German sociologist Ferdinand Tönnies to describe the personal and social interactions and the roles, values, and beliefs that create community as a result.

Gender: The social construction of our sex, based on physical and behavioral representations of the self, attitudes, power differentials, and the ways in which males and females are conceptualized in society through culture.

Gender queer: A term that refers to both a social movement resisting gender binaries as well as those who identify outside the male/female binary.

Genre: A contract between popular culture producers and consumers, with certain expectations on each side of the equation that adapt and shift in response to historical, ideological, and cultural contexts.

Gesellschaft: Term used by German sociologist Ferdinand Tönnies to describe the formal and indirect social interactions that govern societal roles, values, and beliefs.

Globalization: Migration, integration, and interaction of peoples and goods, stimulated by international trade and advances in technology and modes of communication.

Holiday: From "holy day," a day dedicated to observing religious beliefs and values.

Hegemony: Form of social control where those in power maintain their authority through coercion and consent as opposed to physical violence.

Hero: An individual who achieves greatness through some form of achievement, action, or deed.

Heteronormativity: Used to describe the belief that heterosexuality—sexual relations between a man and a woman—is "natural" and that sexual practices outside of this paradigm are seen as deviant.

Hypo-descent: Assigning race based on an individual's socially subordinate heritage.

Icon: The material objects of popular culture which serve as tangible representations of a culture's ideologies, values, and beliefs.

Ideology: The beliefs, practices, and principles that inscribe meaning, wield power, and shape society through a collective adherence of shared values.

Industrialization: Describes the shift from an agricultural to a manufacturing society, and the resultant economic and cultural transformations related to these technological advances.

Institution: The systems, organizations, or practices linked to established bodies of power.

Intersectionality: A frame of analysis that takes into account the ways that elements of identity such as race, gender, and sexuality mutually construct one another.

Liminality: The period in a rite of passage where individuals are in a state of "betwixt and between," occupying a transitional space between their old and new identity.

Liminoid: Term coined by Victor Turner to describe liminal-like experiences that are temporary suspensions of the mundane, but do not signify major life transitions from one stage to the next.

Mainstream culture: Culture that most closely resembles and follows the beliefs, values, and myths of a specific group of people coexisting in a particular place and time.

Market segmentation: A process for shifting the production of goods and culture to specific groups and lifestyles in order to target distinct cultural tastes and specialized audiences.

Marxism: Named for Karl Marx, the study of society examining class struggle and social control with respect to the way capitalism governs economic exchange and structures social life.

Material culture: The physical and tangible (material) objects members of a particular culture use on a regular basis; provide insight into the way of life and beliefs of those individuals.

Microaggressions: Casual disrespect or insult displayed in a nonaggressive and/or subconscious way by dominant groups against marginalized groups in society.

Mindset: The habits and beliefs that shape how one sees the world.

Myth: A shared belief in the symbolic representation of a culture's mindset, identity, and way of life.

Nationalism: Any ideology of pride in one's nation and national identity, as well as the ways nations and individuals work to promote the mindset, values, and beliefs of their country.

Neoliberalism: Economic and political theories associated with free-market capitalism, deregulation, privatization, and reduced expenditures for social and public goods.

Online community: Regular group interactions and relationships that exist through mediated forms rather than in-person connections.

Performance: Stylized, repetitive acts that communicate the expression of self or the enactment of beliefs to audiences.

Planned obsolescence: A strategy of production where products are purposefully designed in such a way that they will become out-of-date and in need of replacement in a short, predetermined time period and/or before the actual need for a new replacement product.

Popular culture: The activities, objects, distractions, and/or focus of daily life.

Post-racial: Belief that a society has moved past racism and/or the belief that discrimination based on the color of one's skin does not exist.

Privilege: An advantage one has based on the circumstances of their birth and factors to which the individual has no control.

Production: Refers to the creation of popular culture products and texts, as well as the media ownership, values, and processes that influence and contribute to their construction.

Pseudo-individualization: Process by where individuals assert false displays of individual identity through the consumption of products altered in a way to appear unique, but are at their core identical.

Racialization: The process by which individuals, social practices, and cultural processes are given racial identity.

Representation: Refers to the ideas, beliefs, and values that are supported, promoted, and perpetuated through popular culture texts and practices. Representation uses symbolism in the creation of cultural myths in order to reflect and fortify ideology.

Rites of passage: The events that mark an individual's movement from one status or stage of life into another.

Ritual: Rigidly structured, actions and performances that, throughout their enactment, carry meaning.

Semiotics: The study of sign systems.

Sex: The biological identity of an individual assigned at birth, based on physiological factors such as reproductive organs and hormones.

Social construction: Theory that identities do not have a fixed, biological basis, but are rather constructed through societal institutions.

Society: The institutions, structures, and organizations that govern the interactions of groups of people geographically and/or culturally linked together.

Stereotypes: Preconceived ideas or notions related to the perceived characteristics of a group of people, the result of which indicates larger power relations in society.

Subculture: A group or subset of a larger culture that shares its own interests, practices, and beliefs, that, while unique, are not in opposition to the dominant culture.

Superstructure: Marxist economic term for the cultural and ideological manifestations of a nation's economic base.

Transgender: Gender identity or gender expression that is different than what was sexually assigned at birth.

Transsexual: An outdated term used to refer to individuals who have undergone medical interventions, such as hormone therapy or surgery, in order to alter their gender identity.

Use value: The value attached to a commodity in terms of its utility.

White privilege: The way in which white as a racial category is taken for granted as the norm in American society.

Bibliography

20/20. "Bruce Jenner—The Interview." [TV program], ABC, April 24, 2015.

2013 National Gang Report. Washington: National Gang Intelligence Center, 2013.

Abrams, Rachel and Marc Graser. "Fans Petition Warner Bros. to Remove Ben Affleck as Batman." *Variety*, August 23, 2015. http://variety.com/2013/film/news/fans-petition-warner-bros-to-remove-ben-affleck-as-batman-1200587228/

Alberoni, Francesco. "The Powerless 'Elite': Theory and Sociological Research on the Phenomenon of Stars." Translated by Dennis McQuail. In *The Celebrity Culture Reader*, edited by P. David Marshall, 108–23. New York: Routledge, 2006.

Althusser, Louis. "Ideology and Ideological State Apparatuses (Notes Toward an Investigation)." 1970. In *Media and Cultural Studies: Key Works (Revised Edition)*, edited by Meenakshi Gigi Durham and Douglas M. Kellner, 79–87. Oxford: Blackwell, 2006.

Altman, Rick. "A Semantic/Syntactic Approach to Film Genre." *Cinema Journal* 23 no. 3 (1984): 6–18.

Altman, Rick. *Film/Genre*. London: British Film Institute, 1999.

American Psychological Association. "Think Again: Men and Women Share Cognitive Skills." August 2014, http://www.apa.org/action/resources/research-in-action/share.aspx

Aristotle. *Poetics*. Edited with critical notes by S. H. Butcher. New York: Macmillan, 1902.

Arnold, Matthew. *Culture and Anarchy*. Edited by Samuel Lipman. NH: Yale University Press, 1994.

Associated Press. "President Obama Responds to #OscarsSoWhite Controversy." *The Hollywood Reporter*, January 27, 2016, http://www.hollywoodreporter.com/news/obama-responds-oscarssowhite-controversy-860008

Bakhtin, Mikhail. *Rabelais and His World*. Translated by Helene Iswolsky. Bloomington: Indiana University Press, 1984.

Barger, Ralph "Sonny" with Keith and Kent Zimmerman. *Hell's Angel: The Life and Times of Sonny Barger and the Hell's Angels Motorcycle Club*. New York: Perennial, 2001.

Barthes, Roland. *Mythologies*. Translated by Annette Lavers. New York: Hill and Wang, 1972.

Bauman, Richard. "Differential Identity and the Social Base of Folklore." In *Toward New Perspectives in Folklore*, edited by Americo Paredes and Richard Bauman, 40–53. 1972. Bloomington: Trickster Press, 2000.

Ben-Amos, Dan. "Toward a Definition of Folklore in Context." In *Toward New Perspectives in Folklore*, edited by Americo Paredes and Richard Bauman, 3–19. 1972. Bloomington: Trickster Press, 2000.

Boorstin, Daniel J. "From Hero to Celebrity: The Human Pseudo-Event." In *The Celebrity Culture Reader*, edited by P. David Marshall, 72–90. 1962. New York: Routledge, 2006.

Bordo, Susan. *Twilight Zones: The Hidden Life of Cultural Images from Plato to OJ.* Berkeley: University of California Press, 1997.

Braudy, Leo and Marshall Cohen. *Film Theory and Criticism*, 5th edn. 1974. New York: Oxford University Press, 1999.

Breech, John. "Super Bowl 49 Watched by 114.4M, Sets US TV Viewership Record." *CBSSports.com*, February 2, 2015. http://www.cbssports.com/nfl/eye-on-football/25019076/super-bowl-49-watched-by-1144m-sets-us-tv-viewership-record

Bridges, Judith S. "Pink or Blue: Gender Stereotypic Perceptions of Infants as Conveyed by Birth Congratulations Cards." *Psychology of Women Quarterly* 17, no. 2 (1993): 193–205.

Bronner, Simon J. "The Intellectual Climate of the Nineteenth-Century American Folklore Studies." In *One Hundred Years of American Folklore Studies: A Conceptual History*, edited by William Clements, 6–7. Washington: American Folklore Society, 1988.

Brown, Linda Keller and Kay Mussell, eds. *Ethnic and Regional Foodways in the United States: The Performance of Group Identity*. Knoxville: The University of Tennessee Press, 2001.

Browne, Ray. *Against Academia*. Bowling Green, OH: Bowling Green State University Popular Press, 1989.

Browne, Ray. "Myths." In *Profiles of Popular Culture: A Reader*, edited by Ray B. Browne, 13–15. Madison: The University of Wisconsin Press, 2005.

Browne, Ray. "The Many Faces of American Culture: The Long Push to Democracy." In *Ray Browne on the Culture Studies Revolution: An Anthology of His Key Writings*, edited by Ben Urish, 27–39. Jefferson, NC: McFarland & Company, Inc., 2011.

Browne, Ray. "The Theory Methodology Complex: The Critics' Jabberwock." In *Ray Browne on the Culture Studies Revolution: An Anthology of His Key Writings*, edited by Ben Urish, 94–103. Jefferson, NC: McFarland & Company, Inc., 2011.

Bush, George W. "Address to the Joint Session of the 107th Congress." *Selected Speeches of President George W. Bush*. https://georgewbush-whitehouse. archives.gov/infocus/bushrecord/documents/Selected_Speeches_George_W_ Bush.pdf

Butler, Judith. *Gender Trouble: Feminism and the Subversion of Identity*. New York: Routledge, 1999.

CBS News. "60 Minutes/Vanity Fair Poll: The American Dream." *CBSNews.com*, April 6, 2015. http://www.cbsnews.com/news/60-minutesvanity-fair-poll-the-american-dream/

Campbell, Joseph. *The Hero with a Thousand Faces*. Princeton, NJ: Princeton University Press, 1972.

Catfish [Film]. Directed by Henry Joost and Ariel Schulman. USA: Rogue Pictures, 2010.

Cawelti, John. *Adventure, Mystery, and Romance: Formula Stories as Art and Popular Culture*. Chicago: University of Chicago Press, 1976.

Cawelti, John. *Mystery, Violence, and Popular Culture*. Madison: University of Wisconsin Press, 2004.

Certeau, Michel de. *The Practice of Everyday Life*. Translated by Stephen Rendall. Berkeley: University of California Press, 1984.

Clark, John, Stuart Hall, Tony Jefferson, and Brian Roberts. "Subculture, Cultures and Class." In *Resistance Through Rituals: Youth Subcultures in Post-War Britain*. 2nd edn. 1976. Edited by Stuart Hall and Tony Jefferson, 3–59. Reprint, New York: Routledge, 2006.

Coleman-Jensen, Alisha, Matthew Rabbitt, Christian Gregory, and Anita Singh. "Household Food Security in the United States in 2015." *Economic Research Report No. 215*, USDA, 2016. https://www.ers.usda.gov/publications/pub-details/?pubid=79760

Collins, Patricia Hill. *Black Feminist Thought: Knowledge, Consciousness, and the Politics of Empowerment*. Boston: Unwin Hyman, 1990.

Crenshaw, Kimberlé. "Demarginalizing the Intersection of Race and Sex: A Black Feminist Critique of Antidiscrimination Doctrine, Feminist Theory and Antiracist Politics." *University of Chicago Legal Forum*, 1, Article 8 (1989): 139–67.

Davis, Lennard. *Enforcing Normalcy: Disability, Deafness, and the Body*. 1995. London: Verso, 2000.

DeGraaf, John, David Wann, and Thomas H. Naylor. *Affluenza: The All-Consuming Epidemic*. 2nd edn. San Francisco: Berrett-Koehler, 2005.

Dormehl, Luke. "Forget Breaking the Internet, Kim Kardashian Broke the App Store." *Cult of Mac*, December 22, 2015. http://www.cultofmac.com/403244/forget-breaking-the-internet-kim-kardashian-broke-the-app-store/

Dorson, Richard. "Current Folklore Theories." *Current Anthropology* 4, no. 1 (1963): 93–112.

Douglas, Susan. *Enlightened Sexism: The Seductive Message That Feminism's Work Is Done.* New York: Henry Holt, 2010.

Dreamgirl. "Hot on the Trail Dress." http://www.amazon.com/Dreamgirl-Trail-Dress-Brown-Medium/dp/B007N1CY1C/ref=sr_1_46?s=apparel&ie=UTF8&qid=14573 66709&sr=1-46&nodeID=7141123011&keywords=native+american+costume

Du Gay, Paul and Stuart Hall. *Questions of Cultural Identity.* 2nd edn. 1996. Los Angeles: Sage, 2011.

Dundes, Alan. "Folk Ideas as Units of Worldview." In *Toward New Perspectives in Folklore,* edited by Americo Paredes and Richard Bauman, 120–34. 1972. Bloomington: Trickster Press, 2000.

Dundes, Alan. *International Folkloristics: Classic Contributions by the Founders of Folklore.* New York: Rowman & Littlefield Publishers, Inc., 1999.

Dundes, Alan. "Who Are the Folk?." In *Interpreting Folklore,* edited by Alan Dundes, 1–19. Bloomington: Indiana University Press, 1980.

Durham, Meenakshi Gigi and Douglas Kellner. *Media and Cultural Studies: Keyworks.* Malden, MA: Blackwell, 2006.

Dyer, Richard. *Heavenly Bodies: Film Stars and Society.* 2nd edn. 1986. Reprint, New York: Routledge, 2004.

Eisenhower, Dwight D. "Farewell Address." January 17, 1961. https://www.eisenhower. archives.gov/research/online_documents/farewell_address/Reading_Copy.pdf

Elliot, Anthony. *Identity Troubles: An Introduction.* Abingdon: Routledge, 2015.

Elliott, Anthony and Charles Lemert. *The New Individualism: The Emotional Costs of Globalization.* New York: Routledge, 2016.

Federal Communications Commission. "About the FCC." fcc.gov

Ferriss, Suzanne and Mallory Young. *Chick Flicks: Contemporary Women at the Movies.* New York: Routledge, 2008.

Ferriss, Suzanne and Mallory Young. *Chick Lit: The New Woman's Fiction.* New York: Routledge, 2006.

Fiske, John. "The Cultural Economy of Fandom." In *The Adoring Audience: Fan Culture and Popular Media,* edited by L. A. Lewis, 30–49. London: Routledge, 1992.

Foucault, Michel. *Discipline and Punish: The Birth of the Prison.* Translated by Alan Sheridan. New York: Vintage, 1975.

Fox and Friends [TV program]. Fox, February 8, 2016.

"Fox News Poll: The American Dream Is Alive—For Now." *Fox News,* October 23, 2014. http://www.foxnews.com/politics/2014/10/23/fox-news-poll-american-dream-is-alive-for-now.html?intcmp=latestnews

Freud, Sigmund. *On Metapsychology: The Theory of Psychoanalysis*. 1914. Reprint, Harmondsworth: Pelican, 1984.

Freund, Hugo A. "Cultural Evolution, Survivals, and Immersion: The Implication for Nineteenth-Century Folklore Studies." In *One Hundred Years of American Folklore Studies*, edited by William Clements, 12–14. Washington: American Folklore Society, 1988.

Frye, Northrop. *Anatomy of Criticism*. 1957. Reprint, Princeton, NJ: Princeton University Press, 1990.

GLADD. 2015 "Where We Are On TV." *GLADD.com*, December 2015. http://www.glaad.org/files/GLAAD-2015-WWAT.pdf

Gallup, Alec and Frank Newport. *Gallup Poll: Public Opinion 2007*. Lanham: Rowman & Littlefield, 2008.

Gamson, Joshua. *Claims to Fame: Celebrity in Contemporary America*. Berkeley: University of California Press, 1994.

Garza, Alicia. "Herstory." *Black Lives Matter*, 2016. http://blacklivesmatter.com/herstory/

Gennep, Arnold van. *The Rites of Passage*. Chicago: The University of Chicago Press, 1960.

Giannetti, Louis D. *Understanding Movies*. 12th edn. 1972. Reprint, Englewood Cliffs, NJ: Prentice-Hall, 2011.

Giddons, Anthony. *Modernity and Self-Identity: Self and Society in the Late Modern Age*. Stanford: Stanford University Press, 1991.

Glassie, Henry. *Material Culture*. Bloomington: Indiana University Press, 1999.

Glassie, Henry. *The Potter's Art*. Bloomington: Indiana University Press, 1999.

Goffman, Erving. *The Presentation of Self in Everyday Life*. New York: Anchor Books, 1959.

Gramsci, Antonio. *Selections from the Prison Notebooks of Antonio Gramsci*. Edited and Translated by Quintin Hoare and Geoffrey Nowell Smith. New York: International Publishers, 1971.

Grant, Valerie J. "Sex of Infant Differences in Mother-Infant Interaction: A Reinterpretation of Past Findings." *Developmental Review* 14, no. 1 (1994): 1–26.

Grider, Sylvia. "Salvaging the Folklore of "Old English" Folk." In *One Hundred Years of American Folklore Studies: A Conceptual History*, edited by William Clements, 26–28. Washington: American Folklore Society, 1988.

Hall, Edward T. *Beyond Culture*. New York: Anchor Press/Doubleday, 1976.

Hall, Stuart. "Notes on Deconstructing 'The Popular.'" in *People's History and Socialist heory*, edited by Raphael Samuel, 222–40. New York: Routledge & Kegan Paul, 1981.

Hall, Stuart. "The Question of Cultural Identity." In *Modernity: An Introduction to Modern Societies*, edited by Stuart Hall, David Held, Don Hubert, and Kenneth Thompson, 595–634. Malden, MA: Blackwell, 1996.

Hall, Stuart and Tony Jefferson. *Resistance Through Rituals: Youth Subcultures in Post-War Britain.* 2nd edn. 1993. Reprint, New York: Routledge, 2006.

Hall, Stuart, David Held, Don Hubert, and Kenneth Thompson. *Modernity: An Introduction to Modern Societies.* Malden, MA: Blackwell, 1996.

Harris-Lopez, Trudier. "Genre." In *Eight Words for the Study of Expressive Culture*, edited by Burt Feintuch, 99–120. Chicago: University of Illinois Press, 2003.

Harzewski, Stephanie. "Tradition and Displacement in the New Novel of Manners." In *Chick Lit: The New Woman's Fiction*, edited by Suzanne Ferriss and Mallory Young, 29–46. New York: Routledge, 2006.

Hebdige, Dick. *Subculture: The Meaning of Style.* 1979. Reprint, New York: Routledge, 2002.

Holt, Fabian. *Genre in Popular Music.* Chicago: University of Chicago Press, 2007.

Horkheimer, Max and Theodor W. Adorno. "The Culture Industry: Enlightenment as Mass Deception." 1944. In *Media and Cultural Studies: Key Works (Revised Edition)*, edited by Meenakshi Gigi Durham and Douglas M. Kellner, 41–72. Oxford: Blackwell, 2006.

Huffington Post. "Kim Kardashian's Rules on How to Take the Perfect Selfie." *Huffingtonpost.com*, December 2, 2013. http://www.huffingtonpost.com/2013/12/02/kim-kardashian-selfie-rules_n_4372892.html

Hurston, A. C. "Sex Typing." In *Handbook of Child Psychology: Vol. 4. Socialization, Personality and Social Development*, edited by E. Mavis Hetherington, 387–467. New York: Wiley, 1983.

Jenkins, Henry. *Convergence Culture: Where Old and New Media Collide.* New York: New York University Press, 2005.

Jenkins, Henry. *Textual Poachers: Television Fans & Participatory Culture.* New York: Routledge, 1992.

Johnson, Lauren. "231 Million People Talked About Pokemon Go on Facebook in July." *Adweek*, August 9, 2016. http://www.adweek.com/news/technology/231-million-people-talked-about-pokemon-go-facebook-and-instagram-july-172891

Kapchan, Deborah A. "Performance." In *Eight Words for the Study of Expressive Culture*, edited by Burt Feintuch, 121–45. Chicago: University of Illinois Press, 2003.

Kendall, Diana. *Framing Class: Media Representations of Wealth and Poverty.* Lantham: Rowman & Littlefield, 2011.

Krause, Jim. *Photo Idea Index*. Cincinnati, OH: HOW Books, 2005.

Lacan, Jacques. "The Mirror Stage as Formative of the Function of the I." 1949. In *Ecrits: A Selection*. Translated by Alan Sheriden. New York: Norton, 1977.

Leavis, F. R. *Mass Civilization and Minority Culture*. Cambridge: Minority Press, 1930.

Lévi-Strauss, Claude. *The Raw and the Cooked: Mythologiques Volume 1*. 1969. Reprint, Chicago: The University of Chicago Press, 1983.

Lévi-Strauss, Claude. *The Savage Mind*. Chicago: University of Chicago Press, 1966.

Lévi-Strauss, Claude. "The Structural Study of Myth." *The Journal of American Folklore* 68, no. 270 (1955): 428–44.

Long, Lucy M. *Culinary Tourism*, edited by Lucy M. Long. Lexington: The University Press of Kentucky, 2004.

Lorde, Audre. "Age, Race, Class, and Sex: Women Redefining Difference." In *Sister Outsider: Essays and Speeches by Audre Lorde*, 114–23. Berkeley: Crossing Press, 1984.

Macdonald, Dwight. "A Theory of Mass Culture." In *Mass Culture: The Popular Arts in America*, edited by Bernard Rosenberg and David Manning White, 59–73. New York: The Free Press, 1957.

Malone, Bill C. *Don't Get Above Your Raisin': Country Music and the Southern Working Class*. Chicago: University of Illinois Press, 2003.

Marcuse, Herbert. *One-Dimensional Man: Studies in the Ideology of Advanced Society*, Boston: Beacon Press, 1964.

Marshall, P. David, ed. *The Celebrity Culture Reader*. New York: Routledge, 2006.

Marshall, P. David. *Celebrity and Power: Fame in Contemporary Culture*. Minneapolis: University of Minnesota Press, 2014.

Marx, Karl and Friedrich Engels. *The German Ideology*. London: Lawrence & Wishart, 1970.

Marx, Karl and Friedrich Engels. *The Manifesto of the Communist Party*. 1848. Translated by Samuel Moore. Marxists Internet Archive, 2010. https://www.marxists.org/archive/marx/works/download/pdf/Manifesto.pdf

Mazza, Cris. "Who's Laughing Now? A Short History of Chick Lit and the Perversion of a Genre." In *Chick Lit: The New Woman's Fiction*, edited by Suzanne Ferriss and Mallory Young, 17–28. New York: Routledge, 2006.

McCarthy, Justin. "Americans Losing Confidence in All Branches of US Government." *The Gallup Poll*, June 30, 2014. http://www.gallup.com/poll/171992/americans-losing-confidence-branches-gov.aspx

McIntosh, Peggy. "White Privilege and Male Privilege: A Personal Account of Coming to See Correspondences Through Work in Women's Studies." *Working Paper No. 189*. Wellesley: Center for Research on Women, Wellesley College, 1988.

Miller, Daniel. *Stuff*. Malden, MA: Polity, 2009.

Min, Lillian. "Oscars 2014: Ellen's #Selfie Wins Internet. Breaks Twitter." *Yahoo Movies*, March 2, 2014. https://www.yahoo.com/movies/bp/oscars-2014–ellen-s-selfie-wins-internet-breaks-twitter-034518537.html

Morris, Wesley. "The Year We Obsessed Over Identity." *New York Times*, October 6, 2015. http://www.nytimes.com/2015/10/11/magazine/the-year-we-obsessed-over-identity.html?_r=0#

Mulvey, Laura. "Visual Pleasure and the Narrative Cinema." *Screen* 16, no. 3 (1975): 6–18.

NBC. "Nationwide Explains Depressing Super Bowl Ad." *NBC News*, February 2, 2015. http://www.nbcnews.com/storyline/super-bowl-xlix/nationwide-explains-depressing-super-bowl-ad-n298181

Nachbar, Jack and Kevin Lause. *Popular Culture: An Introductory Text*. Bowling Green: Bowling Green State University Press, 1992.

Nayar, P. K. *Seeing Stars: Spectacle, Society and Celebrity Culture*. New Delhi: Sage Publications Pvt. Ltd, 2009.

Newport, Frank. "Fewer Americans Identify as Middle Class in Recent Years." *The Gallup Poll*, April 28, 2015. http://www.gallup.com/poll/182918/fewer-americans-identify-middle-class-recent-years.aspx

Nissenbaum, Stephen. *The Battle for Christmas: A Cultural History of America's Most Cherished Holiday*. New York: Vintage Books, 1997.

Noyes, Dorothy. "Group." In *Eight Words for the Study of Expressive Culture*, edited by Burt Feintuch, 7–41. Chicago: University of Illinois Press, 2003.

Noyes, Dorothy. "Humble Theory." *Grand Theory* special issue of *Journal of Folklore Research* 45, no. 1 (2008): 37–43.

Nye, Russel. *The Unembarrassed Muse: The Popular Arts in America*. New York: The Dial Press, 1970.

O'Brien, Susie and Imre Szeman. *Popular Culture: A User's Guide*, 3rd edn. 2004. Toronto: Nelson, 2014.

O'Neil, Lorena. "#DeflateGate Trends on Social Media After Patriots Investigated for Deflated Footballs." *The Hollywood Reporter*, January 19, 2015. http://www.hollywoodreporter.com/news/deflategate-trends-social-media-patriots-764672

Oring, Elliott. "On the Concepts of Folklore." In *Folk Groups and Folklore Genres: An Introduction*, edited by Elliott Oring, 1–22. Logan: Utah State University Press, 1986.

Oxfam International. "An Economy for the 99%." *Oxfam.com*, January 16, 2017. https://www.oxfam.org/en/research/economy-99

Parks and Recreation. "Galentine's Day." NBC, February 11, 2010. Pew Research Center. "The American Middle Class Is Losing Ground." *Pew Research Center*

Social and Demographic Trends, December 9, 2015. http://www.pewsocialtrends.
org/2015/12/09/the-american-middle-class-is-losing-ground/

Radway, Janice A. *Reading the Romance: Women, Patriarchy, and Popular Literature.*
Chapel Hill: University of North Carolina Press, 1984.

Raymond, Diane. "Popular Culture and Queer Representation: A Critical
Perspective." In *Gender, Race, and Class in Media: A Text Reader*, edited by Gail
Dines and Jean M. Humez, 98–110. Thousand Oaks: Sage, 2003.

Reuters. "Goodbye Beyoncé, Hello Sasha Fierce." *Today.com*, October 22, 2008.
http://www.today.com/popculture/goodbye-beyonce-hello-sasha-fierce-
wbna27330555

Roberts, Warren E. *Log Buildings of Southern Indiana*. Bloomington: Trickster Press,
1996.

Rojek, Chris. *Celebrity*, London: Reaktion Books, 2001.

Roszak, Theodore. *The Making of a Counter Culture: Reflections of the Technocratic
Society and Its Youthful Opposition*. New York: Anchor Books, 1969.

Roosevelt, Franklin D. "Address to the Boy Scouts of America and Some
Observations on the Constitution." *National Public Radio*. August 21, 1935.

Samuels, Allison. "Rachel Dolezal's True Lies." *Vanity Fair*, July 19, 2015. http://
www.vanityfair.com/news/2015/07/rachel-dolezal-new-interview-pictures-
exclusive

Santino, Jack. *All Around the Year: Holidays and Celebrations in American Life.*
Chicago: University of Illinois Press, 1994.

Santino, Jack. *Halloween and Other Festivals of Death and Life*. Knoxville: The
University of Tennessee Press, 1994.

Santino, Jack. "The Folk *Assemblage* of Autumn: Tradition and Creativity in
Halloween Folk Art." In *Folk Art and Art Worlds*, edited by John Michael
Vlach and Simon J. Bronner, 151–69. Logan: Utah State University Press,
1992.

Saturday Night Live. "The Day Beyoncé Turned Black" [TV program]. NBC,
February 13, 2016.

Saussure, Ferdinand de. *Course in General Linguistics*. Edited by Charles Bally and
Albert Sechehaye. Translated by Wade Baskin. New York: The Philosophical
Library, 1959.

Sbacker. "Catfish." *Urban Dictionary*, July 22, 2010. http://www.urbandictionary.com/
define.php?term=catfish

Shukla, Pravina. *The Grace of Four Moons: Dress, Adornment, and the Art of the Body
in Modern India*. Bloomington: Indiana University Press, 2008.

Siebers, Tobin. *Disability Theory*. Ann Arbor: University of Michigan Press, 2008.

Target Corporate. "What's in Store: Moving Away from Gender-Based Signs." *Target. com*, August 7, 2015. https://corporate.target.com/article/2015/08/gender-based-signs-corporate

Taylor, Alan. "Occupy Wall Street." *The Atlantic*, September 30, 2011. http://www.theatlantic.com/photo/2011/09/occupy-wall-street/100159/

Timmerman, Kelsey. *Where Am I Eating?: An Adventure Through the Global Food Economy*. Hoboken, NJ: John Wiley & Sons, 2013.

Timmerman, Kelsey. *Where Am I Wearing: A Global Tour to the Countries, Factories, and People That Make Our Clothes*. Hoboken, NJ: John Wiley & Sons, 2012.

Tönnies, Ferdinand. *Community and Civil Society*. 1887. Translated by Jose Harris and Margaret Hollis. Cambridge: Cambridge University Press, 2001.

Turner, Graham. *Understanding Celebrity*. London: SAGE Publications, 2004.

Turner, Victor. *From Ritual to Theatre: The Human Seriousness of Play*. New York: PAJ Publications, 1982.

Turner, Victor. *The Ritual Process: Structure and Anti-Structure*. Chicago: Aldine Publishing Company, 1969.

United Nations. "Convention on the Rights of Persons with Disabilities." *UN Division for Social Policy and Development: Disability*, 2006. http://www.un.org/disabilities/convention/facts.shtml

Veblen, Thorstein. *The Theory of the Leisure Class*. 1899. Reprint, New York: A.M. Kelley, Bookseller, 1965.

Wakeman, Jessica. "Kill Me Now, Please: JC Penney's 'I'm Too Pretty to do Homework' T-Shirt for Girls —UPDATE." *The Frisky*, August 31, 2011. http://www.thefrisky.com/2011-08-31/kill-me-now-please-jc-penneys-im-too-pretty-to-do-homework-t-shirt-for/

Wells, Juliette. "Mothers of Chick Lit? Women Writers, Readers, and Literary History." In *Chick Lit: The New Woman's Fiction*, edited by Suzanne Ferriss and Mallory Young, 47–70. New York: Routledge, 2006.

Wilson, Ryan. "Richard Sherman: 'Thug' Is Accepted Way of Calling Someone N-Word." *CBSSports.com*, January 22, 2014. http://www.cbssports.com/nfl/news/richard-sherman-thug-is-accepted-way-of-calling-someone-n-word

Wolf, Gary I. "Homepage." *Quantifiedself.com*, http://quantifiedself.com

Wolf, Naomi. *The Beauty Myth: How Images of Beauty Are Used Against Women*. New York: W. Morrow, 1991.

Zeman, Ned. "The Boy Who Cried Dead Girlfriend." *Vanity Fair*, April 25, 2013. http://www.vanityfair.com/culture/2013/06/manti-teo-girlfriend-nfl-draft

Ziv, Stav. "Marshawn Lynch Gets Trademark Approved for 'I'm Just Here So I Won't Get Fined.'" *Newsweek*, December 31, 2015, http://www.newsweek.com/marshawn-lynch-gets-trademark-approved-im-just-here-so-i-wont-get-fined-410657

Index